Inequality, Democracy, and Growth in Brazil

Inequality, Democracy, and Growth in Brazil

A Country at the Crossroads of Economic Development

Por Que o Brasil Cresce Pouco? Desigualdade, Democracia e Baixo Crescimento No País Do Futuro

Marcos Mendes
Doctor in Economics
University of São Paulo
Economic Consultant at the Brazilian
Federal Senate Advisory Board
Brazil

AMSTERDAM • BOSTON • HEIDELBERG • LONDON
NEW YORK • OXFORD • PARIS • SAN DIEGO
SAN FRANCISCO • SINGAPORE • SYDNEY • TOKYO
Academic Press is an imprint of Elsevier

Academic Press is an imprint of Elsevier
32 Jamestown Road, London NW1 7BY, UK
525 B Street, Suite 1800, San Diego, CA 92101-4495, USA
225 Wyman Street, Waltham, MA 02451, USA
The Boulevard, Langford Lane, Kidlington, Oxford OX5 1GB, UK

British Library Cataloguing in Publication Data
A catalogue record for this book is available from the British Library

Library of Congress Cataloging-in-Publication Data
A catalog record for this book is available from the Library of Congress

ISBN: 978-0-12-801951-1

For information on all Academic Press publications
visit our website at http://store.elsevier.com/

Typeset by SPi Global, India

Printed and bound in The United States
14   15   16   17   10 9 8 7 6 5 4 3 2 1

Contents

Foreword

Marcos Mendes has done an exhaustive work. He proposes a hypothesis regarding the functioning of the Brazilian social contract and its dysfunctions that, as we know, have resulted in a political balance of low growth and some reduction in inequality. To support his arguments, Mendes has made exhaustive use of recent literature on economic growth and political economy and has compiled an impressive collection of data and empirical evidence.

The basic argument is that inequality creates a great deal of pressure for redistribution. In very unequal societies, the average income is much above that of the typical voter. It is natural that the voter will usually vote to increase the tax burden and transfers.

This natural result of the democratic process is qualified by Brazilian history. Before being democratic, we were all unequal. Inequality in aristocracies produced innumerable transfer mechanisms for the middle and upper strata of society who had access to the king.

Political democratization produced equal access to state rent. The result was a growing tax burden, mediocre growth, and the creation of a myriad of benefits and transfers to social groups under the most diverse criteria. At times this was done in a transparent and meritorious way, such as with the *Bolsa Família* Program. However, it usually was murky, not clear as to the costs and benefits and with no evaluation mechanism. Such is the case, for example, with subsidies to companies that receive loans from the National Bank for Economic and Social Development (BNDES).

The book ends with a question: Will the Brazilian society and political system be able to process this myriad of rents, separate the wheat from the tares, what is meritorious from what is not, in such a way as to provide space in the budget to build physical infrastructure and improve the quality of healthcare, education, justice, and public security?

Or, will the way Brazilian political system works place the country on a dysfunctional trajectory of repeated rounds of tax increases with reduced growth and a greater deterioration of the infrastructure? In this case, will Brazil enter a trajectory of increased polarization and social tension with destructive effects the like of which the recent wave of protests followed by destruction of public property was only the beginning?

Notwithstanding the depth of the theme, the book is written in an easy to read style that appeals to the general public. It is a required reading for anyone who, whether they agree with the author or not, wishes to understand the challenges Brazilian society will face in the coming decades.

São Paulo, Brazil   **Samuel Pessôa**[1]
April 2013.

---

1. Samuel Pessôa is a researcher at the Getúlio Vargas Foundation Institute of Brazilian Economics.

Disclaimers

Institutions and authors quoted in this book do not necessarily agree with the ideas proposed by the author.

All quotes originally in Portuguese were freely and accurately translated by the author.

Monetary values provided in the text are expressed in Brazilian Reais, which are followed by an approximate US Dollar equivalent. Currency conversion was performed using the average commercial exchange rate for the year in question to which the Real amount refers. The reader should understand this as an approximate value for reference purposes only.

About the Author

Marcos Mendes was born in Rio de Janeiro, Brazil. He has a doctorate in economics from the University of São Paulo, Brazil, and a master's and bachelor's in economics from the University of Brasilia. Mendes has extensive experience as a public sector economist, having worked 25 years at Brazilian federal agencies such as the Central Bank and the Treasury Department. Since 1995, he has served as an economic consultant for the Brazilian Senate, being responsible for, among other things, studying the economic impact of bills under congressional debate. A specialist in public finance, he has produced several recognized studies on public policy, fiscal federalism, and budgetary and fiscal policy in Brazil where he analyzes their political and economic aspects. His papers cover such varied topics as the type of fiscal policy that helps elect a mayor in a Brazilian town; the effects of traffic legislation on automobile accident mortality rates; evaluations of large public projects such as the World Cup stadiums and high speed trains; regulatory issues in infrastructure concession to private management; and the opportunistic creation of municipalities in Brazil in past decades. Since 2011 he has been one of the editors of the highly recognized site *Brazil, Economics and Government* (Brasil, economia e governo – www. brasil-economia-governo.org.br), which, in association with the Fernand Braudel Institute (a think tank), seeks to offer didactic explanations for economic themes important to the development of the country.

Acknowledgments

I began to write this book in August 2012, when I started my eight-month stay as a *visiting fellow* at the *London School of Economics and Political Science –* Department of Economics. I would like to thank Professor Francesco Caselli for the invitation and opportunity to take advantage of the productive academic atmosphere at the university. Many people contributed to the writing of this work. Marcos Kohler and Alexandre Rocha are "almost co-authors" because they reviewed the text, debated ideas, and made suggestions along these many months. Fábio Giambiagi, Samuel Pessôa, and Marcos Lisboa heartily encouraged me take the project forward and has made contributions as well. I would like to offer my thanks for the comments, tips, and bibliographical references offered by Naércio Menezes, Fernando Veloso, Leonardo Monastério, Emanuel Ornelas, Everardo Maciel, Gilberto Guerzoni Filho, Rafael Silveira e Silva, Raul Velloso, Marcelo Abi-Rama Caetano, Carlos Mussi, Ricardo Nunes de Miranda, Fernando Álvares Correa Dias, Fernando Lagares Távora, João Ricardo Faria, Jorge Arbache, Gharad Bryan, José Roberto Afonso, and Rozane Siqueira. However, none of these people are responsible for any eventual errors in the text.

I am also thankful for the comments by participants at seminars held by FGV-EBAP (Rio de Janeiro), UnB-Departamento de Economia (Brasilia), ECLAC-OCDE (Santiago, Chile), and the Fernand Braudel Institute of World Economics (São Paulo), where I had the opportunity to expose the book's central ideas.

Débora Costa Ferreira and the research support team at Brazilian Senate Advisory Board, led by Wesley Dutra de Andrade, provided efficient aid in collecting information.

The friendship of Eduardo Nascimento, Tatiana and Walter Deperon, Kátia and Amaro Gomes, Camila and Carlos Mauro and Daniela and Emanuel Ornelas helped me through the long winter.

Dedication

TO *ANA ALBA*

Introduction

With 3.09 million square miles, Brazil has the largest geographical area in Latin America and the 5th largest in the world. In 2014, its GDP should remain in the 7th position in world, ranking at about 2.2 trillion dollars. However, its *per capita* income puts the country in the middle-income range, positioning it at number 60 among the almost 200 countries in the world. It is even behind many Latin America countries, such as Chile, Mexico, Venezuela, Uruguay and Argentina.[1]

The country is certainly a political and economic leader in Latin America, but has never attained a prominent position on the world scene, be it as an economic power or as a country with a high level of human development. It went through a period of intense growth between the end of the 1960s to the mid-1980s, but was immersed in a deep economic crisis in the second half of the 1980s. Such crisis was composed not only of negative GDP growth rates, but also by a hyperinflationary process. Only at the end of the 1990s did the country begin to recover.

Brazil is known by the nickname "country of the future" for showing extremely favorable development conditions: no external conflict, great availability of natural resources, no incidences of catastrophic natural phenomenon (earthquakes or hurricanes, for example), a good climate, one language used in all of the national territory and a large internal market. However, the country is also characterized by one of the most unequal income distributions in the world.

In the over 500 years since its discovery, this country has not been able to fulfill the destiny expected of it. Many academicians, some cited throughout this book, try to understand why Brazil has had an economic and social path so different from that of the United States, since both nations began their lives as colonies, had similar incomes during the early years (actually, Brazil was richer), were colonized at about the same time in history and both have large territories.

Along the 20th century, Brazil has been overtaken, in terms of per capita income, by other nations that had been poorer than it, such as South Korea, Taiwan, or Chile. During the first years of the 21st century, Brazil came back into "vogue." Several analysts came to believe, once again, in the idea of the "country of the future." The nation was internationally celebrated as an emerging power and appeared to be a case of economic success. Placed with China, India, and Russia in the group known as BRIC, it was called *"South America's*

---

1. Source: Cia Factbook

emerging superpower[2] by *Foreign Policy* magazine. *The Economist* even wrote an optimistic cover article entitled, *"Brazil Takes Off,"* illustrated by a suggestive image of *Cristo Redentor* (Christ the Redeemer), the statue symbol of the city of Rio de Janeiro, taking off as a powerful rocket.[3]

Auspicious growth and consumption data, poverty reduction and the accelerated expansion of the middle class created the idea that the country was entering a new era. Many optimistic books predicting a positive economic and political future for the country were published.[4] The government offered to be host for high cost international sporting events – the 2014 soccer World Cup and the Olympic Games of 2016 – building stadiums to be shown off by international broadcasters: a portrait of a new, powerful economy.

The optimism, once again, seems to have lasted little. Political leaders were surprised when, in June 2013, thousands of demonstrators took to the streets, irate over the vision of billionaire soccer stadiums standing next to decrepit hospitals with no equipment, an inefficient and insufficient public transportation system, precarious dwellings balancing on hillsides and public schools that taught little.

International risk evaluation agencies, after successive frustrations with the country growth rate, came to see what many analysts of the Brazilian economy had been saying for a long time[5]: it isn't possible for a country to grow at such high levels for many years with a precarious infrastructure (transportation, energy, and communication), poorly qualified labor, barriers to international trade, quickly growing public expenditure, a jammed court system, and high taxes and interest rates much above the international average.

As time goes by, it becomes clearer that the per capita GDP growth rates seen in the 2004-2010 period, which are not striking (3.3% per year), but are, however, above the mediocre performance from previous years (0.8% per year between 1985 and 2003), were quite influenced by the commodities *boom* experienced by the world economy, which generated great benefits for Brazil and Latin America in general. This extraordinary condition having abated, the country returned to its long-term low growth trajectory (1.0% yearly per capita GDP growth in 2011-2013).

This book analyzes economic growth from a long-term perspective. What is standard for Brazil is not the relatively high growth of 2004-2010, but the low growth of 1985-2007 and 2011-2013. A period of accelerated growth associated with the reduction in income inequality created an optimistic environment

---

2. Foreign Policy, 28/2/2012.

3. The Economist, 12/11/2009.

4. Among these, see, for example, "Starting Over: Brazil since 1985," by Albert Fishlow, "Brazil: Reversal of Fortune," by Albert Moreno, "The New Brazil" by Riordan Roett and "Brazil on the Rise," by Larry Rother.

5. See, for example, Pinheiro and Giambiagi (2006), Mendes (2010), Velloso *et al.* (2012), Hausmann (2009), Hausmann *et al.* (2005).

among entrepreneurs, politicians, and many academicians. With the cooling of the international commodities market, the old problems have returned to be an active restriction and the country is back to its pace of low growth.

In spite of near unanimity regarding the need to control public expenditure and reduce and rationalize the tax burden, as well as rationalize excessive economic regulation, little has been done to reach these objectives by the parties that have governed the country since 1985. Year after year, increases in current expenditures are accompanied by tax increases. Likewise, bad roads, unfinished railroads and congested ports are all part of an almost immutable landscape. Equally unchanging seems to be the sluggish court system, the interventionist labor law, and the protection of specific markets against international competition.

There is a political bottleneck that blocks the advance of solutions to structural problems in the Brazilian economy, which has hampered economic growth. The central argument of this book is that an important cause for this political bottleneck is the co-existence of a democratic environment (instituted in 1985) with high economic inequality.

The mission of this book is to present existing evidence for this causal connection: high inequality plus democracy is equal to low short-term and midterm growth. It is not, however, to be taken as a pessimistic message, to say that there is no hope for Brazil and to simply stand in contraposition to the optimism that has hovered over the country for the last few years.

Curiously, the brake on economic growth generated by the combination of inequality and democracy can, in the future, be a stimulus for growth. If Brazilians can reduce inequality enough, without deteriorating the public budget or creating excessive inefficiency in the economy, a more equal country will immerge in the future, unlocking the political restraints that today impair growth. If it is possible to place the country on a virtuous cycle of inequality reduction and growth acceleration, then the low growth experienced since democratization in 1985 will be the cost paid so that, in the future, Brazilians can have a nation with a high degree of development with less inequality.

Such a virtuous cycle, however, is not guaranteed. It is possible that the country will continue being locked in a high inequality–low growth equilibrium, which would result in repeated economic crises. Both positive and negative paths are possible. Whichever route taken by the country depends on the political choices made by the population and the ability of the next governments to promote strategic political and public policy reforms. This book intends to show what type of reforms and policies will increase the odds of launching a virtuous cycle and leave behind a past of inequality and instability.

Brazil has one of the most unequal income and wealth distributions. Even after significant reductions in inequality indicators during the first years of the 21st century, it continues at the top of the world inequality *ranking*. This has been a unique characteristic of Brazilian society since the first years of colonization. Inequality began with the unequal distribution of land among the first colonizers and has been perpetuated during the long economic cycles of commodities production based on large estates and slave labor. Inequality persisted even after the abolition of slavery, industrialization, and urbanization.

Such a remarkable and persistent social and economic characteristic of a country has a significant impact on the organization of society and, especially, on the economy. Despite this, analysts interested in the Brazilian economy, even today, have shown little interest in investigating how inequality affects the prospects of the economic development of the country.

Studies about Brazilian inequality have always been performed based on the presupposition that extreme inequality is an evil in and of itself and that, therefore, it should be reduced. Such studies search for the immediate causes for the problem as well as propose the proper public policies to reduce it. Certainly, extreme inequality, and the consequent poverty of a large part of the population, are undesirable and need to be remedied. The studies that seek to understand such a phenomenon, and propose ways to overcome it, are fundamental contributions to economic knowledge and public policy.

There is, however, another way to study inequality: seek to understand how it affects the economic performance of a country. Given that inequality exists, and has persisted over time, one should investigate how it affects economic performance. What influence does inequality bring to the perspectives of a country's development in the short, mid, and long terms? Economic theory, even though far from a consensus, has advanced much in the analysis of the causal relationship between inequality and growth. What this book seeks to do is use such literature as a tool to understand the Brazilian case. It is a reading of the economic facts observed since 1985, supported by theoretical and applied literature from different areas of research, such as political economy, macroeconomics, and development economics.

To academic readers, an explanation is due. There is no intention to propose a general economic theory regarding the relationship between democracy, inequality, and economic growth that would be valid for any part of the world. It is a specific analysis of the conditions that prevail in a country during a given historical period. Certainly, the analysis made here will be useful as a support to understand the situation in other countries that, by chance, have economic and social issues similar to those of Brazil, or to stimulate insight for research in inequality and growth.

The search for a general theory regarding the theme has been one of the most difficult challenges for the academic community. Statistical and measurement difficulties, as well as reverse causality and non-linearity, have hindered economists up to the present from making categorical statements, such as "inequality blocks (helps) economic growth" or "democracy hinders (helps) economic growth." The situation is even more complex when one analyzes the combined effect of democracy and inequality. The very difficulty of generating a general theory regarding the theme makes case studies, such as the one presented in this book, to be a more modest, however productive, way to advance in the analysis of the question.[6]

---

6. For a literature review on the relationship between inequality and economic growth, see Mendes (2013).

Qualitative data and evidence are shown that support the argument. However, the additional step of trying to prove, with econometric tools, the existence of the causal relationship between inequality and growth is not taken. This task remains a challenge for researchers. The role of this book is to propose the hypothesis and show initial evidence that the argument deserves to be researched in more depth, at least in the Brazilian case.

To argue that democracy could be responsible for low growth may cause the incorrect and discomforting idea that one is proposing its suppression as a way to make the country grow more. That is not the intention of this book. First, democracy has value in itself: freedom of expression, choice, and political participation are fundamental values for well-being in a modern society. Second, because the Brazilian dictatorial experience was not able to promote development in the country. As will be seen in Chapter 1, the military government from 1964-1984 created several distortions that even today impede rapid growth in the country. Third, because democratic institutions, such as freedom of the press and the checks and balances exercised by the Public Prosecutor's Office, justice and police institutions, are fundamental to reduce the capture of the state by interest groups, corruption, and bad public policy.

To say that the combination of inequality and democracy generates growth problems is an evaluation based on objective reality. What to do with this fact, in terms of policy and reform proposals, is another question. The book faces such a question by defending the maintenance and deepening of democratic institutions, while at the same time seeking to understand what can be done to permanently reduce inequality in a way so as to minimize the harmful side effects to economic growth.

There are not many studies that point toward the co-existence of democracy and inequality as a central cause for low growth in Brazil. Samuel Pessôa, macroeconomist from the Fundação Getúlio Vargas, recognizes that high inequality is an exogenous factor that shapes public expenditure and economic policy after re-democratization:

> *In the social contract currently in place, economic growth has been a residual variable. The observed growth is the one that is possible after attending the demands of welfare programs. (...) The intense demand for the increase of social assistance is due to high income inequality and, especially, educational inequality, which is also very high.*[7]

Lee Alston, along with Brazilian co-authors, from the University of Colorado, published a paper in 2012 arguing that there was a change in "beliefs" within Brazilian society. The frustration with low growth and high inflation resultant from the crisis that defeated the military regime was responsible for the formation of a public consensus revolving around the "redistribution of income with fiscal responsibility."[8]

---

7. Pessôa (2011, p. 207)
8. Alston *et al.* (2012)

In their bestseller *Why Nations Fail*," Daron Acemoglu and James Robinson devote some pages to comments about the Brazilian democratization process. They present a benevolent view, arguing that it broke the monopoly that the national elite exercised over government, giving the *Partido dos Trabalhadores* (Worker's Party) access to power. This party, in their view, was committed to the creation of "inclusive institutions," based on the equality of opportunity, democracy, respect for property rights, provision of efficient public services for all, etc., which would be the key to economic development. As a consequence, Brazil would be on a sure road to rapid growth and inequality reduction.

Even though the arguments developed in this book share some aspects of the previously cited studies, it does not agree with the benevolent interpretation that the Brazilian society decided, in a harmonious and consensual way, that it needs to be less unequal. According to this view, democratization, in and of itself, broke the political dominance by the economic elite and this was sufficient to provide a way for development.

What will be argued in the following pages is that there is no broad social consensus that makes society as a whole search for greater equality. Furthermore, the economic elite have not lost their grip on governmental decisions. Yet, there is a great conflict between the many heterogeneous social groups, each trying to obtain more benefits, more regulatory protection, and less tax from the state. In this climate of social conflict, in a society where social groups are hugely different one from the other, different policies that favor some groups, but hurt collectively, have been put into practice, impairing efficiency and economic growth.

The fact that one can see a reduction in inequality since the beginning of the 21st century does not mean that the entirety of society has decided to be more equal. It should be seen as a result of the distributive conflict being more advantageous for the poorer groups of society. In addition to this, developments in the international economy associated with demographic changes have caused the job market to generate results that, almost by chance, have promoted the reduction of inequality.

Borrowing an expression used by Lee Alston and his co-authors, we could say that Brazil is living in a situation of "**dissipative redistribution**"[9]: there is some income distribution for the poorer, however economic resources dissipate, be it by economic inefficiency that results from redistributive policies, be it by appropriation of part of the public resources by those of high and middle income, which refrains redistribution and raises fiscal and economic costs of a given reduction of inequality. The result is, therefore, **an economic model of low growth with dissipative redistribution.**

The ex-Secretary of Economic Policy in the first presidential mandate of Lula da Silva, Marcos Lisboa, in partnership with macroeconomist Zeina Latif[10] emphasizes the environment of conflict, arguing that there exists a high degree of *rent seeking* in Brazil, this being the fundamental cause for low growth. The

---

9. Alston *et al.* (2012)
10. Lisboa and Latif (2013)

analysis made in this book coincides with these authors, however, it goes a step further by proposing the hypothesis that *rent seeking* is a consequence of the combination of **inequality** and **democracy.** Additionally, we analyze the long-term perspective, which could have a good outcome in which the reduction of inequality could dissolve the causes for *rent seeking*, providing for greater economic growth and less inequality.

It certainly is possible, in an unequal society that has attained a middle level of production and economic sophistication, to reduce poverty by means of redistribution of wealth. It could, over the years, reduce poverty by distributing the existing wealth. This is what Brazil successfully did during the first decade of the 21st century. Income for the poorest of society grew at an accelerated rate, while the income of the rich increased at a slower rate. The result was decreased inequality (which is still high) and an expanded middle class. It created an optimistic environment, despite the growth rate being unimpressive.

However, in the long term, the jump to a high level of development, where almost all the population has a middle or high income and poverty comes to be a residual problem, requires that redistributive policies be aligned with conditions that lead to economic growth. Brazil will not become a developed country if its per capita income continues to grow to the paltry rate of 1.4% per year, which was the average for the period of 1985-2014.

This book innovates in showing how various Brazilian economic problems from the 1985-2014 period, usually analyzed alone, could have a common cause (but not necessarily the only one) in the extreme inequality associated with a democratic political environment. Looking at it from this perspective, it is possible to put together a puzzle where the important pieces are: lagging education, excess in public expenditures of questionable quality, frailty of regulatory agencies, closure of the economy to international commerce, high interest rates, high tax burden, actuarial imbalance of social insurance, sluggish courts, government subsidy for large companies, informal businesses, insufficient infrastructure, and long strikes by civil servants. All these characteristics are **symptoms** or **proximate causes for** the **low growth with dissipative redistribution model**. A deeper cause would justly be the coexistence of inequality and growth.

It is worth noting that there is a positive aspect in this policy of distributing state benefits and regulatory protection for different social groups. After all, by mediating the distributive conflict and avoiding that only one social group be the uncontested winner in this conflict, the successive Brazilian governments of the new democratic era were able to make democracy survive. With no social group clearly identifying itself as the loser in the distributive conflict, chances are less that these groups will unify in order to overthrow the government by non-democratic means. Democracy has survived for 30 years with no coup attempts and a growing institutional stability, which is a long time by Brazilian standards.

The book is organized into six chapters. A summary of each chapter follows. Such summaries are a guide for the development of the argument presented in the book.

CHAPTER 1

Chapter 1 begins with a brief summary of the determining factors for economic growth. It shows that the driving factors are the accumulation of physical capital (machines, equipment, infrastructure) and human capital (quantity and training of available laborers), as well as the increase of productivity, which is the efficiency with which workers use the available physical capital to produce.

Following, the general characteristics of the political and economic models used by the Brazilian military regime (1964-1984) are described. It was a closed regime with restrictions on franchise; a high level of intervention in the economy; closure of the country in relation to international trade; a deepening of the model of import substitution by means of protecting the industry that produced raw materials and equipment; no concern for social policies or the education of the poor; and an increase of economic inequality. Much of the economic model of the military regime remained after democratization.

The next section shows that Brazil has grown little since democratization. Ten stylized facts that may be considered causes of low growth are analyzed. Such characteristics hinder the accumulation of physical and human capital as well as interfere with an increase in productivity, resulting in low potential for economic growth. The 10 stylized facts are:

- Steady growth of public current expense;
- Ever increasing tax burden;
- Low savings;
- High interest rate;
- Infrastructure bottlenecks;
- Increase in minimum salary above the increase in labor productivity;
- Closure of economy to international trade;
- Judicial uncertainty and weak property rights protection;
- Proliferation of small and informal businesses;
- Low educational performance, especially in public schools.

In general, economists point to these factors as the **causes** of low growth in Brazil. What the book argues is that, actually, these are **proximate causes or symptoms** associated with a deeper cause: the coexistence of high inequality and democracy, which leads to an inefficient dispute for income among different groups.

Before developing this argument in detail, the book analyzes the characteristics of Brazilian inequality. Since this is a fundamental variable for the analysis, it is necessary to know it better.

CHAPTER 2

This chapter presents the evolution of inequality since 1985 as measured by the Gini Index. It will be first shown how inequality is a phenomenon that has been persistent over time: countries that were unequal in the past tend to be the same now. This persistence through time is an indication that inequality creates conditions for its own perpetuation. This point will be analyzed in Chapter 3.

Then it will be argued that the reduction in inequality observed in the initial years of the 21st century is not only due to government redistributive policies, nor was it exclusive to Brazil, being observed in almost all countries in Latin America. It is also due to factors out of the control of government authorities, as, for example, the emergence of favorable conditions in the labor market. The *boom* in *commodities* prices in the international market seems to be an important source of inequality reduction.

Even having decreased, Brazilian inequality continues to be quite high when compared to the rest of the world. Also, this reduction does not mean that the government redistribution policy is efficient. Actually, federal government social disbursements are highly concentrated in expenses such as social insurance and government payroll, which has a regressive effect, while it dedicates fewer resources to programs with greater redistributive impact.

More concerning yet is the fact that the trend of inequality reduction is decelerating during the second decade of the 21st century, and may stall at a still high level. The country lives, therefore, in a "cup half full" or "cup half empty" situation. Effectively, there was a reduction in inequality and poverty. However, there are no guarantees that it will be possible to continue this redistributive trajectory nor that it will be possible to avoid in the future a significant part of the families in the new middle class sliding back to poverty. On one hand, the expansion of the middle class creates conditions for this group to demand better public services and greater economic growth. On the otherhand, the persistence of low growth and a still large number of poor households tends to reinforce the present model of dissipative redistribution that ends in low growth.

CHAPTER 3

Chapter 3 begins the analysis of how inequality could be behind the 10 stylized facts that block economic growth.

In an unequal society, there is typically a nucleus of very rich people, with economic power and political influence that can be used to bypass the law and make possible the appropriation of rent by that group.

The very rich have more liquidity and working capital, which allows them to keep a long judicial dispute active without going broke. They also have greater financial capability and better political connections, which allows them to pay good lawyers and guarantee that there will not be regulatory changes contrary to their interests.

In unequal societies, there is a high probability that the judicial, political, and regulatory systems are not able to restrain the ability of the very rich to do things such as disrespect the rules of commerce or influence peddling. Property rights, laws, and rules tend to be weak and do not offer proper protection to other members of society, who are subject to being expropriated by the very rich.

Inequality has the ability to reproduce over time. It produces weak institutions that are biased in favor of the rich. This reinforces inequality by means of concentrating investments, human capital and access to credit, and wealth and power. That would be the cause of the persistence of inequality over time (documented in Chapter 2): societies that begin unequal in their inception tend to remain unequal throughout history.

Two stylized facts shown in Chapter 1 are directly connected to the predominance of interests of the high-income strata and help explain the model of low growth with dissipative redistribution.

The first is closure of the Brazilian economy to international trade (Stylized Fact 7), which represents the ability of national producers to obtain government protection for their businesses and profit in relation to international competition. This hinders the productivity gains that could be provided by greater competition as well as reduce firms' access to better quality imported supplies at lower prices.

The second is judicial uncertainty and the fragility of property rights (Stylized Fact 8), which materialize in the form of sluggish and uncertain justice and in regulatory agencies that are fragile and susceptible to political influence. This opens a breach for dominance by those who hold greater political and economic power.

Such judicial uncertainty makes the participation of the private sector in infrastructure investments more difficult. As this sector involves high front-end costs and long-term contracts, potential investors fear that the fragile legal base will be altered during the term of the contract, damaging them. This explains, in part, another stylized fact: the infrastructure bottlenecks.

Other stylized facts are also associated with the pro-rich bias of unequal societies. The steady growth of public expenditure (Stylized Fact 1) has as one of its causes the subsidies and advantages the rich extract from the government: financing by public banks with subsidized interest, concession of selective tax benefits, and forgiveness of debts guaranteed by the government and others. As we will see in Chapters 4 and 5, there is pressure for spending directed towards the poorer and middle-income groups as well, which results in a high level of current expenditure.

The increase of public expenditures generates some other stylized facts: increase in the tax burden (Stylized Fact 2); increase of public deficit (Stylized Fact 3); increase in interest rates (Stylized Fact 4); and a cut in public investments and infrastructure (Stylized Fact 5). All these facts have direct negative consequences on economic growth.

CHAPTER 4

While the previous chapter analyzes how the concentration of power in the hands of the very rich can lead to stylized facts associated with low economic growth, this chapter focuses on the other extreme of income distribution. It shows that the co-existence of a high degree of inequality within a democratic political regime leads to the adoption of public policy directed towards the redistribution of income and poverty reduction.

In a democracy, politicians can only keep their careers if they have the votes. In an unequal society, typically there are a great number of poor voters. It is natural for the political class to meet the demands of the poor in exchange for a large number of votes. The motto during the military regime was, "make the product grow before redistributing it."[11] After democratization the political slogan of the new government changed to "everything for social justice," a phrase quoted repeatedly by the first president of the democratic era, José Sarney.

Public redistributive policies are made by means of: (a) public expenditures for programs directed toward the poor, and (b) economic regulation (laws dealing with the minimum wage and labor rights, for example). It so happens that, even while being successful in reducing inequality, these policies can generate effects that are harmful to economic growth.

They cause the increase of government expense (Stylized Fact 1 from Chapter 1), driving other stylized facts that undermine economic growth: increased tax burden, reduction of public savings, increase in interest rates, and cuts to public investment in infrastructure.

The increase in minimum wage (Stylized Fact 6) has been an important component in the policy to reduce poverty and inequality. It so happens that it generates effects that are pernicious to growth. First, it accelerates the increase of public expenditure (since many social benefits paid by the government are tied to minimum wage), which feeds the tax increase cycle and cuts into infrastructure investments. Second, the persistent yearly minimum wage increase causes it to rise to a level incompatible with the productivity of workers that receive such remuneration, which reduces the profitability expected from companies. The result is a reduction in the incentives business owners have to invest in increasing production, which hinders growth.

What is more, high taxes and excessive labor market regulation (another instrument used in redistributive policy) induce businesses to remain small and informal (Stylized Fact 9). Being informal, the business does not pay taxes or worker benefits. And, being small, they remain nearly invisible to Federal Revenue or Labor Ministry inspectors, as well as other control mechanisms. It so happens that small businesses are systematically less productive than larger ones. Less productivity necessarily leads to lower economic growth.

As shown in Chapter 2, redistributive policies that favor the poor, even though not singly responsible for inequality reduction, help in the process. However, they have a harmful effect on growth.

For this reason, redistribution to the poor, together with redistribution to the rich, act in a way to generate low growth with dissipative redistribution.

---

11. Phrase credited to Delfim Netto, minister in several economic areas during the military regime. For a summary of the controversy surrounding the concentration of income during the military regime, see Baer (2009).

CHAPTER 5

Chapters 3 and 4, as described above, show that in the democratic environment inaugurated in 1985, two large redistributive tendencies operate in Brazilian society: one in favor of the rich and the other for the poor. These extreme poles on the income pyramid have enough political capital to be favored in the allocation of public spending and regulation. Chapter 5 describes how redistributive pressure also appears among middle-income groups. The participation of the middle class in the distributive conflict intensifies the dispute for income in society and its adverse effects on economic growth.

Redistribution to the poor is a new event in the country's history and begins with the inauguration of democracy. Redistribution to the rich is old, going back to the early years of the colonization and occurs independent of the current political regime. Be it during authoritarian periods or democratic periods, strong economic groups and high-income individuals have privileged access to power and are capable of molding institutions in their favor.

The middle-income strata combines characteristics of individuals situated at the extremes and is formed by distinct and heterogeneous groups. There are middle-income individuals who, like the rich, have privileged access to government decision processes (high-ranking civil servants and public company managers, for example) and are able to influence political decisions in their favor, even before democratization.

At the same time, there are some groups with characteristics closer to those at the base of the pyramid, even though they have income levels that do not permit them to be classified as poor (organized industrial union members, for example) and who, with democratization, came to have greater organizational power through unions and associations. They were able, therefore, in the new democratic environment, to exert pressure on government to receive benefits by means of collective action (strikes, publicity campaigns, lobbying, etc.).

In the new democratic environment, intermediate income groups that have an advantage are: (a) those that have large numbers and who vote in a homogenous way (elderly, ethnic, or religious groups); (b) those that are able to organize themselves into unions and associations; (c) those that live in the same social environment as politicians (civil servants, for example); and (d) those that have the power to vote in contrast to those groups who do not vote (for example, elderly and youth *versus* children).

The increase of political power in some intermediate income segments could induce a movement in the direction of dismantling privileges created for the rich or to restrict policies in favor of the poor. This would reduce the adverse effects of redistributionism on economic performance. However, economic theory shows that, in the presence of significant inequality, it is difficult for society to come to a consensus regarding reforms that, if approved, would dismantle privileges and benefit the majority.

Given the impossibility of forming a consensus to revoke policies and institutions that benefit some groups and hurt society as a whole, the rational strategy for each group is to demand more benefits for themselves. Since each group cannot enjoy the benefits of accelerated economic growth, at least they try not to be the losers in the redistributive game.

Therefore, a confusing web of public programs is created, financed by taxes, public deficit, and cross-subsidies. At the end of the day, it is unclear as to who are the real winners and losers. Many families receive benefits and pay the bill at the same time. Such uncertainty makes it even more difficult to dismantle the whole system since it is unclear who will win and who will lose in such a reform.

For this reason, the tendency is for the dispute for income to increase over time and for the established privileges and rents to perpetuate. The pressure on public coffers and the harmful effects of excessive regulation on the economy curb the potential for economic growth.

In any country, in any political regime, redistribution to the poor, and to some extent the protection of rents for rich and middle-income groups, is normal. What seems to make the Brazilian situation *sui generis* is the fact of high inequality, coupled with the liberty to organize and make demands that exist in a democracy, intensify the incentive of these practices and take redistributive pressure to a very high level, able to hinder the operational capacity and solvency of the state, as well as affect economic growth.

CHAPTER 6

This chapter seeks to analyze the long-term effects of the low growth with dissipative redistribution model. Even if such redistribution provokes a reduction in economic growth in the short and mid-term, it can have a beneficial long-term effect.

The main argument presented in this book is that inequality is at the root of the low-growth problem. It happens that, as shown in Chapter 2, inequality is falling. So, despite the dissipation of resources, the continued fall of inequality could in the long-term achieve such a low level that the distributive conflict comes to extinguish or moderate itself.

This scenario, which we will call a **virtuous cycle**, would show a gradual increase in the middle class and a reduction of the poor in need of public redistributive policies. The middle class, more interested in a healthy business environment where they can venture and prosper, would pressure the government to reduce privileges conceded to the rich and offer quality public services, such as education and infrastructure, which would foster growth.

This change in voter preference would stimulate politicians to dismantle part of the redistributive policies (for the rich, middle class, and poor) and concentrate on a government more focused on providing high-quality public services, which would promote gains in economic productivity. With less inequality, *rent seeking* would naturally lose power.

Also, the reduction of poverty, concurrent to the fall of inequality, would free a large part of the poor from the credit restrictions that prevent them from financing a new business or educating their children. This would open new opportunities for social mobility by means of the private market, reducing the importance of social policies as an instrument to reduce poverty.

By freeing themselves from poverty, people free themselves from the harshness of daily survival and acquire the ability to plan for the future. They no longer need to focus their attention on providing their next meal. They can plan for permanent improvement for themselves and their children. Therefore, they adopt behaviors that aid in economic growth, such as greater investment in education of their heirs and an increase in the family savings account.

This means that the low growth resulting, in part, from the redistributive policy for the poor, could come to be considered a cost to be paid in the short and mid terms, but that generates long-term fruit. There would be an automatic conversion from the low growth and dissipative redistribution model to a high growth and low inequality model.

This virtuous cycle, however, is far from being a guaranteed trajectory for Brazil. The country can take a less healthy path and remain for a long period in the **vicious cycle** of low growth with dissipative redistribution. The maintenance of the current, high-cost redistributive policy can result in unsustainable costs. In this negative scenario, there would be no long-term gains. The country would remain locked in the distributive conflict, with alternating periods of modest growth, when external markets were favorable, and political crises in the descendent economic cycles, when there would be a lack of resources to pay for all the benefits demanded by social groups.

Brazil seems to oscillate between optimistic and pessimistic trajectories, such as an indecisive driver regarding which way to go at a crossroad. On one side, there is the decrease in inequality and poverty of the recent past (Chapter 2), which creates hope that there could be a change in the demands of the "ex-poor" regarding what they will be provided by the public sector. The demonstrations held in June 2013, which protested against the poor quality of public services and corruption, could be an indication of such.

However, those demonstrations could simply be a symptom of the political crisis that comes as a result of the lack of resources to maintain the generalized distribution of public benefits to everyone. In this case, the demonstrations could be considered an uncoordinated action by various groups, each of which wants to receive more and pay less without being concerned with the consistency of their demands, deepening the conflict that leads to the low growth with dissipative redistribution model.

Furthermore, as shown in Chapter 2, there are signs that the rate of inequality reduction is losing momentum and tending to stagnate. A large part of the "ex-poor" could still be considered vulnerable to a return to poverty, not having attained the economic stability typical of the middle class. Several years of frustrating GDP performance, added to the stagnation in the reduction of inequality, could return this population to poverty or maintain them in a vulnerable position and, therefore, dependent on welfare programs. Unable to free themselves from the barriers that hinder their access to credit, open new opportunities for new business and better education, these groups would perpetuate a strong demand for social assistance.

Another possibility for change in the direction of a less redistributive model and more favorable to growth comes from the possible weariness of the current model. A fiscal or a balance of payment crisis, a long period of low growth, and the decrease of public services to below a supportable standard could generate sufficient political conditions to end privileges and promote reforms. This would allow the creation of redistribution policies more focused on the poorest, reducing the economic costs of redistribution. The recent history of the country shows that the two main movements for institutional reform (1965-1967 and the second half of the 1990s) came after hard economic crises. This, however, is a risky path for it could involve a rupture with the current democratic system. However, outside crisis periods, broad reforms do not seem viable, because of the entrenched interests that block it.

Summarizing, Brazilian society is faced with two alternative routes. It can take the virtuous road of inequality reduction and gradual acceleration of growth, or it can follow the undesirable path of stagnation, fiscal imbalance, inflation, interruption of the reduction of inequality, and political and institutional crises. Many years of low growth could even create a political rupture and put democracy at risk.

Both paths are open and depend not only on the internal political debate, but also on the effects of the international economy on the country.

REFERENCE

Mendes, M.J., 2010. Controle do Gasto Público: Reformas Incrementais, Crescimento e Estabilidade Macroeconômica. CLP Papers n. 4, Available from http://www.clp.org.br/2013/wp-content/uploads/2012/11/CLP-Paper-n%C2%BA4-Mendes.pdf.

Chapter 1

Low Economic Growth and its Proximate Causes

Chapter Outline

1.1 INTRODUCTION

The main goal of this chapter is to show that the average economic growth rate in Brazil since the mid-1980s has been disappointing. It presents ten stylized facts on the Brazilian economy that constitute the immediate causes for this poor performance.

To introduce the question of economic growth, the chapter begins with Section 1.2, which summarizes the theoretical foundations of economic growth and development. After that, Section 1.3 presents a brief review of the Brazilian economic policy during the military regime, (1964-1984), showing how such a policy conditioned the choices made after the 1985 democratization. Section 1.4 shows data on economic growth, highlighting the poor Brazilian performance in terms of long-term growth since 1985. Section 1.5 focuses on the 10 Stylized Facts that explain the low growth. The final section of the chapter presents the main thesis of this book, which is: an important cause for low growth in Brazil is the coexistence of acute inequality in income and assets distribution with a democratic political regime. All 10 Stylized Facts that constitute proximate causes for low growth are, to a large extent, consequences or symptoms of this deeper cause.

1.2   SOURCES OF ECONOMIC GROWTH[1]

Economic growth basically results from the accumulation of: (a) physical capital (machinery, roads, ports, land, etc.); (b) labor (number of workers available to be employed in the productive process); (c) human capital (the ability of workers, which usually increases with their level of education); and (d) productivity (more productive economies are able to create more units of product for each unit of capital and labor employed in the productive process).

It is easy to see that production grows when more machinery and workers are employed in the productive process. It is also clear that better trained workers are able to provide more and better goods and services. Furthermore, an economy that is able to produce more than others, using the same amount of workers and physical capital (higher productivity) will tend to achieve a higher level of per capita income.

Therefore, economic growth tends to be intense in countries where private sector companies show a high rate of investment in machinery and equipment and the public and private sectors invest in infrastructure in order to make the production and sales of goods and services (energy, transportation, communications) easier. Moreover, in this ideal country there is a large number of working-age citizens available to be employed in productive activities. Workers have been educated in high-quality schools, which enable them to perform complex tasks.

It is important to note that investing in physical and human capital, in order to foster growth, comes at the cost of reducing consumption or increasing debt. Money used to finance the purchase of equipment or monthly tuition payments is the same that finances the purchase of consumer goods. Therefore, the decision to invest should be accompanied by a decision regarding the origin of the

---

1. Ray 1998 and Jones 2002 are undergraduate-level textbooks on development and growth. Acemoglu 2000 is a more advanced book on the topic.

funds used to finance the investment: reduction in consumption or increase in debt. Considering the economy as a whole, the savings accumulated by some people can be lent to others who desire to invest an amount greater than their financial resources. Therefore, the greater the level of consumption and the smaller the level of savings in a society, the less available capital there is to finance investments.

A society that, in aggregate terms, consumes a greater part of the income it generates has the option of financing investments through loans from abroad, or rather, borrowing from countries with populations that save more. One could say that using this mode of financing is equal to the use of "external savings." Opting to use external savings means accepting the fact that the country's foreign debt increases. As this debt is incurred in international currency (dollars, pounds, yens, etc.) and the national currency of developing countries, such as Brazil, is not accepted internationally, a high foreign debt brings the risk that at some time the country may not have enough international currencies on hand to pay its foreign debt.

Although necessary, high investment levels and the availability of high levels of capital (physical and human) and labor are not sufficient for a country to grow quickly and achieve a high level of development. The literature on growth and development shows that different availability of physical capital, human capital, and labor do not explain the large difference in the per capita level of income among countries. (See, for instance, Caselli, 2005.) For instance, the per capita GDP in France is 98 times higher than in Zimbabwe, and the United States is 32 times richer than The Gambia, while differences in capital and labor availability among these countries are not that high (Heston, Summers and Aten, Penn World Table Version 7.1, Center for International Comparisons of Production, Income and Prices at the University of Pennsylvania, Nov. 2012.). What makes the United States, France and other developed countries much richer than underdeveloped nations is their *productivity*: developed countries are able to use their inputs much more efficiently in order to obtain higher production levels.

Productivity depends on the level of technology adopted and how the production factors are allocated. It is not easy to explain why some countries can use better technology or can make better use of their capital and labor. Generally speaking, one can say that such countries have good "institutions" or good "social infrastructure"(Jones, 2002).

These are social norms that are business friendly and offer incentives and safety to those that intend to invest and work hard: contracts are easily enforced; the judicial system is agile and able to preserve the rule of law; companies face low administrative costs and bureaucratic requirements; the labor market is flexible (it is easy to hire and dismiss workers, without costs or penalties); creating or closing a business does not involve complex bureaucratic procedures or costs; there are no barriers to trade, such as high tariffs on external trade; taxation imposed on firms and families is not high and is evenly distributed among households; the government regulates natural monopolies and imposes rules that protect competition by means of antitrust legislation. This list is not complete and economists are far from agreeing on the conditions that are most relevant to foster productivity and growth.

However, it is easy to see why productivity tends to flourish under the conditions described above. Firms can import the best machinery available in the world, since there are no import restrictions. Banks lend at low interest rates because they are sure they can count on the courts to recover their money in case of default. As a consequence, cheap money is available to finance investments. In a fair, competitive environment, less productive firms are excluded from the market, releasing productive factors (capital and workers) that are available for employment by more productive companies. Companies do not waste time and resources on unproductive activities, such as attending to bureaucratic government procedures or paying for accounting services to perform the complex calculations required under a dysfunctional tax system.

Productivity is also determined by the allocation of resources among the three main sectors of the economy: agriculture, industry, and services. In general, the agriculture and service sectors tend to be less productive than industry because the industrial sector uses streamlined production processes and allows the easier diffusion of technology while the other two sectors usually rely on traditional production methods, especially in less developed countries. This means that the natural development process, in which industry gains importance and agriculture reduces its participation in total national production, tends to accelerate economic growth. In a second phase, when the service sector expands and industry participation in GDP shrinks, economic growth decelerates.

In a similar fashion, the age pyramid affects the evolution of *per capita* GDP. In countries where children represent a large portion of the population, there will be few adults working to provide goods and services for the whole population. The natural demographic trend of countries is to reduce the number of children per woman, which increases the proportion of adult population in relation to youth. This "demographic transition" results in a higher per capita GDP since there will be a higher percentage of the population working and creating goods and services while fewer individuals depend on the production of others. A similar phenomenon occurs when female participation in the labor market grows. On the other hand, when the majority of the population ages, per capita GDP tends to reduce since a smaller adult working population must provide goods and services to be consumed by the elderly.

Finally, it is important to notice that, from a long-term perspective, economic growth is essential to move a country to a higher level of development. Although the quality of life of the poor may improve by means of income and assets redistribution, long-term growth in *per capita* income is essential to make everybody in that society better. An economy that redistributes, but doesn't grow, will tend to be one where everybody is equal, but equally poor.

This brief description of the economic growth process is useful to understand the causes of low growth in recent Brazilian economic history. However, before presenting the stylized facts that characterize the Brazilian low-growth scenario, it is worth considering the historical background that influenced the design of the main social and economic features of the recent Brazilian democratic era, beginning in 1985, or rather, after the military dictatorship of 1964-1984, 20 years that conditioned the political choices made after democratization.

1.3   THE BRAZILIAN ECONOMY DURING THE MILITARY GOVERNMENT (1964-1984) AND THE TRANSITION TO DEMOCRACY

From 1964 to 1985 Brazil was under military rule and the right to choose political leaders was quite restricted. Main offices, such as the president of the republic, state governors and mayors of capitals, were filled by means of indirect elections overseen by military leadership.

Governing with no political pressure from voters or opposition, the military rejected liberal economic measures implanted soon after the military coup and decided to implement a nationalist development model based on the protection of national industry: state-centralized planning and forceful governmental interference and market regulation. They followed a tendency that had prevailed in the country since at least the 1940s and that was carried out in both the democratic periods as well as by the Getúlio Vargas dictatorship (1937-1945): induce industrialization by means of import substitution. In fact, they broadened this policy by closing the economy not only to industrialized consumer goods (as had been done in previous decades), but also to the import of machinery, computers and high-tech inputs (chemicals, for instance), in an attempt to foster local production.

Furthermore, the military regime expanded public infrastructure by means of public investment (mainly through the creation or expansion of state owned enterprises – SOEs). Export-led agriculture, based on large-scale commodity production, remained an important source of foreign currency. Rural political leaders, especially in backward regions, were pleased by the military, not only because of their strategic role as foreign currency providers, but also as conservative leaders that outweighed the opposing power of the urban middle class.

This type of economic policy and political strategy created a privileged class of industrial businesspeople and landowners who had access to public subsidies, political influence on economic policymaking and protection against foreign competition. National industries had a guaranteed large profit margin and no incentives to invest in quality or innovation.

On the other hand, the government neglected the basic education of the masses and invested in (tuition-free) public universities. Middle- and high-income students had the advantage in entrance exams for a seat in public universities since their families could afford good, private elementary and secondary schools, which prepared them to take the exams. This kind of policy amplified an already historically high income and wealth inequality, making Brazil one of the most unequal countries in the world.

Governmental assistance to the poor was miniscule. Public health, unemployment insurance and retirement plans were accessible only to workers employed in the formal sector, which excluded a large number of unemployed, self-employed, and workers without a formal job contract. Rural workers were especially harmed by the ongoing social policy due to their precarious and seasonal job contracts. There was no large-scope public program to assist vulnerable social groups such as the elderly, poor children, or the disabled.

From 1968 to 1980, Brazil experienced high growth rates, which resulted basically from a combination of: (a) state-induced industrialization and government investments and (b) the transition of workers from agriculture to the industry and service sectors, which raised the average productivity of the economy. The abundance of credit in international financial markets guaranteed funds for private and public investment, especially in infrastructure (at the cost of an increasing foreign debt). Improvements in human capital and technological development were not relevant sources of growth.

In the mid-1980s, the last years of military rule, Brazil was considered a successful case in economic growth (average of 6.5% PY from 1970 to 1985) but a failure in terms of income distribution, social assistance, and poverty alleviation. The Gini Index of income inequality was about 0.60 (http://www.ipeadata.gov.br) in 1985, one of the highest in the world. Eighty-three percent of the population had no more than a primary education (worse than Sub-Saharan countries such as Congo and Gabon whose indexes were 63% and 75%, respectively) (Barro and Lee, 2010). Life expectancy at birth was about 64.4 years: 170th out of 221 countries. No less than 42% of the population was poor and 18% extremely poor (http://www.ipeadata.gov.br).

To describe extreme inequality, Edmar Bacha, a Brazilian economist, created a nickname for Brazil that became famous: "Belindia" – a country that had citizens with a quality of life similar to that of Belgium, but a large amount of people living like the poor of India (Bacha, 1974).

At the end of the 1970s, and more intensely during the beginning of the 1980s, economic growth collapsed due to a perverse combination of: (a) international shocks (two oil crises and an increase in international interest rates that hurt a highly indebted government); (b) the fading out of the labor-force transition from agriculture to urban professions; (c) macroeconomic mismanagement; (d) inability of the "self-sufficient import substitution economic model" to effectively foster a productive and competitive national industry; and (e) low level of human capital.

The intense use of public resources to stimulate the economy generated chronic public deficits that, in turn, led to high inflation. High inflation and economic stagnation deepened poverty and deteriorated middle-class standards of living, which weakened political support for the military regime. A transition to democracy began in 1979. In 1985, for the first time in 20 years, a civilian president was elected by the Federal Congress, which began the transition to democracy.

The new democratic era started within the context of a huge social demand to alleviate poverty, and to provide jobs, education, and health services. Those demands, blocked during the military regime, could now be expressed by the population within the new context of free speech and the formation of political parties, labor unions, and social organizations. This is a common phenomenon in societies in the process of democratization, as expressed by the historian James Robinson:

> ... the move from non-democratic political systems (...) to more democratic systems, ought to have the effect of broadening the basis of political power.

Since, prior to the onset of democracy, power was in most cases monopolized by the richer segments of society, one would naturally conjecture that this movement would have led to pressure for policies and regulations that would be relatively favorable to the newly enfranchised, and would thus involve some redistribution of income towards the relatively poor. In short, we would expect democracy to reduce inequality relative to the levels experienced under non-democratic regimes (Robinson, 2008, p. 2).

In 1988, a new constitution was approved, expanding voting rights to all citizens over 16, including the illiterate.[2] The new constitution was a political construct that tried to balance conflicting interests inherited from the military period: (a) the demand of the poor (now empowered by vote and with a voice) for redistribution of income and poverty relief, after 21 years of weak governmental attention to these issues; and (b) pressure by high-income groups that fought to preserve the privileges obtained by means of favored access to the decision-making process, not only during the military regime, but also in the history of the country, beginning with its colonization.

The new constitution is replete with declarations regarding civil rights, but without clearly defining how to finance the necessary expense to guarantee such rights. For example:

- Article 3. The fundamental objectives of the Federative Republic of Brazil are: (...)
  - III – to eradicate poverty and substandard living conditions and to reduce social and regional inequalities; (...)
- Article 6. Education, health, food, work, housing, leisure, security, social security, protection for mothers and children, and assistance to the destitute are social rights, as set forth by this Constitution.
- Article 196. Health is a right of all and a duty of the state and shall be guaranteed by means of social and economic policies aimed at reducing the risk of illness and other hazards and the universal and equal access to actions and services for its promotion, protection, and recovery.

---

2. In fact, an amendment to the previous constitution, approved in 1985, gave voting rights to the illiterate and citizens between 16 and 18 years old. Before that amendment, the voting age was 18.

- Article 203. Social assistance shall be rendered to whoever may need it, regardless of contribution to welfare (…)
- Article 205. Education, which is the right of all and duty of the state and of the family (…)
- Article 215. The state shall ensure to all the full exercise of cultural rights and access to the sources of national culture and shall support and foster the appreciation and diffusion of cultural expressions.

This new constitutional order is <u>now</u> almost 30 years old, during which time there has been democratic stability. This is a long period by Brazilian standards. In the Republican era (beginning in 1891), the longest-lived constitution lasted 43 years (from 1891 to 1934). From 1934 to 1988, three other constitutions were approved and revoked, always in the midst of political conflict.[3]

It is not easy to maintain political stability and democratic liberties in a society where inequality is as high as in Brazil, especially after two decades of neglecting poverty relief, health and educational policies. Inequality is an obvious source of distributive and social conflict. (See, for instance, Easterly, 2001 or Rajan, 2006.) The poor, having the majority of votes, tend to pressure the government to deal with their needs and to redistribute income, wealth, and property. The rich, on the other hand, tend to use their economic power to try to maintain their privileges. Political and social stability was maintained by the public sector that distributed benefits in favor of high- and low-income groups, thereby softening conflicts. Since their demands are being gradually met by social and redistributive policies, the poor have no reason to support revolutionary or extreme populist movements. Thanks to these policies, the regime has not gone further to the left, as in countries such as Venezuela, Ecuador, and Bolivia. On the other hand, the economic elite see no reason to oppose redistributive policies because they are able to maintain their privileges.

A collateral effect of this political balance is that the demand for public benefits and subsidies expanded to the intermediate strata of society, which by means of organized interest groups, increased their access to benefits paid by public coffers. During the military government, middle-income groups enjoyed privileges, such as labor legislation that protects workers in the formal sector and tuition-free higher education. After democratization, new government benefits for this group were created, such as welfare benefits and increases in high-salary civil servant employment.

The government came to function as an income clearinghouse and protective regulator for different social groups. Public expenditure skyrocketed. Public budget and economic regulation became the main tools for income and asset distribution in favor of the poor (welfare policies), the rich (industrial policies), and middle-income groups (public service, privileged public welfare, etc.).

---

3. One of them – the 1967 constitution – was extensively rewritten 2 years after of its ratification.

In the initial years (1985-1994) of the recent democratic era, this redistributive movement occurred in an uncoordinated manner. Pressure on the National Treasury increased the inflation rate towards hyperinflation. In 1994, after five unsuccessful plans to stabilize the economy, Brazil managed to control inflation. Some institutional improvements allowed the implementation of a new fiscal regime in 1999, which was based on fiscal balance at all levels of government, improved public account transparency and an active monetary policy. An acute economic crisis forged consensus in favor of economic reforms.

This means that after a period of learning by doing, the new democratic regime was able to find a coordinated way to finance the expansion of public expenditures caused by the redistributive drive of public policy. Hyperinflation was then replaced by an ever-increasing tax burden that was capable of financing, at least in part, the expansion of public expenditure. As such, the life of the state as a distributor of privileges to different classes was prolonged.

At this point in our argumentation, we come to the central point of the book: political and social stability in Brazil has been achieved at the cost of good economic growth. High-income and asset inequality generate demand for a constantly expanding public sector (in terms of expenditure, taxes, and regulation) that seeks to maintain political and social stability.

A **low growth with dissipative redistribution model** was created. State expansion and the regulation that generated distortions weakened economic growth. The way these tensions could develop in the next decades, including a surprising reversal in direction and the acceleration of long-term growth, constitutes an interesting question to be covered in Chapter 6.

1.4   LOW GROWTH

The Brazilian economy has shown poor performance in terms of economic growth in the recent democratic era. Figure 1.1 illustrates the yearly average rate of per capita GDP growth, which is about 1.4%. For the golden years of the international commodities market (2004-2010), the figure shows a higher mean growth rate (2.8% PY).

In 2009, the world economic crisis had a profound impact on the country's growth rate. However, the prompt reaction of China's economy kept commodity prices at high levels, allowing the recovery of the Brazilian growth rate. The high rate observed in 2010 is a combination of the Chinese performance with the loose fiscal and monetary policies adopted in Brazil, which allowed a recovery from the 2009 recession by means of the occupation of the idle productive capacity left by the 2009 crisis. However, in 2011 and 2012, restrictions on the supply side of the economy brought back the low growth pattern, despite the continuation of fiscal and monetary stimuli.

How good or bad are these figures? Figure 1.2 compares the Brazilian performance with a representative set of countries for the 1985-2010 period. This set includes: Latin American neighbors; some Asian countries that represent

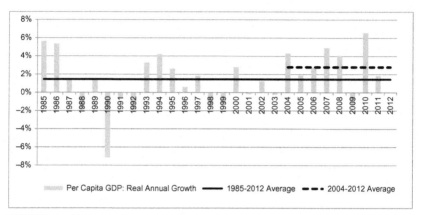

FIGURE 1.1 GDP per capita in Brazil: Annual Growth Rate (1985-2012) (%). *(Source: Central Bank of Brazil (Banco Central do Brasil). Prepared by the author.)*

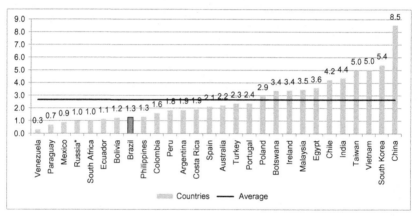

FIGURE 1.2 GDP per capita in Selected Countries: Annual Growth Rate (1985-2010) (%). *(Source: Heston, Summers and Aten, Penn World Table Version 7.1, Center for International Comparisons of Production, Income and Prices at the University of Pennsylvania, Nov. 2012. (*) Average for the 1991-2010 period. Prepared by the author.)*

success cases in terms of economic growth; an Asian country that has not been as successful as its neighbors (Philippines); members of the so-called BRIC group; a developed country whose economy is heavily dependent on commodity exports, as well as Brazil (Australia); emerging European economies hit by the 2008 crisis (Portugal, Spain, and Ireland); and other relevant middle-income countries (Turkey, Poland, and Egypt).[4] This group will be used as a comparison group throughout this chapter.

---

4. The acronym BRIC refers to Brazil, Russia, India and China. Most recently, South Africa has been included in the group. The term was created by Jim O'Neil, a Goldman Sachs executive, to denominate those countries considered emerging powerful nations.

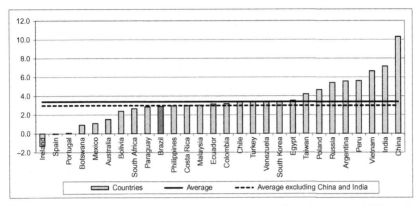

FIGURE 1.3 GDP per capita in Selected Countries: Annual Growth Rate (2004-2010) (%). *(Source: Heston, Summers and Aten, Penn World Table Version 7.1, Center for International Comparisons of Production, Income and Prices at the University of Pennsylvania, Nov. 2012. Prepared by the author.)*

It is easy to see that the Brazilian performance is not great. It is far below the group mean (straight line). Even Argentina, a country famous for wasting growth opportunities throughout history, achieved a higher mean growth. If Brazil had grown at the same pace as, for example, Costa Rica (1.9% PY) during the 26 years considered in the figure, its GDP today would be 17% higher than it now is.

Even if we consider only the best Brazilian economy sub-period of (2004-2010), the country does not appear in a prominent position, and stays below the group mean, as shown by Figure 1.3. For this period Spain, Portugal, and Ireland, heavily affected by the Euro-crisis, pulled the group mean down. However, it was not enough to put Brazil above the mean. It is important to comment on this point: we took the most favorable period in the Brazilian economy, one in which other economies in the comparison group were affected by a crisis, and despite this biased comparison in favor of the country, there is still an average growth rate under the group mean. To create an even stronger bias in favor of Brazil, we could drop two countries with high growth rates in the 2004-2010 period from the group (China and India). Even in this case, the new group mean (3.0%) is slightly higher than the Brazilian mean (2.9%).

Therefore, we can conclude that Brazilian growth performance has been poor in the last three decades.

1.5 PROXIMATE CAUSES FOR LOW GROWTH IN 10 STYLIZED FACTS

This section intends to show 10 stylized facts that characterize the Brazilian economy in the post-1985 democratic period. Taken together, these facts provide a consistent explanation for the poor growth performance during the period.

As said before, the next chapters will argue that these facts are, in reality, proximate causes for low growth since they result from a deeper cause: the coexistence of inequality and democracy.

1.5.1   STYLIZED FACT 1: Current Governmental non-Financial Expenditures have Steadily Grown

Figure 1.4 shows the real evolution of the current federal government expense between 1980 and 2012, excluding interest paid on public debt. It covers federal government expenditure with personnel, state, and municipal transfers and other ongoing expenses, such as daily administrative expenses, credit subsidies, welfare payments, etc. It is worth highlighting that government investments are not included.

What is worth noting in this figure is that the expense in 1984 was only 8% higher than that of 1980. After 1985, the year of democratization, one notices an increase in spending. In 1986, expenses were already 46% higher than in 1980 (35% higher than in 1984) and the tendency to increase persisted over three decades. In 2012, spending levels were seven times higher than in 1980. The data, therefore, is compatible with the idea that pressure from social groups in a politico-electoral democratic system makes the expansion of spending feasible, which leads to the growth of public expense.

Though illustrative of the strong general tendency for the expansion of ongoing expenses, Figure 1.4 is not precise. This is because of the intense inflationary process up to 1994 (during which there were five changes in the monetary

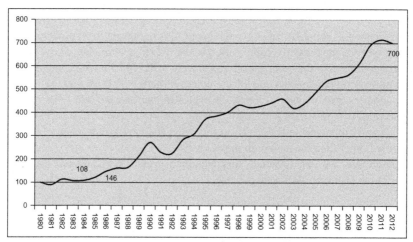

FIGURE 1.4   Current Federal Government Non-Financial Expenditures in Brazil (1980-2012) (% of GDP). *(Source: National Treasury Department (*Secretaria do Tesouro Nacional*) – Expenses of the Federal Government Grouped by Nature of Expense. Deflator: IGP-DI. Prepared by the author. Note: Includes transfers to state and municipal governments.)*

standard) and the low quality of fiscal statistics prior to 1990, reducing the trustworthiness of data referring to the 1980s and the first half of the 1990s.[5]

For this reason it was opted, as praxis in fiscal analysis of the Brazilian economy, to work with data relative to the so-called "central government primary expense," accounted for by the National Treasury as of 1997,[6] when price stability was a reality. Figure 1.5 shows that such expenses clearly grew, going from 14% to 18.3% of the GDP between 1997 and 2012. In 15 years, central government expense rose no less than 4.3 percentage points of the GDP.

The same pattern has been followed by state and municipal governments. Figure 1.6 presents the evolution of the current non-financial expenditures of the Brazilian sub-national governments between 1995 and 2011: expenses as a fraction of GDP in 2011 were 5.8 percentage points higher than in 1995.

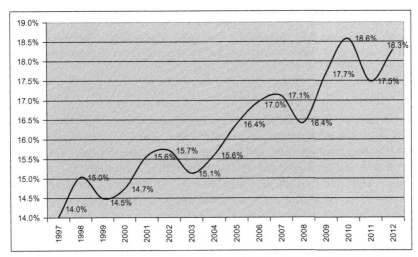

FIGURE 1.5 Current Central Government Non-Financial Expenditures in Brazil (1995-2011) (% of GDP). *(Source: National Treasury Department (Secretaria do Tesouro Nacional) – Deflator: IGP-DI. Prepared by the author.)*

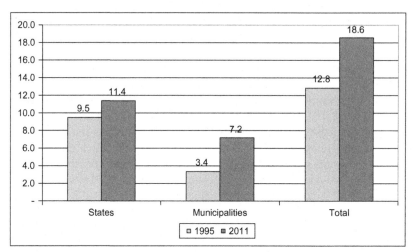

FIGURE 1.6 Current State and Municipal Governments Non-financial Expenditure in Brazil: 1995 vs. 2011 (% of GDP). *(Source: National Treasury Department (*Secretaria do Tesouro Nacional*). Prepared by the author.)*

This is not to condemn any and all public expense, considering it bad in and of itself. No doubt, as we will see in the next chapters, a significant part of the expansion of public expenditure has had positive effects in improving the quality of life for the poor and has helped reduce inequality, with positive effects for society as a whole. However, there are also many examples of resources captured by high-income groups, inefficient public programs and poor allocation of resources and expenses for which the only justification was to generate rent for pressure groups.

Figure 1.7 puts Brazilian public expenditures in an international perspective. It shows that Brazil is not only above the mean of the comparison group, but it is also close to countries that are facing tough economic crises due to high public expenses (Portugal, Spain, and Ireland) – whose GDP shrank, producing a high ratio of expenses to GDP – and to countries that took advantage of high international oil prices to finance high public expenditures (Russia, Venezuela, and Ecuador).

Therefore, the non-financial current public expense in Brazil is not only high, it is also growing. As has been previously stated, the central argument of this book is that this is a direct consequence of the coexistence of high-income inequality and ample democratic freedom. These two characteristics in Brazilian society place the Brazilian state at the center of a distributive conflict in which social group pressures for expenditures in its favor. The politicians, who depend on the vote to survive in the democratic environment, try to please their respective electoral niches and, doing so, increase public expenditure. The sum of the demand of all pressure groups is a high and ever increasing bill to be paid by taxpayers.

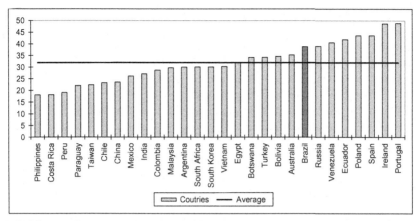

FIGURE 1.7   Government Expenditure in Selected Countries (2012) (% of GDP). *(Source: Heritage Foundation – Index of Economic Freedom (http://www.heritage.org/index/explore) Prepared by the author.)*

1.5.2   STYLIZED FACT 2: The Tax Burden had to be Raised to Finance Increasing Expenditures

The increase in public expenditures shown above was one of the causes of the hyperinflation that struck Brazil in the late 1980s. (For the Brazilian hyperinflation and the Real Plan, see Arida and Resende, 1985; Franco, 1995; Giambiagi, 2008.)

The inexistence of fiscal revenue to pay for the ever-increasing expenditure forced the government to finance it by printing money. Control of hyperinflation was achieved in 1994-1995 through the implementation of a stabilization plan called "The Real Plan," after five failed attempts.

The sudden fall in inflation rates required an increase in tax revenues for two reasons. First, because there was a reduction in the inflation tax collected by the government (currency in the hands of the population was no longer quickly devaluated by inflation): therefore the inflation tax had to be replaced by "regular" taxes. Second, because under high inflation the government could reduce the real value of its expenses by simply postponing payment for a few days. It was just a matter of letting inflation erode part of the value of the financial obligation. In the new low-inflation scenario this would no longer be possible: to finance the ever-increasing public expenditures, government had to extract more and more taxes from taxpayers.

To stabilize inflation, Brazilian society had to promote institutional improvements in order to abandon inflation as the main mechanism to finance public expenditure increases. Many hard-to-approve reforms were put in place, such as the Fiscal Responsibility Law (in 2000) and an International Monetary Fund (IMF) style bailout of sub-national debts, which imposed a credible fiscal adjustment program on those governments. (For the fiscal crisis and adjustments in the states and municipalities, see Pellegrini, 2012; Salviano, 2004; Nascimento and Debus, 2002.)

At that historic moment, the pressure exerted by the fiscal and economic crisis gave the President of the Republic the opportunity to use a heavy hand in fiscal control over states and municipalities, in spite of the political power of their representatives in Congress. As will be argued in this book, the moments of acute economic crisis have been, in Brazil, windows of opportunity for unpalatable reforms that reduce benefits enjoyed by some groups.

Given that the current expense continued its growth trajectory, the new regime of fiscal balance consisted of raising taxes. Figure 1.8 illustrates the ascending trajectory of the tax burden. In 2011 it achieved 33.5% of GDP, nine percentage points higher than in 1991. There was a jump in tax collections just after the Real Plan (1994) and the rising trend continues up to 2008, when the economic world crisis caused the government to refrain from tax increases in order to stimulate economic activity.

The level of the Brazilian tax burden is quite high when compared to countries in the comparison group. As one can see in Figure 1.9, it only loses to Argentina.

In summary, Stylized Facts 1 and 2 show that the Brazilian fiscal regime, in the new democratic era, is one of fastest increasing current public expenditures followed by increasing taxation, in an attempt to accompany the rhythm of the growth of expenses and avoid increasing the national deficit.

According to traditional growth models, high taxes impair the growth rate. Since the net return of capital after tax is reduced when taxes increase, there will be fewer stimuli to invest in physical or human capital accumulation. The pace of accumulation of those factors slows when taxes are high, affecting growth. Moreover, high taxes discourage investments in new technologies since the expected profits generated by innovation will be captured by the government.

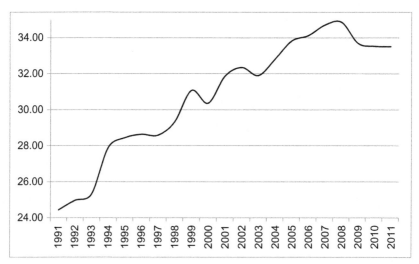

FIGURE 1.8   Overall Tax Burden (Federal, State, and Municipal) in Brazil (1991-2011) (% of GDP). *(Source: Brazil Ministry of Finance (2011) and http://www.ipeadata.gov.br. Prepared by the author.)*

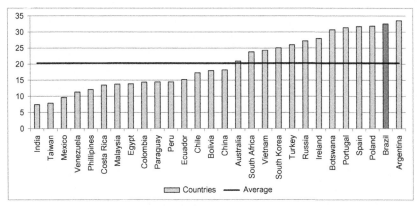

FIGURE 1.9   Tax Burden in Selected Countries (2012) (% of GDP). *(Source: Heritage Foundation – Index of Economic Freedom. Available at: http://www.heritage.org/index/explore. Prepared by the author.)*

Furthermore, in an open economy, where capital can easily migrate to countries with lower taxation, it is a disadvantage to maintain a high level of taxation.

The negative effect of taxation on investment and growth may also come through other channels that affect productivity. (See Pagés, 2010, Chapter 7 for a review on the causal relationship between high taxation and low productivity.) A good tax system explores three types of tax bases: income, consumption, and property. If taxes are restricted to these three bases, it is possible to minimize the impact of the tax system on economic decisions and, therefore, reduce efficiency distortion and welfare losses. (For a general view of the theory on taxation and economic distortions, see Stiglitz, 2000. For a specific analysis of the Brazilian case, see Biderman and Arvate, 2005.) Consumption taxation, for instance, may be done by means of a value added tax (VAT) method, that allows the discount of tax paid in previous transactions, so that the retail price is not inflated by taxes accumulated throughout intermediate transactions.

However, when a government desperately needs to increase its revenues, it tends to worsen the quality of the tax system. The main objective of the government becomes to raise money. Considerations regarding the negative impact of taxation on economic efficiency become secondary. If economic distortion is the price to be paid in order to finance the ever-growing public expenditure, government is willing to pay such a price. It is better to have fiscal stability with a tax system that hurts productivity than to have a good tax system, but that does not collect enough.

In order to maximize fiscal revenue, new tax bases started to be exploited, such as financial transactions, payroll, gross revenue, and exports, among others. Such "heterodox" taxation brings negative consequences, such as relative price distortion and misallocation of economic resources. (For more details regarding the distortions caused by cumulative taxes and the Brazilian experience with these taxes, see Varsano et al., 2001; Afonso and Araujo, 2005.) For instance, when government creates or increases payroll tax, it cannot be charged on intermediate transactions, and products that have a large chain of production (more steps between raw material production and final consumption) become more expensive than others that go direct from the producer to the consumer. Industrialized and sophisticated goods tend to become more expensive than raw products. For example, an apple goes from the producer to the final consumer by means of some intermediaries (wholesaler and retailer). On the other hand, an automobile begins the manufacturing process with the extraction of iron ore, which goes through steel mills and design studios. It involves the confection of seats, windows, etc. There is a long chain of negotiations before arriving in the showroom. At each step, tax is levied and that tax will be included in the price charged for the next step in the production chain, inflating the final product price.

This kind of taxation causes changes in the relative prices between imported and locally produced goods as well. Imported goods do not pay a cumulative tax in their country of origin; therefore they are cheaper than an equivalent good produced within the country. This fact causes national producers to pressure for commercial protection, which usually causes a new round of higher taxes by means of higher import tariffs.

Another kind of distortion is the incentive to consolidate the production of a good in one single firm, in order to avoid commercial transactions with third parties and reduce tax payments. A firm will produce something internally that could be bought from another company at a lower price and of higher quality. One company cannot be good at everything. To maximize its productivity, it must concentrate on the activities that it is good at and outsource supplies and services. Specialization has been recognized since Adam Smith as the fundamental tool to obtain increases in productivity. An economy where there are companies that specialize in tires, another in engines and still others in windshields, all of which sell to automotive manufactures, tends to be more productive than another economy where the automotive manufacturer fulfills all roles alone. In this way, a poor quality tax system interferes with the efficient allocation of resources, with a negative effect on productivity and growth.

Seeking revenue, and disregarding fairness and efficiency issues, the government tends to overtax activities that are easy to tax. In Brazil there is a concentration of tax on public utilities, company payrolls, beverages, tobacco, cars, and financial operations (Pinheiro and Giambiagi, 2006). Once more, there is an interference in relative prices that distorts incentives to invest and prevents the efficient allocation of resources.

Furthermore, as a tax system becomes more complex and focused in maximizing revenue, taxpayer compliance costs go up. There are more rules with which to comply, and the high total cost of paying taxes makes it worth the expense to hire specialized lawyers to exploit loopholes in legislation and reduce tax payments.

The high level of taxation also creates room for political demand and lobby for special treatment and tax exemptions. At the end of the day, the tax system becomes more and more complex, full of exceptions and special treatments.

Company administrative costs go up and productivity goes down. Those firms that succeed in avoiding taxes gain a competitive edge in relation to those that are fully taxed. This advantage reduces their incentives to invest in technology and product improvements, since they can earn profits above the market average without making any extra effort. Once more productivity and growth take a back seat.

Brazil is a typical case of a country whose tax system prioritizes the maximization of revenue in detriment of the neutrality of taxation. There are plenty of unconventional tax bases, cumulative incidences, and complex legislation. A prime example is the fact that receipts generated by taxes that have a cumulative effect on the production chain went up from 2.77% of GDP in 1985 to 6.71% in 2011 (Afonso and Araujo, 2005 and Receita Federal do Brasil – Estudos Tributários, *Carga Tributária Brasileira* 2011. Taxes considered: COFINS, PIS-PASEP, CPMF, ISS, IOF and Single Taxes on energy, fuel and minerals.)

Table 1.1 presents the number of hours a medium-size company needs to prepare, file and pay three major types of taxes and contributions (World Bank, 2013a, p. 122).

TABLE 1.1 Time Required to Comply with Three Major Taxes in Selected Countries (2012) (hours per year)

Country	Hours per Year
Ireland	80
Australia	109
Malaysia	133
Botswana	152
Spain	167
Russia	177
Philippines	193
South Africa	200
Colombia	203
South Korea	207
Taiwan	221
Turkey	223
Costa Rica	226
India	243
Portugal	275

Continued

TABLE 1.1 Time Required to Comply with Three Major Taxes in Selected Countries (2012) (hours per year)—cont'd

Country	Hours per Year
Poland	286
Chile	291
Peru	293
Mexico	337
China	338
Paraguay	387
Egypt	392
Argentina	405
Ecuador	654
Venezuela	792
Vietnam	872
Bolivia	1025
Brazil	**2600**

Source: The World Bank – Doing Business http://www.doingbusiness.org/data. Prepared by the author.

In Brazil a firm spends 2600 hours per year dealing with tax procedures. The country is last among the 28 countries in the comparison group. In fact, in this item, Brazil ranks as the last of all 180 countries considered in the World Bank's *Doing Business* database. The country that is situated just above Brazil in this ranking (Bolivia) spends less than half of the time consumed in Brazil.

The federal government has made three major attempts to rationalize the fiscal system: 2003, 2008, and 2012, all of which were buried by Congress. In the proposed 2008 reform, the Ministry of Finance (Brazil Ministry of Finance, 2008) published a study that detailed the distortions and inefficiencies in the current system and estimated that the reform could lead, in the long term, to a GDP 12% greater than the one that would be produced by maintaining the *status quo*.

One of the main reasons for the failure of many reform attempts is the simple fact that rationalization results in lower revenue, and the players involved in the negotiation (states, municipalities, the federal government) fear losing their most needed revenue, without which they are unable to attend to the persistent pressure for expenditures (Stylized Fact 1).

Since the political priority is to keep expenditures high, every bill proposal that intends to reform the tax system does not survive the political vetoes.

In summary, tax policy is endogenous to the political decisions of expenditure increase. (For a description and analysis of tax reform attempts, see Varsano and Afonso, 2004; Zouvi et al., 2008; Giambiagi, 2008; Varsano, 1997; Friedmann, 2011.)

1.5.3   STYLIZED FACT 3: Tax Increases were not Sufficient to Finance Growing Expenditures and, as a Consequence, Public Sector Savings became Negative

In spite of efforts by tax-collection institutions, revenues did not accompany the rate of expense growth. As a consequence, a gap remained between the two, which represented a fiscal deficit, as shown in Figure 1.10. During the new democratic era, the public sector has presented a deficit in its accounts, which is the same as saying that there is a negative savings in the public sector.

When the public sector drains part of society savings to finance its current expenditures, there are fewer resources available to finance private sector investments. Consequently, economic growth recedes, because less investment leads to a slower rate of fiscal capital accumulation.

There are three sources of savings in an economy: foreign savings, domestic public savings, and domestic private savings. When public savings are low or negative, investments must be financed by foreign or domestic private savings. External savings are nothing more than the deficit of a country in its current transactions account abroad, which causes international resources to flow into the country. Since Brazil only issues Reais, any devaluation of the national

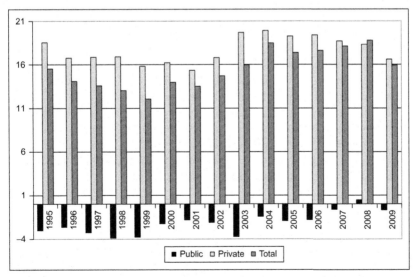

FIGURE 1.10   Public, Private, and Total Savings in Brazil (1995-2009) (% of GDP). *(Source: Levi and Giambiagi 2013. Prepared by the author.)*

currency makes the foreign debt more expensive, which could financially strangle companies and public entities.

This means that the country cannot rely heavily on this source of savings due to the risk of an unsustainable increase in its external debt. During the military regime, Brazil used external savings intensively and became vulnerable to external crises. The same happened again in the 1990s. Therefore, the dangers and restrictions involved in the use of foreign savings are clear to politicians and policymakers.[7]

Due to limitations in the use of external savings and the negative balance in government savings, private domestic savings become the main source of financing for physical capital. If these savings are insufficient to sustain an adequate level of investments, economic growth is threatened.

Hausmann, Rodrik, and Velasco created a method to diagnose the fundamental causes for low growth in some economies. They consider that, in Brazil's case, the lack of savings is a fundamental cause of sluggish growth:

> *[Brazil] has been trying to cope with the paucity of domestic savings by both attempting to attract foreign savings and by remunerating domestic savings at very high real rates. Over time, the country has borrowed so much from abroad that it has been perceived as being on the brink of bankruptcy, (as indicated by the spread on its foreign debt). In addition, Brazil's growth performance has moved pari passu with the tightness of the external constraint. **When the external constraint is relaxed** say, because of an increase in the general appetite for emerging market risk or because of **higher commodity prices**, as in recent months, the economy is able to grow. But when the external constraint tightens real interest rates increase, the currency depreciates and growth declines. **This suggests that growth is limited by the availability of savings**. (Hausmann et al., 2005, p. 13; emphasis added.)*

The dependence on external savings for Brazilian growth, due to the lack of internal savings, is reflected above in Figure 1.1. As commented, the average growth rate goes up as of 2004 in response to the improvement in terms of trade due to the boom in the commodities market, which relieved the restriction on external savings for the country, allowing higher growth.

Figure 1.11 shows this relationship in a clearer way: the real GDP variations follow *pari passu* the variations in terms of trade (price of exports in relation to price of imports). There is a positive correlation (0.61) between the two series.

Ex-Central Bank president, Affonso Celso Pastore, interprets this correlation in one of his habitual journalistic articles:

> *Causality tests applied to these two series show that the changes in commodities prices are what caused variations in the GDP, not vice versa, and the positive,*

---

7. Besides the specific country restriction on the use of foreign savings, it is important to emphasize that, worldwide, investments are closely related to domestic savings, as shown by the seminal contribution of Feldstein and Horioka, 1980.

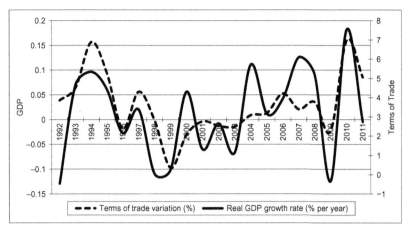

FIGURE 1.11 GDP and Terms of Trade in Brazil: Annual Rate of Change (1992-2011) (%). *(Source: World Bank database (http://data.worldbank.org/) and http://www.ipeadata.gov.br. Prepared by the author.)*

*high, stable correlation between the two attests that the acceleration in commodities prices causes acceleration in GDP growth. Both the increased growth in the 2006-2008 period and the strong recovery in 2010 are, in large part, fruit of an accented growth in commodities. (...) increases in commodity prices lead to gains in terms of trade, which **allows investment growth above national savings, which are small,** leading to the absorption of external savings by means of net imports, without current accounts being excessively pressured. (Pastore, 2013; emphasis added.)*

Therefore, there is evidence that the scarcity of savings is an active restriction that limits investments in the Brazilian economy and, with that, restricts GDP growth. The takeoff of public expenditure (Stylized Fact 1), insufficiently covered by the expansion of revenue (Stylized Fact 2), raised the public deficit, creating a negative public savings and, therefore, sharpening the scarcity of savings.

By the law of supply and demand, when there is a scarcity of savings, the price of this scarce "merchandise" increases. The "price" of savings is the interest rate: whoever desires to borrow money to make an investment will pay dearly for it. This is the next Stylized Fact to be analyzed.

1.5.4   STYLIZED FACT 4: High Interest Rates

One of the most remarkable features of the Brazilian economy is the high level of interest rates. Figure 1.12 shows the real interest rate in bank-lending operations. Although there has been a consistent reduction in that rate throughout the years, it is still very high. In 2011, the last year of the series, it was about 34.5% per year.

Figure 1.13 contrasts Brazilian interest rates with the comparison group in 2010-2011. It is clear that the Brazilian rate is an outlier. Even if one takes the

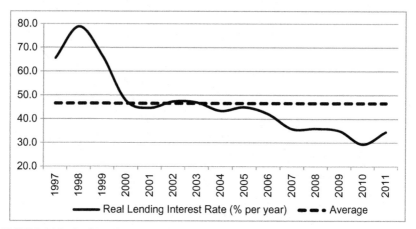

FIGURE 1.12   Real Lending Interest Rate in Brazil (1997-2011) (% PY). *(Source: World Bank database (http://data.worldbank.org/). Note: Inflation measured as the GDP deflator. Prepared by the author.)*

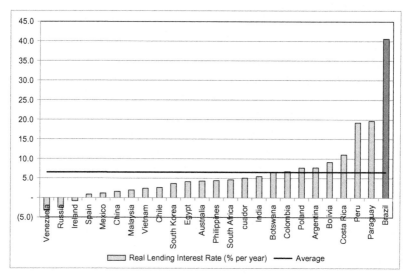

FIGURE 1.13   Real Lending Interest Rate in Selected Countries: Average for 2010-2011 (% PY). *(Source: World Bank database (http://data.worldbank.org/). Note: Inflation measured as the GDP deflator. There is no available data for Portugal, Turkey, and Taiwan. Prepared by the author.)*

lowest rate observed in Brazil since 2000 (29% in 2010) it is still much above the figures in other countries.

This remarkable feature of the Brazilian economy has, for many years, been considered the main, exogenous cause for low growth. Many politicians and economists argued that it was ideological shortsightedness by the Central Bank to set high interest rates in its operations with the banking sector. This "error" in economic policy was, in their view, responsible for the low rate of investment.

Actually, high interest rates are nothing more than a consequence of a low savings rate in the economy. It is a symptom of the low growth problem and not a cause.

The recent economic history of the country shows that interest-rate increases are consequences of one of two factors: (1) balance of payment crises, in which interest goes up in order to attract foreign money; and (2) inflationary pressure due to aggregate demand expansion.

Both phenomena are consequences of the high rate of increase in government non-financial expenditures (Stylized Fact 1). This chronic expansionary fiscal policy permanently pressures aggregate demand and erodes aggregate savings (Stylized Fact 3). Balance of payment crises are a result of the excessive use of external savings (due to the scarcity of internal savings), and the excess of aggregate demand is a direct result of government expenditures, which represents a push in aggregate demand for goods and services.

A recent econometric analysis of the question by Alex Segura-Ubiergo clearly makes this point. The text, which has the suggestive title of "The Puzzle of Brazil's High Interest Rate," shows the importance of low domestic savings, especially low savings in the public sector, as the cause of high interest rates:

> ... *increasing domestic savings would seem to be the single most important factor to reduce real interest rates in Brazil over time. This is the variable that has potentially the most promising effect because Brazil still has a low level of domestic savings and there is therefore substantial room for this variable to expand. Raising domestic savings to the level of Mexico would reduce the average difference with the rest of the IT emerging markets by almost 50 percent.*
>
> *Increasing domestic savings through an improvement in the fiscal position is likely to produce potentially larger effects. (Ubiergo, 2012, p.16; emphasis from the original.)*

In other words: the central cause of high interest rates is the low Brazilian savings rate, especially a low public savings rate (Stylized Fact 3). As proposed before, low public savings comes from the ever-increasing current non-financial expenditures (Stylized Fact 1). Although taxes had been raised (Stylized Fact 2), it was not enough to balance the public budget. High interest rates are a symptom of the problem, not its cause.

1.5.5   STYLIZED FACT 5: Infrastructure Bottlenecks

There is an outstanding shortage of infrastructure services in Brazil. Table 1.2 shows that the country is the 107th out of 140 nations in a ranking of overall infrastructure quality: it is in the 8th decile of the distribution. Among the 28 countries in the comparison group, Brazil repeats its bad performance: 21st of 28; still in the 8th decile.

TABLE 1.2 Overall Quality of Infrastructure: Ranking of Selected Countries (2012-13)

Country	Ranking
Portugal	11
Spain	18
South Korea	22
Taiwan	27
Malaysia	29
Chile	31
Turkey	34
Australia	36
Ireland	37
South Africa	58
Botswana	64
Mexico	65
China	69
Poland	79
Ecuador	85
India	87
Egypt	88
Costa Rica	95
Philippines	98
Russia	101
Brazil	**107**
Colombia	108
Peru	111
Argentina	112
Bolivia	118
Vietnam	119
Venezuela	135
Paraguay	140

Source: The World Economic Forum. The Global Competitiveness Report. Prepared by the author.

TABLE 1.3 Brazilian Rank in The World Economic Forum Index of Infrastructure Quality (2012-2013)

	Highways	Railways	Ports	Air Transport	Energy Supply
Comparison Group (28 Countries)	22	23	26	27	13
All Countries in Sample (144 Countries)	123	100	136	134	68

Source: The World Economic Forum. The Global Competitiveness Report. Prepared by the author.

Transportation infrastructure is a special concern. As show in Table 1.3, Brazil is among the worst countries in terms of roads, ports, airports, and railroads. Even in a sector where the country has comparative advantages, such as electric supply (there are plenty of rivers that can be used to generate hydroelectric power), the country scores no higher than an intermediate rank.

Between 1940 and 1990 Brazil built an integrated system of hydroelectric power generation that allowed the country to provide an efficient system of energy distribution to the different areas of the country. However, limited resources to maintain and expand the system resulted in underinvestment. An energy crisis due to insufficient supply erupted in 2001, causing extensive losses in terms of economic growth. Twelve years after that traumatic energy supply crisis, the country still walks on the razor's edge: slight reductions in rainfall trigger concerns about shortages in energy supply.

Sanitation is another area of concern, especially in metropolitan areas where large numbers of inhabitants live in slums. Although there is not an international comparison for some relevant statistics in sanitation, the fact that 53.3% of the population is not connected to a sewer network and that 62% of the collected sewer is not treated reveals that there is much to be done in this area (Frischtak, 2013; original source: National Water Agency (ANA)).

Public and private investments in infrastructure have been kept at low levels for a long time. Table 1.4 shows that until 1980, Brazil had a relatively good level of infrastructure investment, above 5% of GDP. During that period, before the huge fiscal crisis that occurred at the end of the military government, those investments were basically made by public entities (central and state governments, public enterprises). After 1980, the level of investment fell and is currently around 2% of GDP.

The reduction in public investment was not accompanied by a parallel increase in private investment, causing a slowdown in the supply of infrastructure

TABLE 1.4 Infrastructure Investment in Brazil by Economic Sector (1971-2010) (% of GDP)

	1971-1980	1981-1989	1990-2000	2001-2010
Electricity	2.13	1.47	0.76	0.67
Telecomunications	0.8	0.43	0.73	0.64
Transportation	2.03	1.48	0.63	0.64
Water and Sewer	0.46	0.24	0.15	0.19
TOTAL	5.42	3.62	2.27	2.14

Source: Frischtak (2013).

services. Table 1.5 shows that private investment fluctuates at around 1% of GDP for the whole period, while public investment fell from more than 3% to near 1% of GDP.

Cláudio Frischtak, an economist specialized in infrastructure, estimates that Brazil should invest at least 3% of its GDP in order to: (a) preserve the existing infrastructure capital stock (1% of GDP); (b) cope with population growth (1.3% of GDP); (c) offer a 100% coverage of water and sanitation services in a 20-year span; and (d) offer 100% coverage of electric supply in a 5-year span (Frischtak, 2008). Therefore, keeping infrastructure investment around 2% of GDP, as shown in Table 1.5, is clearly insufficient. The same author estimates that Brazil would need infrastructure investments of 5% to 7% of GDP to catch up to South Korean standards.

Efficiency in infrastructure service provision depends on the complementary actions of public and private providers. For instance, privately managed ports will be able to receive large ships only if the public sector provides adequate

TABLE 1.5 Infrastructure Investment in Brazil by Ownership (1981-2011) (% of GDP)

	1981-1986	2001-2006	2007	2008	2009	2010	2011
Public	3.6	1.15	0.92	1.12	1.48	1.43	1.08
Private	1.54	0.97	0.94	1.37	1.02	0.92	0.97
TOTAL	5.15	2.11	1.86	2.49	2.5	2.35	2.05

Sources: Calderon and Servén, 2010; Frischtak, 2013.

dredging and rock removal services. The construction of hydroelectric power dams by the government may include the construction of sluices that allow for the private construction of waterways. A centralized government energy distribution system may be required to maximize efficiency in the use of energy generated by many private firms.

In fact, World Bank economists César Calderon and Luís Servén, who did research in an attempt to evaluate the causal nexus between infrastructure availability and economic growth worldwide, argue that there is a positive correlation between private and public infrastructure investment in Latin America. Countries such as Chile and Colombia have high levels of public and private infrastructure investment, while Brazil, Peru, and Mexico face low levels in both types of investment (Calderon and Servén, 2010).

In addition to this complementarity, the government also has an important role in stimulating private infrastructure services that create positive externalities for society. For instance, some diseases are controlled by sanitation; pollution is reduced when public transportation substitutes cars; company productivity is enhanced when traffic jams are reduced, etc. Since private infrastructure services providers are not concerned with these externalities (profit is their main objective), the level of service they provide tends to be lower than the social optimum. For instance, there is no incentive to offer private sanitation to poor areas where the population cannot afford the service. Therefore, government must interfere through subsidies, direct public provision or regulation, in order to amplify the service supply.

Furthermore, an efficient infrastructure network requires large doses of long-term planning and coordination, which are intrinsically a government task: interconnection of different modes of transportation, choosing between two competitive and mutually exclusive options of investment; inventory of available sources of hydropower and other natural resources, etc.

Therefore, a good infrastructure, one that includes private sector participation, requires intense governmental participation. Specifically, it requires a government that: (a) has present and future funds available to make complementary investments and to subsidize fees when externalities and distributive issues are relevant; (b) can provide stable and efficient regulatory institutions (regulatory agencies, judiciary, audit agencies); and (c) has public agencies specialized in infrastructure planning and coordination.

How does Brazil fit into these requirements? The quality of regulation, judiciary efficiency and respect for the rule of law and property rights are questions that will be analyzed below (Stylized Fact 8). For now, suffice it to say that these institutions are far from perfect and, in fact, represent obstacles to a deeper involvement by the private sector in the provision of infrastructure.

The availability of funds is a central issue. Since current expenditure skyrocketed after democratization (Stylized Fact 1), investments became secondary. A pivotal institutional change against infrastructure investments was the abolition of the earmarking of funds for that kind of investment. This earmarking clause was part of the 1967 Federal Constitution and was abolished by the new 1988 Constitution. Tax revenues that were previously reserved to finance infrastructure investment were transferred to a common pool and became available to finance current expenditures. This was a preview of the major changes in political priorities in public resource allocation that would occur in the following years: a shift from investments to current expenditures.

The intense pressure to remedy poverty and social needs, in the new democratic era, in which politicians depend on a popular vote, was a central cause for this change in priorities. Infrastructure investments have a positive impact on poverty reduction on a long-term horizon, but the pressure for immediate changes and the election calendar could not wait that long. (Frischtak, 2013 summarizes the literature on the causal relationship between infrastructure investment and economic growth and provides bibliographical references.)

More than two decades of compressed public and private investment in infrastructure resulted in the scrapping of public institutions devoted to planning and coordinating those investments. A symbol of this reality is the extinction of the Brazilian Transportation Planning Company (GEIPOT), a public enterprise where a team of highly-skilled engineers were in charge of defining the main guidelines of the national transportation network. The extinction or privatization of companies in areas such as telecommunications and energy also reduced the ability of the government to plan and coordinate, since these companies were managed under strict central government control, and their professionals could interact with each other in the design of nationwide projects. It does not mean that they were perfect or efficient planning and coordination instruments. But there was some centralized planning that was disassembled in the 1990s and not replaced by any other public agency able to strategically analyze future needs in terms of infrastructure.

Anand Rajaram and his colleagues from the World Bank (Rajaram et al., 2008) set up a guide to evaluate the quality of public investment management. The World Bank (World Bank, 2009) applied such an evaluation to Brazil. Almost all potential problems listed by Rajaram et al. are found in the Brazilian case: inability to select priority projects and discard those less important (including the waste of public money in building "white elephants"); delays in all phases of project planning and execution; corruption and inefficiency in procurement; cost overruns; many unfinished and abandoned projects; and inability to efficiently operate and maintain the existent infrastructure.

In the mid-1990s, Brazil implemented an extensive privatization program. Following a world trend, the country tried to insert profit motive in the infrastructure sector in order to stimulate efficiency and productivity and, at the same time, solve the problem of the lack of government funds.

Privatization allowed improvement in some areas. Telecommunications is the main success story. Once technological innovations reduced the natural monopoly features in this sector and introduced the potential for competition, there was a noticeable improvement in the coverage and quality of service. However, whenever regulation and coordination issues are relevant, problems appear, since the regulatory governmental body is kept politically and technically weak (as shown in Chapter 3). For instance, there are problems in areas such as: the use of infrastructure owned by one company by its competitors; licenses to install antennas in public areas and the enforcement of quality standards and consumer rights.

There was progress in the privatization of roads, but only those that were located in the more developed regions of the country, especially in the state of São Paulo. The quality and availability of privatized roads improved, but there are political conflicts concerning toll prices. Given that this is an explicit expense (users feel it in the wallet every time they pass the toll booth), several politicians have found a political niche in the criticism of tolls as a way to garner votes, pressuring for the reduction of the prices charged. This led to a federal highway privatization program with an emphasis on charging cheap tolls, which has reduced incentives for the private sector to invest in road improvements (this issue will be taken up again in Chapter 5).

Summarizing, Brazil faces infrastructure bottlenecks due to a combination of: (a) political preferences for current expenditures in detriment to public investment; (b) lack of government ability to plan and coordinate; and (c) political and financial frailty of regulatory agencies and other institutional weaknesses that interfere with active participation by the private sector.

Insufficient infrastructure inhibits economic growth in Brazil for several reasons. It is intuitive that good infrastructure: (a) opens new markets (for instance, connecting faraway cities to dynamic economic centers); (b) reduces costs (transportation, communication); (c) increases worker productivity (health improvement, fast urban transportation); (d) amplifies production scale by reducing average costs (large ports); (e) makes essential inputs available at affordable prices (energy, water); and (f) intensifies competition (easier access of imports to the internal market). (Pagés, 2010 extensively demonstrates the mechanisms that connect infrastructure to economic productivity.)

In the Brazilian case, there is evidence that infrastructure shortage is in fact a real constraint to economic growth. The already mentioned economic downturn caused by the 2001 energy crisis is a clear example. In 2014 the country was again under an energy shortage threat, which shows the persistence of the problem for more than a decade.

Transportation is another field where the impact of insufficient infrastructure seems strong. Commodities are quite important items in Brazilian exports. They usually have low unitary prices and are heavy. Therefore, commodity exports require transportation of large amounts of heavy cargo, which means that freight is an important cost item. Soy exports are an interesting example. Brazil is probably the most efficient producer in the world. However, transportation costs erode this advantage.

Carmen Pagés conducted an extensive study of the Inter-American Development Bank (IADB) regarding Latin American economy productivity. This research shows that transportation costs represent 32% of the total cost of Brazilian soy against only 18% of the cost of the soy produced in the United States. Consequently, the total production and transportation costs together are the same in both countries, despite the fact that the cost before transportation is much lower in Brazil. While in the United States producers may choose between rail or highway transportation, in Brazil, bumpy roads are the only option (Pagés, 2010, p. 132).

Another study of the IADB by Maurício Marques Mesquita and co-authors (Mesquita et al., 2008) shows that infrastructure deficiency is more harmful to Brazilian exports than the commercial protection of developed countries or the unavailability of general trade agreements. Fernando Lagares Távora came to the same conclusion after developing a microeconomic model to study the international soybean market (Távora, 2008).

Urban traffic congestion is another clear example of how insufficient infrastructure precludes productivity gains and efficiency. A study done by the Brazilian government in 1999 concluded that traffic congestion in the city of São Paulo raises public transportation operational costs by 15.8%, while in Brasilia (a city with more fluid traffic) it represented only 0.9% of total costs (Pagés, 2010, p. 131).[8]

The continental dimension of the country is another factor that makes transportation a pivotal input. The unavailability of good roads or railways marginalizes cities and regions that are far from developed cities, where a large part of national production is consumed. At the same time, protected by high transportation costs, firms located closer to the consumer market have lower incentives to invest and raise productivity. In contrast to this isolation scenario, the historical experience of the United States shows the importance of an efficient transportation network for interregional trade and production specialization. Furthermore, lower transportation costs make it possible for consumers and companies to buy products and inputs in distant places, increasing competition and productivity (Pagés, 2010, pp. 130-131).

In summary, infrastructure weakness seems to be a real constraint to growth in Brazil. To overcome this problem the country will need to not only stimulate private participation in the sector, but also increase public funds to direct complementary investments, reinforce planning and coordination, and strengthen regulatory bodies. However, the political priority given to current expenditure expansion (Stylized Fact 1) represents a clear constraint to infrastructure development.

---

8. Since the publication of this study, traffic conditions in Brasilia have deteriorated and a repeat of the research would certainly reveal a greater impact of congestion on transport costs in this city as well.

1.5.6 STYLIZED FACT 6: Skyrocketing Minimum Wage

Figure 1.14 shows the evolution of the real value of minimum wage since 1990. From 1990 to 1995 it presents wide oscillations without a clear trend, due to high inflation and short time intervals between the readjustments of the nominal value. The real value oscillated a lot but did not increase over time.

After 1995, hyperinflation was no longer a concern and the real value of the minimum wage began a long-term upward trend. In January 2013 it was 170% higher than in January 1995. This resulted from a deliberate federal government policy. Politicians quickly realized that real increases in a widely known wage parameter were a strong voting incentive for the poor, whose incomes were directly or indirectly influenced by the minimum wage.

Minimum wage was quite low at the end of the 1990s. As such, in the initial years of this policy there were no significant impacts on production costs, since the real value of that wage was low. However, after almost 20 years of successive real increases, the minimum wage began to represent an important source of expense for companies.

Brazil has a large number of workers with a low level of education and no professional training, which results in low productivity. Forcing firms to pay them a minimum wage that is probably above their productive capabilities stimulates companies to restrict demand for low-qualified workers. This could push less qualified labor into the informal market, where they would receive less than the legal limit.

However, there is clear empirical evidence that the minimum wage works as a reference for salary payments, not only in the formal market but in informal

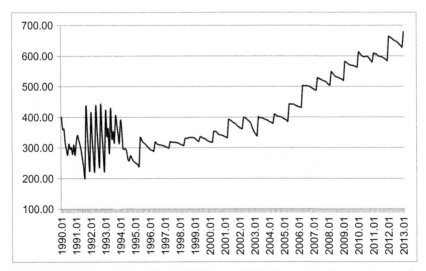

FIGURE 1.14   Minimum Wage in Brazil (R$ of January 2013). *(Source: http://www.ipeadata.gov.br. Deflator: National Consumer Price Index (INPC). Prepared by the author.)*

activities as well. (See, for instance, Neri et al., 2001.) As a consequence, minimum-wage increases create cost pressures not only in formal businesses, but in the informal sector as well. The minimum-wage readjustment is also a reference to update salaries that are higher than the minimum. It is not uncommon for salaries to be indexed to minimum wage: job contracts stipulate that the salary will be, for instance, equal to two or three times minimum wage. Therefore, the mean real salary of the economy tends to rise when minimum wage goes up. (Brazil Central Bank, 2011, pp. 23-25.)

In other words, even though the Brazilian minimum wage represents, in itself, low remuneration (in 2014 it was R$724 per month, or about US$1.97 per hour worked) (considering an exchange rate of R$2.30 per US dollar and 20 working days per month, 8 hours per day), its readjustment impacts the salary structure that goes beyond the group of laborers who receive the minimum, both in the formal and informal market.

Real salary increases that arise from productivity gains do not affect business costs. When salaries grow ahead of productivity for a short period, companies may squeeze their profit margin and the salary increase is absorbed without macroeconomic impacts. However, a long period of salary increases above productivity gains reduces expected profits and, therefore, discourages investments, with a negative impact on economic growth (Brazil Central Bank, 2013, pp. 94-102). Figure 1.15 shows that minimum wage and mean salaries are growing at higher rates than worker productivity. While minimum wage rose by

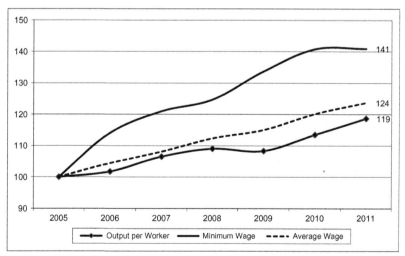

FIGURE 1.15   Minimum Wage, Mean Salary, and Labor Productivity in Brazil: Index of Real Values (2005 = 100). *(Sources: http://www.ipeadata.gov.br: Minimum wage and average wage (deflated using INPC). Average wage is the "usual income from the main occupation for employed people in metropolitan regions – Monthly employment enquires – IBGE"* (rendimento habitual do trabalho principal das pessoas ocupadas em regiões metropolitanas – *Pesquisa Mensal de Emprego – Brazilian Institute of Geography and Statistics (IBGE)).)*

5.9% PY and the mean salary increased by 3.6% PY, worker productivity had a more modest performance, growing by 2.9% PY. Therefore, the public policy of real increases in the minimum wage may be blocking growth by means of lower investments due to low expected profits.

Heston, Summers and Aten, Penn World Table Version 7.1, Center for International Comparisons of Production, Income and Prices at the University of Pennsylvania, Nov. 2012: Worker productivity up to 2009.

IBGE National Accounts and PME – employed population: Worker productivity for 2010-2011.

Even if one considers the Brazilian minimum wage low and incapable of affecting business costs, there is another channel that works through public expenditures. The 1988 Federal Constitution states that social security benefits shall not be inferior to one minimum wage (Brazilian Federal Constitution, Article 201, Paragraph 2). Other social assistance programs define the amount paid to beneficiaries in multiples of minimum wage (in general, they pay exactly one minimum wage).

Figure 1.16 shows the evolution of the share of the federal public expenditures indexed to the minimum wage. Social assistance and social security benefit expenses amounted to 6.6% of GDP in 1998. Fourteen years later they had reached 8.7% of GDP.

Figure 1.16 simulates the evolution of this expenditure in a scenario where benefits were readjusted only by the inflationary index, instead of using the minimum wage as reference. In this case the evolution of expenditures would

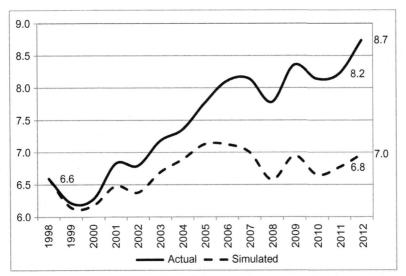

FIGURE 1.16 Social Assistance and Social Security Benefits Indexed or Influenced by the Minimum-Wage Value in Brazil: Observed and Simulated Values (1998-2012) (% of GDP). *(Source: Finance Ministry – Economic Policy Department (SPE).)*

be determined by the increase in the number of benefits paid, since the real value of the unitary benefit would remain constant. In this simulated path, total expenditures in social assistance and social security benefits would total 7% of GDP in 2012: 1.7 percentage points lower than the observed expenditure. Therefore, real increases in minimum wage significantly affected overall public expenditure.

Simulation was made based on the hypothesis that 27% of the social security benefits were equal to one minimum wage in 1998, with an increase of 1 percentage point per year in this proportion. Prepared by the author.

Figure 1.5 (shown above in Stylized Fact 1) shows that the central government's primary expense grew from 15% to 18.3% of GDP between 1998 and 2012, or rather, 3.3 percentage points. Figure 1.16 shows that 1.7 percentage points of the increase were caused by the indexing of some expenditures and social benefits to minimum wage. Therefore, 51% of the increase in primary central government expense was caused by increases in minimum wage. Of course, this is an extremely relevant factor in the generation of expense increase.

In conclusion, we may say that real increases in the minimum-wage tend to negatively affect growth by means of two channels: compression of expected profits and increase of public current expenditures.

Despite this, there is evidence that the increase of minimum wage above inflation has contributed to the reduction of income inequality (as will be shown in Chapter 2). Such benefit, however, is accompanied by negative consequences as seen above. The strong political-electoral appeal of minimum-wage increases prevents a rational evaluation of the cost-benefit of this policy as well as the design of a strategy to reduce real readjustments after so many years of real gains. The presidential candidate who speaks openly about reducing the rhythm of real adjustments to minimum wage will have taken the first step to be defeated. Their adversaries will immediately label them as an "enemy of the poor."

1.5.7   STYLIZED FACT 7: The Brazilian Economy is Closed to International Trade

Figure 1.17 presents a measure of economic openness (exports plus imports as a proportion of GDP). Brazil is the most closed economy in the comparison group.

It is interesting to note that Brazil is in this position despite the fact that in the 1990s there was an important shift in its trade policy, which promoted a significant reduction in trade barriers (Menezes Filho and Kannebley, 2013; Pinheiro and Giambiagi, 2006; Corseuil and Kume, 2003 describe trade liberalization in Brazil). In fact, Figure 1.18 shows an upward tendency of the Brazilian openness index after the late 1980s. However, there was a generalized movement of trade liberalization around the world and, although audacious by national standards, Brazilian liberalization fell short in comparison (Pinheiro and Giambiagi, 2006).

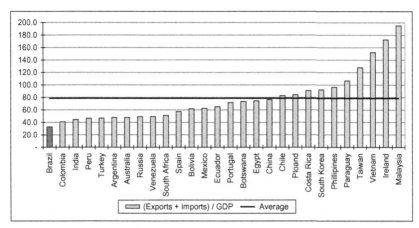

FIGURE 1.17   Trade Openness in Selected Countries: Exports Plus Imports as a Percentage of GDP (2010). *(Source: Heston, Summers and Aten, Penn World Table Version 7.1, Center for International Comparisons of Production, Income and Prices at the University of Pennsylvania, Nov. 2012. Note: Measured at 2005 prices. Prepared by the author.)*

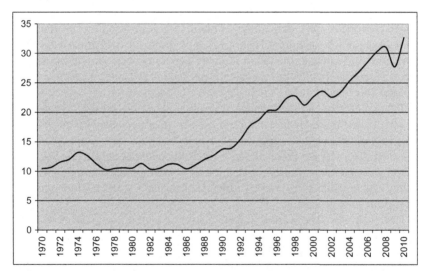

FIGURE 1.18   Trade Openness in Brazil: Exports Plus Imports as a Percentage of GDP (1970 – 2010). *(Source: Heston, Summers and Aten, Penn World Table Version 7.1, Center for International Comparisons of Production, Income and Prices at the University of Pennsylvania, Nov. 2012. Note: Measured at 2005 prices. Prepared by the author.)*

Of course, one should not expect that Brazil, a country of large continental dimensions and population, would be as open as a small, low-population nation. There is a natural tendency to rely on the internal market. However, the set of countries shown in Figure 1.17 has other large area and/or high-population countries, such as Russia, Mexico, and China. All of them are more open than Brazil.

As with many other Latin American countries, Brazil has a history of import substitution policies. As emphasized in the introduction to this chapter, the military government (1964-1985) raised trade barriers beyond the protection of the consumer goods market, and even tried to protect sectors such as machinery, computers, and high-tech industrial inputs. This policy option resulted in a very low level of trade openness in the 1970s (especially after 1974), as can be seen in Figure 1.18 above.

A common argument generally used in favor of this kind of policy is the protection of the national infant industry, which needs to be insulated from international competition for a while, until it can be strong enough to compete. The idea is that industry is a more productive sector than agriculture or services, and economic development is possible only if the country is able to set up a strong industrial sector.

Even though commercial protection can, in fact, have an important role to begin the process of industrialization, the problem is that protection can perpetuate itself along the years. Protection, if exaggerated for an excessive amount of time, will allow companies benefited by it to obtain extraordinary profit without an effort to improve product quality or to control costs. Employees in these companies will also be benefited by excessive and prolonged protection since part of the extraordinary gains can be converted into extra wages or job openings. These groups of employers and employees have an interest in uniting to maintain a closed economy. This is a strong incentive to form a *lobby* for the extension of protection (Chapter 3, Section 3.4.4 explores this idea).

Industrialization formed under protection tends to present accelerated growth due to the simple fact that rural laborers migrate to the city. As productivity in agriculture tends to be lower than in industry, the transition to industrial jobs raises the average productivity. Even if the national industry is less productive than its international competition, it is more productive than the rural sector, which justifies government support of industry at the beginning of the industrialization process.

However, when the worker transition from agriculture to industry is complete, there is no other source of productive gain, since the local protected industry has no incentives to seek more productive methods, and the economy stagnates. This is basically what happened to the Brazilian economy from the 1960s to the 1980s: a growth process followed by stagnation.

An additional argument in favor of trade restrictions is related to protection of the internal market. Large countries with large populations tend to have large internal markets. A kind of mercantilist reasoning argues that the local market has to be preserved for local firms, since these are the companies that create jobs for the local population.

However, this argument fails to explain that the jobs created and protected by trade barriers will be unproductive, since protected companies will not have incentives to work efficiently or to update their technology. As a result, productivity goes down and so do average salaries. Furthermore, a closed economy misses the opportunity to open new markets and create new jobs. For instance, if the computer industry is protected and cannot produce up-to-date equipment, many new jobs related to the creation and operation of new machines will not exist in the country. Take, for example, the quantity of new products and professions that arose with digital expansion and the Internet: web designers, online commerce, etc. All of this is delayed when equipment is outdated and more expensive, the connection speed is low and the options of equipment brands and models are restricted.

In fact, economic literature points out four main channels through which open trade may foster economic productivity and increase long-term economic growth (Pagés, 2010; Menezes Filho and Kannebley, 2013 present a summary of these theories): (a) natural selection, (b) access to better technology and inputs, (c) increased competition, and (d) expansion of exports.

The "natural selection" argument means that low-productivity companies will not resist the competition of imported goods produced by more efficient international firms. When these low-productivity companies close, they release productive factors (labor, capital, credit) to be used by more productive companies, which results in an increase in the average productivity of the economy.

The second channel – access to better technology and inputs – comes from the cost reduction that results from trade liberation. High-quality, imported machinery and intermediate inputs allow companies to adopt new production techniques.

The third channel, increase in the availability of imported alternatives to domestic production, stimulates local companies to invest in technology and to adapt their productive process to a more competitive environment. Companies that succeed in this reshaping are able to survive the natural selection process and become more productive.

Finally, open trade makes it easier for local companies to access external markets. In general, open trade is a two-way road, and trade agreements between two countries tend to open both markets. Once a company starts to be an exporter, it may absorb new techniques and standards of quality from their international clients. It may amplify its operational scale and reduce average costs, as well.

Although small by international standards, the opening of the Brazilian economy seems to have brought a significant improvement in industrial productivity. In one of the many studies performed by Brazilian economists to measure this phenomenon, Ferreira and Rossi show robust evidence of productivity improvement after trade liberalization in the 1990's (Ferreira and Rossi, 2003).

Menezes Filho and Kannebley Jr. (Menezes Filho and Kannebley, 2013) provide a summary of studies regarding this theme. They argue that three of the four channels described above helped improve total factor productivity in Brazil as a consequence of trade liberalization: natural selection, increased competition, and access to inputs. They do not find evidence that Brazilian companies had increased access to the export market.

The lesson learned by the 1990s liberalization experience is that trade openness is a way to increase long-term growth in Brazil. Since the country remains closed, despite recent liberalization, it seems to be worth deepening trade openness. However, Brazilian industries and industrial labor unions are politically powerful and able to block these initiatives. They have also been successful in inducing government to compensate them by means of tariff barriers and commercial regulation (such as tax deductions) that recover their protection and restrain Brazilian international trade expansion (more on this in Chapter 3, Section 3.4.4).

1.5.8   STYLIZED FACT 8: Judicial Uncertainty and Poor Protection of Property Rights

Since 2003 the World Bank has been doing broad research to assess how difficult it is to manage businesses in different countries. This project, called *Doing Business*, "measures business regulation and the protection of property rights – and their effect on businesses, especially small and medium-size domestic firms."[9] It tries to capture four different dimensions: complexity of regulation, time and cost of achieving a regulatory goal or complying with regulation, the extent of legal protection of property, and the tax burden on business.

Brazil appears in an unfavorable position. In the most recent ranking (*Doing Business 2013*, based on 2012 data) it is ranked as 130 among 180 countries: it is in the 8th decile. Table 1.6 shows the position of the 28 countries in the comparison group. The disadvantageous position of Brazil is glaring: 23 of 28 countries (9th decile).

Among the 11 dimensions evaluated by the aggregate *Doing Business* index, the poor position of Brazil is related to its tax system (156 of 185 countries: 9th decile), an issue already analyzed in Stylized Fact 2. However, the country shows bad performance in some other important items, especially on those related to the legal protection of property rights. It is worth taking a closer look.

Table 1.7 shows the *Doing Business* ranking on contract enforcement. It measures the efficiency of the judicial system in resolving a commercial dispute. The index is formed by three dimensions: time, cost, and procedures. "Time" measures the number of days necessary to resolve a commercial sales

---

9. All descriptions of *Doing Business* indicators presented throughout this section are transcriptions of the World Bank "data note," a chapter on the *Doing Business* 2013 main report – World Bank 2013a, pp. 106-130.

TABLE 1.6 Ease of Doing Business Ranking: Selected Countries (2013)

Country	All Countries Ranking (180 Countries)	Comparison Group Ranking (28 Countries)
South Korea	8	1
Australia	10	2
Malaysia	12	3
Ireland	15	4
Taiwan	16	5
Portugal	30	6
Chile	37	7
South Africa	39	8
Peru	43	9
Spain	44	10
Colombia	45	11
Mexico	48	12
Poland	55	13
Botswana	59	14
Turkey	71	15
China	91	16
Vietnam	99	17
Paraguay	103	18
Egypt	109	19
Costa Rica	110	20
Russia	112	21
Argentina	124	22
Brazil	**130**	**23**
India	132	24
Philippines	138	25
Ecuador	139	26
Bolivia	155	27
Venezuela	180	28

Source: World Bank – Doing Business (http://www.doingbusiness.org/data). Prepared by the author.

TABLE 1.7 *Doing Business Ranking on Contracts Enforcement: Selected Countries (2013)*

Country	All Countries Ranking (185 Countries)	Comparison Group Ranking (28 Countries)	Time		Cost		Procedures	
			Days	Ranking (28)	% of Claim	Ranking (28)	Number	Ranking (28)
South Korea	2	1	230	1	10.3	1	33	8
Russia	11	2	270	2	13.4	4	36	12
Australia	15	3	395	3	21.8	10	28	2
China	19	4	406	5	11.1	2	37	16
Portugal	22	5	547	14	13.0	3	32	7
Malaysia	33	6	425	8	27.5	17	29	4
Turkey	40	7	420	7	24.9	12	36	12
Vietnam	44	8	400	4	29.0	20	34	10
Argentina	48	9	590	16	16.5	5	36	12
Poland	56	10	685	22	19.0	9	33	8
Ireland	63	11	650	21	26.9	15	21	1
Spain	64	12	510	11	17.2	7	40	21
Botswana	68	13	625	20	28.1	18	28	2
Chile	70	14	480	10	28.6	19	36	12
Mexico	76	15	415	6	31.0	22	38	18

Venezuela	80	16	510	11	43.7	27	30	6
South Africa	82	17	600	19	33.2	23	29	4
Taiwan	90	18	510	11	17.7	8	45	27
Ecuador	99	19	588	15	27.2	16	39	20
Paraguay	106	20	591	18	30.0	21	38	18
Philippines	111	21	842	24	26.0	13	37	16
Peru	115	22	428	9	35.7	25	41	24
Brazil	**116**	**23**	**731**	**23**	**16.5**	**5**	**44**	**26**
Costa Rica	128	24	852	25	24.3	11	40	21
Bolivia	136	25	591	18	33.2	23	40	21
Egypt	152	26	1010	26	26.2	14	42	25
Colombia	154	27	1346	27	47.9	28	34	10
India	184	28	1420	28	39.6	26	46	28

Source: World Bank – *Doing Business* (http://www.doingbusiness.org/data). Prepared by the author.

dispute in the courts. It measures the time needed to: file and serve the case, trial and obtaining judgment, and enforce the judgment. "Cost" measures the percentage value of the claim that is spent by the plaintiff paying all court costs. "Procedures" is the number of interactions between the parties or between them and the judge or court officer necessary to enforce a contract through the courts.

Table 1.7 presents the Brazilian position among all 185 nations evaluated by research and among the 28 countries of the comparison group. It also shows the numerical value of each of the three indicators (time, cost, and procedure) and the respective country rank in the comparison group for each indicator.

Brazil ranks as 116 among 185 countries (7th decile). Its relative position among the comparison group is even worse: 23 of 28 (9th decile). The country performs badly in two of the three dimensions measured by the index: *procedures* and *time*. The *cost* paid for court procedures doesn't seem to be a major problem.

The Brazilian data seems to portray a backlogged judiciary system. One takes a long time and has to deal with a lot of bureaucracy in order to settle an issue though the courts.

Notice that the "cost" dimension measured by this index takes into account only the direct costs in a judicial dispute. It does not consider the opportunity cost involved in a long judicial dispute (for instance, the delay in receiving payment when there is a judicial dispute, the time and effort the company has to employ in judicial disputes).

When the judicial system is slow there are opportunities for obtaining advantage in business by not complying with contracts. In financial terms, it is worth delaying payment and force the creditor to seek their rights in the courts. The long time period in fulfilling the court decision to pay allows the debtor to have cash on hand to apply in their business, receiving interest and allowing inflation to corrode the real value of the debt.

This incentive represents a risk to any company that comes to find itself in a creditor position, reducing expected profit due to the high probability of loss from non-payment by debtors. An immediate consequence is the need to carefully select commercial partners, which increases company operational costs due to the need to hire specialized professionals and invest in the analysis of the ability of potential clients to pay. Also, companies will tend to prefer doing business with known partners, losing the opportunity to purchase better or less expensive supplies from other suppliers that are not part of their circle, which causes negative effects on profits and productivity.

A similar picture emerges when one analyzes the time and cost faced by the creditor of an insolvent company (World Bank, 2013a, p. 126). The *Doing Business* index of *resolving insolvency* measures three dimensions of insolvency proceedings involving domestic entities: time, cost, and the rate of credit recovery. "Time" is the number of years from the company's default until the payment of some or all of the money owned to creditors (delay tactics by the parties, such as dilatory appeals, are taken into consideration). "Cost" represents the direct costs of legal procedures. "Recovery rate" is recorded as cents on the dollar recovered by creditors by means of reorganization, liquidation, or debt enforcement proceedings. The recovery rate also takes into account the depreciation of assets and the amount of time spent in insolvency proceedings.

Table 1.8 shows that Brazil is once more ill positioned in the ranking: 143 of 171 countries (9th decile). (Fourteen of the 185 countries have no index for insolvency resolution.) Among the comparison group, Brazil is 24 in 28 (9th decile). As in the former indicator, direct costs are not the main issue: on average, creditors spend 12% of the credit value in the insolvency proceedings, which puts Brazil in the 12th position among 28 countries.

The main problem is, once again, the "time" dimension: four years are required to settle an insolvency issue, which places Brazil near the bottom of the ranking (22 of 28). The percentage of credit recovery is a problem as well: for each dollar owed by a creditor, only 16 cents are recovered, the 5th worse position among 28 countries.

It is important to highlight that the "recovery rate" dimension takes into account the costs created by the delay in resolving the insolvency process: depreciation of assets and the opportunity cost of the creditor capital involved in the dispute. Therefore, the sluggishness of judicial and bureaucratic procedures plays a crucial role in the risk companies incur in doing business with each other. If one commercial partner becomes insolvent, costs and risks imposed on their partners are far from being irrelevant. It reduces incentives for trading with unknown firms and reduces the possibility of finding new and more efficient suppliers or good clients, with negative effects on profit prospects and productivity gains.

A third important indicator is related to the strength of legal rights in credit operations. It measures the degree to which collateral and bankruptcy laws protect the rights of borrowers and lenders and thus facilitate lending (World Bank, 2013a, p. 116).

Of course, credit is a fundamental tool in economic growth since it allocates available savings to those interested in making investments. It allows companies to overcome investment costs and families to invest in education. The index ranges from 0 to 10, with higher scores indicating that collateral and bankruptcy laws are better designed to expand access to credit.

As presented in Table 1.9 Brazil fulfills only 3 of 10 of the required features of a good credit environment. An inadequate environment in the credit market induces banks and other financial institutions to expand their spreads in order to compensate for unrecoverable credit. Money becomes expensive and many investments that could be profitable with lower interest rates are not made due to credit costs. Moreover, those who pay their obligations on time are bearing the cost created by defaulting debtors.

A fourth important *Doing Business* index measures minority shareholder protection. This index tries to capture the efficacy of instruments that restrain

TABLE 1.8 *Doing Business Ranking on Resolving Insolvency: Selected Countries (2013)*

Country	All Countries Ranking (171 Countries)	Comparison Group Ranking (28 Countries)	Time		Cost		Recovery Rate	
			Years	Ranking	% of Estate	Ranking	Cents on Dollar	Ranking
Ireland	9	1	0.4	1	9	6	87.5	1
South Korea	14	2	1.5	4	4	1	81.8	2
Taiwan	15	3	1.9	11	4	1	81.8	2
Australia	18	4	1.0	2	8	5	80.8	4
Spain	20	5	1.5	4	11	11	76.5	5
Colombia	21	6	1.3	3	6	3	76.2	6
Portugal	23	7	2.0	12	9	6	74.6	7
Mexico	26	8	1.8	9	18	22	67.3	8
Botswana	29	9	1.7	7	15	14	64.8	9
Poland	37	10	3.0	16	15	14	54.5	10
Malaysia	49	11	1.5	4	15	14	44.7	11
Russia	53	12	2.0	12	9	6	43.4	12
Bolivia	68	13	1.8	9	15	14	39.0	13
China	82	14	1.7	7	22	25	35.7	14
South Africa	84	15	2.0	12	18	22	35.4	15

Argentina	94	16	2.8	15	12	12	30.8	16
Chile	98	17	3.2	18	15	14	30.0	17
Peru	106	18	3.1	17	7	4	28.1	18
India	116	19	4.3	25	9	6	26.0	19
Turkey	124	20	3.3	19	15	14	23.6	20
Costa Rica	128	21	3.5	20	15	14	22.5	21
Ecuador	137	22	5.3	27	18	22	17.8	22
Egypt	139	23	4.2	24	22	25	17.6	23
Brazil	**143**	**24**	**4.0**	**22**	**12**	**12**	**15.9**	**24**
Paraguay	144	25	3.9	21	9	6	15.3	25
Venezuela	163	27	4.0	22	38	27	6.4	27
Philippines	165	28	5.7	28	38	27	4.9	28
Vietnam	149	26	5.0	26	15	14	13.9	26

Source: World Bank – *Doing Business* (http://www.doingbusiness.org/data). Prepared by the author.

TABLE 1.9 *Doing Business* Ranking on Strength of Legal Rights in Credit Operations: Selected Countries (2013)

Country	Power of Legal Rights Index (0-10)
Australia	10
Malaysia	10
South Africa	10
Ireland	9
Poland	9
India	8
South Korea	8
Vietnam	8
Botswana	7
Peru	7
Chile	6
China	6
Mexico	6
Spain	6
Colombia	5
Taiwan	5
Argentina	4
Philippines	4
Turkey	4
Brazil	**3**
Costa Rica	3
Ecuador	3
Egypt	3
Paraguay	3
Portugal	3
Russia	3
Bolivia	1
Venezuela	1

Source: World Bank – *Doing Business* (http://www.doingbusiness.org/data). Prepared by the author.

the ability of company directors to misuse corporate assets for personal gain. The index is built on three dimensions: the extent of disclosure required for company operations in which directors have a personal interest; how hard it is to make a director liable for a transaction that harms the company; and shareholder ability to challenge a potentially harmful transaction.

Brazil is a little better in this index, but it does not go beyond an intermediate position: 82 of 185 countries (5th percentile). In the comparison group it ranks as 17 in 28 (7th percentile). Table 1.10 shows the numbers.

All the indexes presented above are related to judicial or legal uncertainty. They measure the extent of the legal property protection (World Bank, 2013a, p. 116). By these indexes, Brazil seems to be a society where the rules of the game change frequently, are sometimes bypassed by some individuals or take a

TABLE 1.10 *Doing Business* Ranking on Protecting Investors: Selected Countries (2013)

Country	All Countries Ranking (180 Countries)	Comparison Group Ranking (28 Countries)
Malaysia	4	1
Ireland	6	2
Colombia	6	2
South Africa	10	4
Peru	13	5
Taiwan	32	6
Chile	32	6
South Korea	49	8
Portugal	49	8
Mexico	49	8
Poland	49	8
Botswana	49	8
India	49	8
Australia	70	14
Turkey	70	14
Paraguay	70	14
Egypt	82	17
Brazil	**82**	17

Continued

TABLE 1.10 Doing Business Ranking on Protecting Investors: Selected Countries (2013)—cont'd

Country	All Countries Ranking (180 Countries)	Comparison Group Ranking (28 Countries)
Spain	100	19
China	100	19
Russia	117	21
Argentina	117	21
Phillipines	128	23
Ecuador	139	24
Bolivia	139	24
Vietnam	169	26
Costa Rica	169	27
Venezuela	181	28

Source: World Bank – *Doing Business* (http://www.doingbusiness.org/data). Prepared by the author.

long time to be enforced. It reduces future predictability and makes investments riskier than in a stable environment: an entrepreneur may believe that investing in a new factory may be profitable, but risks of expropriation and client default, plus the high cost of credit (high spreads compensating credit risk), discourage him from going ahead.

Investments that involve a large share of immobilized assets are especially affected by judicial uncertainty. Take, for example, building a railway or exploring for oil. The railway owner cannot simply pull up the rails and move them to another country if something goes wrong after the investment has been made. Likewise, the oil explorer invests a large amount of money before extracting the first barrels of oil. They have no room to move if something goes wrong after the initial investments are made. A large amount of capital has already been "sunk" into the business and there is no way to protect it from expropriation. For example, if the government decides to expropriate the railroad or to abrogate the concession to explore for oil without paying indemnification, the company has few resources to defend itself. (Pinheiro and Giambiagi, 2006, pp. 192-198; and Pinheiro, 2005 present a summary of the arguments that associate judicial uncertainty with growth and macroeconomic stability.)

Therefore, judicial uncertainty is one more barrier to private infrastructure investment, which makes the infrastructure bottleneck solution (Stylized Fact 5) even more difficult. To make private infrastructure investment attractive it is necessary to raise prices. The private sector will operate infrastructure services only if the profit margin is high enough to compensate for expropriation risks. In this case, judicial uncertainty generates higher production costs, reducing competition in the economy.

The high price for important goods (such as credit and infrastructure) disseminates cost pressures throughout the whole economy, reducing its ability to compete for external markets. The economy loses the opportunity to grow through increased exports.

Furthermore, assets that are not fully protected from expropriation may not be accepted by banks as credit collateral, which reduces the opportunity for taking credit to finance a new activity or investment.

Moreover, in an unstable judicial environment, people allocate their savings based more on safety issues than on expected returns. Buying a minority participation in a promising company may not be a good deal if there is a risk of unchecked misbehavior by the board of directors. It may be preferable to buy real estate and let it remain idle (real estate or gold, for instance) in order to protect assets. Even simple commercial deals, such as offering a house for rent, may be risky if the judicial system is unable to promptly evict a defaulting tenant.

The mean return of investments goes down and economic agents will prefer to allocate their income to consumption instead of to investments and savings, reinforcing the problem of low savings (Stylized Fact 3). Economic growth perspectives go down.

As mentioned before, firms tend to restrict their set of commercial partners, doing business only with those they know better, in order to avoid commercial litigation. Therefore, they miss opportunities to find more efficient partners and better quality inputs. Another common strategy is to internalize commercial transactions: firms sometimes prefer to produce their own inputs in order to avoid commercial relations with third parties. It may reduce efficiency because firms would be more productive if they specialized in areas where they had comparative advantages.

In summary, judicial uncertainty harms investment, productivity, and growth. The data shown in this section are evidence that Brazil is far from offering a stable legal environment, which has probably affected its long-term growth rate.

1.5.9 STYLIZED FACT 9: A Large Number of Small and Informal Companies Drive Average Productivity Down

Brazilian companies are typically small. Table 1.11 shows that 91% of all formally registered companies have no more than nine employees. The manufacturing sector has larger organizations, but even in this case small companies represent 78% of all firms. Considering that these figures come from an inquiry that does not cover informal organizations (usually smaller than registered companies), the average size of all companies is certainly even smaller.

TABLE 1.11 Distribution of Formally Registered Companies by the Number of Paid Employees in Brazil (2010) (%)

	Total	Manufacture	Retail and Vehicle Repair	Lodging and Food
Up to 9	91	78	4	89
10 or more	9	22	6	11

Source: IBGE – Company Demographics (*Demografia das Empresas* – 2010). Prepared by the author.

Unfortunately, there is not much comparative information available for other countries, as in the case of former sections of this chapter. The information that could be obtained from literature was taken from a study done by David Lagakos (Lagakos (2009). The author seeks to understand why less developed countries have low productivity in the retail sector. Lagakos presents a picture where low- and middle-income countries typically have small companies, while in the developed ones, large firms are the majority. Table 1.12 compares employment in small (less than 20 employees) and large retail companies for six countries. While in the United States 67% of employees work for large companies, in middle- and low-income countries this participation reached no more than 23% (21% in Brazil). Lagakos (2009), from which these statistics were taken, argues that Germany, France, the United Kingdom, and the Netherlands present employee distribution similar to that of the United States.

Parallel to the small size of formal companies is the widespread phenomenon of informality, i.e., firms that are not registered and do not pay taxes and fees. The aforementioned study on productivity in Latin America, coordinated

TABLE 1.12 Employment Share in Large and Small Retail Stores: Selected Countries (%)

	Less than 20 Employees	More than 20 Employees
USA (2005)	33	67
Mexico (2005)	77	23
Brazil (2002)	**79**	**21**
Thailand (2002)	81	19
El Salvador (2005)	85	15
Philippines (2005)	85	15

Source: Lagakos, 2009.

by Carmen Pagés, argues that informality and tax evasion are especially high among micro and small companies, achieving 30% to 40% of total sales in Brazil and Panama. The authors also state that in Brazil the probability of paying taxes increases with the size of the company. In Mexico almost 70% of microcompanies declared that they are not formally registered and do not pay taxes. In El Salvador only 3% of all companies are registered.

What causes companies to be small and informal in middle- and low-income countries? The literature offers different explanations that do not exclude each other:

- Excessive bureaucracy and high formalization costs may be a barrier to register a firm, access credit and make business grow (Soto, 2003);
- Low-income levels create demand for low-quality products that can be produced by small firms using unsophisticated production methods (Lagakos, 2009);
- Labor market regulation may create high costs for formal companies, stimulating them to remain informal and to not register their employees;
- Excessive taxation stimulates small, unproductive firms to hide themselves from tax authorities in order to survive; if they had to pay (usually high) taxes they would not be able to stay in the market.

Although the first two explanations may not be disregarded in the Brazilian case,[10] the role of taxation and labor market regulation must be emphasized.

Let us first analyze the tax question. As argued in Stylized Fact 2, the tax burden in Brazil is high and concentrated in some sectors of the economy. The main goal of tax authorities is to maximize revenue so as to cover increasing expenses (Stylized Fact 1). To achieve this goal, the revenue office concentrates its attention on large contributors. This gives opportunity for small companies to evade taxes when they realize that there is a low risk of being fined.

Tax evasion works as a subsidy for small business. They have lower costs when compared to other companies due to not paying taxes or social security contributions. With this, they are able to remain in the market even though being less efficient than their tax-paying competitors.

Labor law affects company size in a way similar as excessive taxation (regarding this point, see Amadeo and Camargo, 1993; Barros and Corseiul, 2001). Brazilian legislation dates back to the 1940s and is focused on protecting the employee by means of strict rules to be followed by the employer. It considers

---

10. For instance, bureaucracy and costs to open a company in Brazil are quite high. In the *Doing Business* ranking of "starting a business" the country is 121 among 185 countries. "Starting a business" measures "the procedures, time, cost, and paid-in minimum capital required for a small or medium-size limited liability company to start up and formally operate". (World Bank, 2013a, p. 56).

the employee unable to negotiate their work contract, be they an illiterate farmer or a financial analyst in a large bank.

The difficulty of Brazilian society to come to a consensus in modernizing this legislation is impressive. Actually, the main alterations made to labor legislation in recent years, especially those introduced in the 1988 Constitution, were in the direction of reinforcing the 1940s model.

Labor legislation is composed of rigid rules that: (a) penalize companies that dismiss employees on "unjustifiable" grounds; (b) strongly regulate the length and flexibility of work hours; (c) limit temporary hiring or outsourcing; and (d) impose fixed, non-negotiable benefits (length of vacation, maternity leave, and required payment for extra hours or night duty).

This means that hiring employees is a risky decision. If, in the future, it is necessary to lay them off due to market changes faced by the company, there will be a high cost to pay. The company will have to opt between layoff costs or maintain an unnecessary employee on its payroll. This does not include legal costs in case the employee goes to court alleging the non-compliance of some labor law regulations. Even when there is no need for layoffs, work-hour inflexibility leads to the occasional seasonal workforce idleness, raising company costs, and reducing work productivity.

Employer obligations in addition to wages (license, gratifications, paid leave, etc.) represent an additional relevant cost. Calculations made by a labor accounting firm indicate that such costs are equal to 64% of the wage (see: http://www.delphin.com.br/orientacao/66-encargos-sociais-sobre-a-folha-de-pagamento).

These costs are added to the tax obligations that, as emphasized in the description of Stylized Fact 2 (high taxes), use payroll as basis for tax calculations. Some of these taxes are tied to worker benefits, such as unemployment compensation or the *Fundo de Garantia do Tempo de Serviço – FGTS* (Time of Service Guarantee Fund), a type of forced employee savings account, which can be withdrawn upon dismissal.

These tax-related employment costs represent 36% of payroll (see: http://www.delphin.com.br/orientacao/66-encargos-sociais-sobre-a-folha-de-pagamento). Added to the costs of the required benefits as described above, to have a formal employee costs the employer the equivalent of about twice what the employee receives as wage.

Labor law specialist, José Pastore, says that such costs are among the highest in the world:

> *The weight of labor legislation in determining if a company hires employees is well known. Brazil is world champion. Hiring legally generates costs of 103.46% of the nominal salary. In France, a highly regulated country, these expenses reach 80%; England, 59%; Italy, 51%, Japan, 12%, Asia, 11% (average); and the United States, a little more than 9% (Pastore, 2005).*

The companies that want to escape the inflexibility of labor legislation, and the associated direct and indirect costs, tend to follow the same line as those who want to escape taxation in general. They remain small and informal, far off the inspection radar, so as to not have to pay taxes or follow labor legislation. The result is that half of the workforce in the country is informal, employed without the benefit of rights guaranteed by legislation (http://www.ipeadata.gov.br).[11]

Therefore, both high taxes and labor legislation tend to induce companies to remain small. The problem is that small companies are typically less productive than larger ones. If most companies are small and less productive, average economic productivity is low, which reduces the potential of long-term growth.

In other words, if the economic inputs (work and capital) were reallocated from small to large companies, average productivity would increase. The country "wastes" work and capital in allocating them to small, unproductive companies. This poor allocation of productive factors is only possible due to the evasion of taxes and employee obligations, which gives spurious competition to these companies.

Why are small companies usually less productive than larger ones? Imagine an economy where every company, large or small, is equally taxed. In this ideal scenario, small, efficient firms will grow while the inefficient won't be able to grow and will eventually perish. As such, when "taking a snapshot" of companies at a determined moment, what one will see is a group of small, medium, and large companies that are in activity at that moment. The medium and large were once small, but due to their efficiency, grew. Therefore, this group has already gone through natural selection because firms that are not efficient cannot grow. In the group of small companies that are in the snapshot, there will be both the efficient that will prosper, and the inefficient that will close. Consequently, the average productivity of the small companies will be lower, for this group is composed of productive and unproductive firms.

However, when small, inefficient companies gain competition because they do not pay taxes or respect labor laws, they are able to remain in the market. This pulls average productivity down.

In addition, given that the companies that evade taxes need to remain small in order to take advantage of their evasion and illegality, they cannot have access to credit (in general, banks demand proof of tax payment to make loans; according to Pagés, 2010, p. 184 access to credit in Brazil is directly correlated to formalization and payment of taxes). This prevents them from taking advantage of opportunities to expand and benefit from economies of scale.

Informal companies live a dilemma between living in the shadows and not growing or becoming formal and having the liberty to expand. They will only choose the second option if they are sufficiently productive to be able to pay wage, tax and regulatory costs, and still generate more profit than if they

---

11. Gonzaga 2003 calls attention to another problem: the compulsory savings mechanism by means of the FGTS induces a high employee turnover, discouraging companies from investing in training. This results in less productivity, limiting economic growth.

remained informal. The higher those costs, the smaller the proportion of companies that will opt for the transition to formality.

The result is that the average company size and average economic productivity fall. Table 1.12 above has already shown that firms are smaller in developing countries. Table 1.13 below shows that small companies in these countries are much less productive than the larger ones. It presents the productivity (output per worker) of small (less than 20 employees) and large retail companies. The productivity in North American companies is taken as a benchmark. The table shows that productivity in small retail firms in Brazil is less than one third that of the large firms in the same country. While large Brazilian companies achieve an output per worker equivalent to 73% of that obtained by US companies, the productivity of small Brazilian firms is equivalent to only 20% of that of US companies. Similar results are found for other developing countries shown in the table.

The Brazilian government tried to attract companies to become formal by offering them a simplified tax system, in which they pay less, with less red tape. Although many small firms indeed formalized their activities and began paying taxes, the new tax system became an extra incentive for companies to remain small. If they were to grow beyond a certain threshold, they would not be able to remain in the simplified system and be required to pay more taxes and complete many more forms. Consequently, companies prefer to stay small or rather pretend that they do not grow (for example, create a second company and manage the business as if they were two different firms, which brings many additional costs and a loss of economies of scale).

Bernard Appy, a former vice-Minister of Finance in the Lula da Silva administration (2003-2010), who championed two ample tax reform attempts, often presents a very interesting example in his conferences: the amount of tax paid by an electrical repairs firm. If this is a large company (with gross revenues higher

TABLE 1.13 Output per Worker in Retail Sector: Selected Countries (US Retail Sector = 100)

	Less than 20 Employees	More than 20 Employees
Thailand (2002)	23	83
El Salvador (2005)	18	80
Brazil (2002)	**20**	**73**
Philippines (2005)	12	72
Mexico (2005)	18	68

Source: Lagakos, 2009.

than a certain threshold), total taxation (paid by the firm and the employee) will represent 43.5% of gross revenues. If the company is eligible for the simplified tax system, the burden falls to 23.5%. There is, however, a third and more attractive option: the electrician may work as an autonomous professional instead of being a company employee. In this case the person may register themself as an "individual micro-entrepreneur" and pay only 1.3%.

There is an obvious incentive for the electrician (and all other types of service providers) to work autonomously. Instead of having medium or large firms that offer electrical repairs, there will be a thousand individual professionals with a mobile phone waiting for a call from their clients. This reduces the productivity of these professionals. Sometimes they will be idle, and sometimes they will not be able to attend two customers simultaneously. A large company could provide its employees training and technical updates and guarantee a higher standard of quality. If electrician A is unavailable when a costumer requires service, the firm may send electrician B instead. However, if electrician A works autonomously, and the consumer doesn't know electrician B (or has no information regarding his abilities), they will need to spend time looking for another electrician, calling friends for recommendations, etc. Furthermore, companies are in a better position than autonomous professionals to take advantage of purchasing in large quantities, providing service warranty and being up to date on new technology.

As argued in Stylized Fact 2, due to ever-increasing expenses, the government always needs more revenue. One way to do that is to attract informal service providers and small businesses to formality, offering them a special tax regulation, despite negative collateral effects in terms of efficiency and productivity. (For an analysis of special, small-business tax regimes, see Pagés, 2010, Chapter 10.)

In a study on the Latin American manufacturing sector produced by the Inter-American Development Bank (IADB), Busso and his co-authors estimate that reallocating capital and labor from unproductive to more productive firms inside sectors of the Brazilian manufacturing industry could increase output by more than 40%. Therefore, unproductive firms put a high burden on the potential production of the economy. (Busso et al., 2012 analyze 10 Latin American countries. By their calculations, Brazil is the country where misallocation of productive factors among high and low productive firms is less severe, even though the absolute value of production loss due to misallocation in the country is high.)

Ferraz and Monteiro (Ferraz and Monteiro, 2009) specifically studied the Brazilian manufacturing industry and found similar results. According to them, productivity in the Brazilian manufacture industry could grow by almost 50% if resources from less productive firms were reallocated to more productive ones. Likewise, the aforementioned IADB study, coordinated by Pagés, calculates that the gap in total factor productivity between formal and informal micro-enterprises in Brazil is about 55% (Pagés, 2010, p. 192).

It is important to note that the above cited studies by Busso and co-authors and by Ferraz and Monteiro use databases that only consider companies with 30 employees or more. Therefore, very small (and unproductive) firms were not considered, which means the impact of low-production firms on potential output is probably even greater.

Another important point to consider is that the manufacturing industry tends to present less variability in productivity against firms in other sectors, such as services. Services are usually non-tradable, which means there are limited possibilities for the competitive pressure exerted by imports, different from manufacturing industries that face external competition. Manufacturing must be sufficiently productive to compete with similar imported products and that are available on the national market. Moreover, geographic location plays an important role (consumers usually call service providers located near their homes or offices).

de Vries studied the productivity of the retail sector in Brazil. He estimates that the reallocation of capital and labor could result in productivity gains of more than 250% in the Brazilian retail sector (de Vries, 2009). Considering that services answer for more than 65% of the country's GDP, the impact of the low productivity by small, informal firms on the potential output may be substantial.

Summarizing, high and distortionary taxation (Stylized Fact 2), including taxation related to labor market regulation (Social Security and other compulsory contributions) and labor market inflexibility, result in companies that are small and informal. This prevents companies from growing, making technological improvements and obtaining productivity gains.

1.5.10 STYLIZED FACT 10: Educational Backwardness

The average level of education in Brazil is quite low. Figure 1.19 shows the average amount of schooling for people over 15 years of age (the age at which they go into the labor market). Brazil appears on the left side of the picture. It is 1.5 years below the group mean or 2.6 years below Chile.

Although it is still behind most countries in the comparison group, Brazil has made impressive progress since the 1980s, as presented in Figure 1.20. In the 30-year period from 1950 to 1980, the average years of schooling had a modest increase of 1.07 years. In the following 30 years, from 1980 to 2010, there was a much larger increase of almost 5 years.

The major achievement has been the universalization of primary education. The coverage of the secondary and tertiary levels, although still narrow, has increased. In one of his several studies on education in Brazil, Veloso shows that the rate of attending youth between 15 and 17 grew from 64% to 85% between 1995 and 2009. (Veloso, 2011, p. 216) However, as the author argues, the progress made in recent years has not been enough to allow the country to catch up with the international mean, according to what Figure 1.21 shows. If Brazil maintains its pace of educational advancement, no less than 15 years will be necessary to achieve the current Chilean level of schooling.

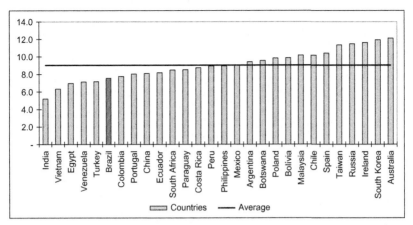

FIGURE 1.19   Average Years of Total Schooling for People Over 15 Years Old in Selected Countries (2010). *(Source: Barro and Lee, 2010. Data available at: http://www.barrolee.com/data/ dataexp.htm. Prepared by the author.)*

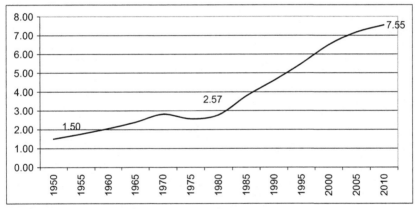

FIGURE 1.20   Average Years of Total Schooling for People Over 15 Years of Age in Brazil (1950 – 2010). *(Source: Barro and Lee (2010). Data available at: http://www.barrolee.com/data/ dataexp.htm. Prepared by the author.)*

Furthermore, the <u>quality</u> of education is a central issue. Brazil usually remains at the lower end of the ranking in international comparisons of student achievements. Table 1.14 presents results of the 2009 edition of the Programme of International Student Assessment (PISA). Sixty-five countries participated in this edition of the evaluation sponsored by the Organization for Economic Co-operation and Development (OECD). Table 1.14 displays the ranking of those countries that belong to our comparison set and participated in the evaluation. Considering all 65 participant countries, Brazil is in the 8th decile in all three subjects evaluated. Among the 15 countries shown in Table 1.14 it ranks in the 9th decile.

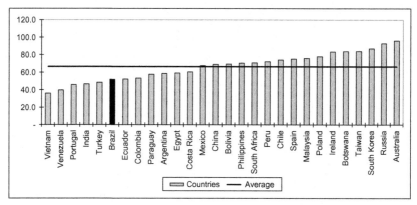

FIGURE 1.21   Percentage of Population Over 15 Years Old that Attended at Least One Year of Secondary Education in Selected Countries (2010). *(Source: Barro and Lee (2010). Data available at: http://www.barrolee.com/data/dataexp.htm. Prepared by the author.)*

TABLE 1.14 Programme for International Student Assessment (PISA): Rank of Selected Countries (2009)

	Reading	Math	Science
South Korea	2	4	6
Australia	9	15	10
Poland	15	25	19
Ireland	21	32	20
Taiwan	23	5	12
Portugal	27	33	32
Spain	33	35	36
Turkey	41	43	43
Russia	43	38	39
Chile	44	49	44
Mexico	48	50	50
Colombia	52	58	54
Brazil	**53**	**57**	**53**
Argentina	58	55	56
Peru	63	63	64

Source: OECD. Data available at: http://www.oecd.org/pisa/46643496.pdf. Prepared by the author.

However, the country has improved its performance over the years. According to Menezes Filho, an economist specialized in education, "between 2000 and 2009 the performance by Brazilian students [had] one of the greatest increases observed among participants." As a country with a very low level, however, "this improvement represents only a partial reduction of the country´s backwardness" (Menezes Filho, 2011, p. 271).

Education or, more broadly, *human capital* is an important engine to place a country at a higher level of development. The main link between education and growth is through productivity gains. More educated workers (in terms of years of education and quality of education) have a wider range of abilities and are able to do things better and faster. The interaction of many educated workers may further improve collective productivity by means of the exchange of knowledge in the workplace.

Barbosa Filho and Pessôa estimate that educational backwardness in Brazil explains 33% of the productivity gap between Brazil and the United States (Barbosa Filho and Pessôa, 2013). Gomes, Pessôa and Veloso (Gomes et al., 2003) estimate that human capital was responsible for 32% of GDP growth per worker between 1950 and 2000. Furthermore, they find that this impact grew over time, achieving 55% in the 1990s. The World Bank stresses that in Brazil, as in most countries, education has the power of raising development on a long-term horizon:

> *Time series data for Brazil over the last fifty years thus appear to be consistent with the main result of cross-country data analysis: countries with higher levels of education, other things being equal, seem to grow faster (...) (World Bank, 2002, p. 43).*

Therefore, educational backwardness seems to be an important factor in blocking long-term economic growth in Brazil.

1.6   THE STORY BEHIND LOW GROWTH

The common point that seems to unite the 10 Stylized Facts seems to be a combination of: (a) democratization of the country in a social and economic context that is characterized by high inequality; (b) terrible social conditions for the poor at the time of transition to democracy; and; (c) rooted privileges for the higher social classes.

An unequal society is typically composed of a mass of poor and a small, very rich group. Along Brazil's history, since the colonial period, the richer groups have used their economic power and old ties to the political elite to create, preserve, and amplify their privileges. The richer segments of society, which control the large companies, have been successful in protecting themselves from the market competition. Fragile judicial and regulatory systems and a closed economy are useful when desiring to block new competition, expropriate minority shareholders or to preserve a monopolistic or oligopolistic situation.

All this weakens competition, discourages investment and the search for gains in productivity, reducing potential growth. Certainly, it is not easy to find empirical evidence to prove that a bad business environment has been created on purpose by the elite. However, such an environment is, at least, useful for those who profit from the preservation of low competition and judicial uncertainty. Also, the rich do not move their economic and political capital in favor of institutional reform aimed at improving the business environment and the leveling of conditions for competition between large and small, new and old companies.

On the other hand, when Brazil was democratized in 1985, the politicians perceived that the majority of votes were in the hands of poor voters. If the immediate interests of this group were not attended, the chances of leaders to remain in power were low. The great demand for politicians to relieve poverty and bad social conditions, accumulated over the military period, created pressure for the provision of welfare policies.

This set in motion the creation and expansion of many programs directed toward the poor: poverty reduction, social assistance, public health, and public education, etc. Public expenditure grew as a result of these policies.

So, with democratization, what was observed was NOT a substitution of spending in favor of the rich for those in favor of the poor. Policies with the latter in mind were added to the old, resistant policies in favor of the first. Therefore, there was a significant increase in public spending (Stylized Fact 1).

Besides spending more on social policies, the public sector came to approve regulations with a view to attract votes from the poor. The most important example is the real increases made to minimum wage (Stylized Fact 6), which not only feeds public spending but also pressures companies, discouraging investments.

These adverse effects on growth were strengthened by the fact that democratization opened space for demands not only by the poor, but also by some middle-income groups. Those especially benefitted were those who took advantage of the ample liberty, conceded by democracy, to organize associations and unions. Also benefitted were groups with privileged access to the political decision process (civil servants who advise on government decisions), and numerous groups that have easily identifiable homogeneous demands (the elderly, religious groups, ethnic groups).

This amplified even more the part of the population with the ability to demand public programs and state regulation in favor of specific interest groups. Examples of policies in favor of the middle-income group are: maintenance and amplification of labor legislation that predominantly protects formally employed union workers; free public university primarily for middle- and high-income students; retirement rules that disproportionately benefit middle-income segments (benevolent pensions in case of death, for example); and many subsidies and benefits for the elderly, with no distinction of income level, attending the elderly with middle and high incomes the same as the poor.

With the addition of large segments of the middle-income group in the redistributive game by means of public policies, there was an additional impulse for public spending and regulation harmful to productivity.

As related, increasing public expenditures led to higher, inferior quality taxes, with a negative impact on investments and productivity (Stylized Fact 2), which reduced the potential for economic growth. Furthermore, the appearance of a chronic public deficit reduced savings associated with the economy, making investment financing more expensive (Stylized Facts 3 and 4). The need to please distinct social groups, transferring income to them by means of subsidies, salaries, and income transfer programs, led to the need to cut investments in infrastructure (Stylized Fact 5), for there simply were not enough resources for everything. Once more, growth was hindered.

In Brazil, a strong stimulus has been created for the *rent-seeking* behavior, where each group tries to extract the maximum possible benefits for itself, while at the same time tries to push the cost of public policies onto others, escaping taxation.

The reaction by the public sector was to try to attend the pressures from all social groups. The young, fragile Brazilian democracy, in its first years, feared that not considering one or more social groups could, in a way, destroy the democracy. The mantra of the first democratic government under the first president, José Sarney (1985-90), was "everything for social justice." Or rather, it did what "society" demanded, at least what the groups with the power to vote demanded. After some years of democracy and the country having faced hyperinflation, a direct result of the excess of demands made on the state, fiscal control institutions were perfected. What did change was that, under obligation to maintain its accounts up to date, the government was forced to greatly increase taxation and cut investments in infrastructure (Stylized Facts 2 and 5).

This sharpened the distributive conflict. From the individual point of view, each group did not feel capable of imposing a policy to cut expenditures made in favor of other groups, in order to reduce the tax burden on themselves. In this way, the optimum strategy of each group is to extract as many benefits as possible from the government, while trying to flee the taxation that paid such benefits.

This behavior is clear in the case of companies that prefer to remain small in order to escape paying taxes and fulfilling labor legislation (Stylized Fact 9). With this, few are able to survive, even being inefficient, bringing down the average economic productivity. Once more, economic growth was hindered.

Brazil could obtain productivity gains and the consequent increase in potential growth by means of improvements in public education. After all, if the politicians are attending demands by the poor and the demand for more public education, there should be a tendency for it to improve. In fact, according to Stylized Fact 10 there was an improvement in the inclusion of the poor in the educational system. However, the distributive conflict between different social groups prevents this improvement from happening more quickly.

The maintenance of free public universities, for example, typically benefits those students from the middle-income group and drains a large part of public education resources – resources that could be invested in the basic levels of public education, which is entirely attended by the poor. What is more, teachers unions (a middle-income group with great organizational power), tend to block educational reform designed to reward those with greater performance and punish absenteeism and low effort. The very demands by the poor appear to be initially concentrated on short-term income gains necessary for survival (income transfers and assistance policies) are detrimental to long-term income gains. This demand profile, perfectly reasonable for the one who does not have their short-term survival guaranteed, tends to change only when the majority of the poor have at least their survival guaranteed, only then being able to plan their long-term life.

From the point of view of the middle-income group, improvement in the education of the poor is not necessarily a good deal. If on one side the middle class would gain because society would have more productive labor and could grow more quickly, on the other side their youth would come to face a more competitive labor market, since the poor would acquire more human capital and be able to compete on equal terms.

The result is that a social consensus is not formed in regards to the need for quick advances in education. The advance is only to the point that the inclusive policies take the poor to school, but improving quality is a much harder challenge.

In summary, the "history behind low growth" seems to be a social conflict, in a very unequal society where different groups pressure the government for distinct policies. The state, in turn, tries to accommodate the conflict by "redistributing income to almost everyone," with perverse effects on the potential for economic growth. Therefore, a model of "**low growth with dissipative redistribution**" is created. It is dissipative, because the redistribution that should be for the poor, seeps, in large part, to the pockets of the rich and middle-income groups. It is dissipative, also, because the distributive conflict creates different sources of inefficiency, which reduces economic productivity and wastes productive resources that could be better employed.

The ten stylized facts, instead of <u>causes</u> for low growth are, actually, <u>symptoms</u> of a deeper cause: the combination of high inequality with democracy.

Along the almost 30 years of democratic regime, it has been possible to balance political pressure and preserve democracy. The economy, however, is overburdened by excessive taxation, bad infrastructure, precarious education, high interest rates, and an inhospitable business environment. The mid-term perspectives of growth are pale.

The good news is that inequality and poverty have been systematically falling since the beginning of the 1990s, partly because of dissipative redistribution.

Even though the fiscal and economic cost has been high, dissipative redistribution has been able to give a sufficiently enough portion to the most poor to help reduce inequality and poverty. If this tendency continues in the future, it is possible that, in the long-term, Brazil will not be so unequal and an ample middle class will form.

If inequality is at the center of the cause for the low growth with dissipative redistribution model, a substantial fall in inequality would tend to undo the model. In fact, it is possible that a more equal society would become less conflicting. The dominance of the middle class would lead to a smaller demand for welfare policies and more demand for conditions favorable for growth and the creation of jobs in the private market. At the same time, this ample middle class would be better informed and more resistant to the privileges given to the rich, which would eliminate political support and such privileges.

There would be, therefore, political support for a state more focused on the provision of efficient public services, including law and contracts enforcement. A high-growth model with low inequality could emerge as consequence of the current model of low growth with dissipative redistribution. In this case, low growth in the first decades of democracy would be the price to be paid for obtaining, in the future, high growth and more equality.

However, this automatic, inertial transition is far from being the only future possibility. There is a negative scenario: the perpetuation of the current dysfunctional model. To enter the virtuous cycle, a big drop in inequality would be necessary. But inequality is still high, even after the reductions of the last decade. Inequality will not necessarily continue to fall. It is possible that it stops falling and stabilizes at a still high level. This would maintain the stimulus for social groups to maintain the behavior that generates the model of low growth with dissipative redistribution.

The remainder of the book tells the story in a more detailed way. Given that inequality is here considered a key variable to explain low growth, the next chapter will examine in detail what the literature has to say regarding inequality in Brazil: its causes, its tendency along the years and the reasons for its fall since the 1990s.

ANNEX 1A.1   THE MAIN ELECTORAL AND POLITICAL INSTITUTIONS IN THE NEW BRAZILIAN DEMOCRACY

This annex aims to briefly describe the main features of the electoral and political systems in Brazil after democratization. This description shows how the political-electoral system fits into the model of dissipative redistribution, being flexible enough to allow the implementation of polices that controlled hyperinflation without disrupting the dissipative redistribution, even after the introduction of a relatively tight fiscal regime at the end of the 1990s. (A synthetic description of the Brazilian political institutions and abundant bibliographical references can be obtained at Cintra, 2004.)

The new constitution did not promote radical change in the political representation system and electoral rules in force during the military regime. It maintained a presidential regime with a two-chamber congress, in which the Chamber of Deputies and the Senate constituted two distinct decisional instances. All items submitted to Congress should be voted in one house and reviewed by the other. The federative system was also maintained, with three levels of government: union, states, and municipalities.

This means that there are several levels of power able to interfere in political decisions. The executive branch, to pass public policy, needs not only to obtain a majority vote in both houses, but also avoid offending the interests of the states and municipalities, which have reasonable influence over the deputies and senators that represent their respective states.

The executive branch, however, has instruments at its disposal that are strong enough to guarantee presidential leadership in political action and fiscal control. The first of these instruments is called the "provisional measure" (*medida provisória*). It is a law, temporary but immediate, that the president can declare without previous congressional approval. Once the provisional measure is instituted, Congress must approve, amend or alter it, within a determined amount of time, making it into a bona fide law. This instrument is an adaptation of the "law decrees" created during the military regime. In the way it was written into the new constitution, provisional measures receive priority consideration by Congress, and, while there are pending provisional measures to be voted, Congress cannot deliberate a large part of other types of bills. This gives the president the power to place its preferred bills at the top of the legislative vote agenda.

The president also has other instruments at his or her disposal in relation to Congress. He can request that a particular bill be considered urgent in nature, making it move to the front of other projects in vote priority. The president also has the exclusive power to present bills dealing with specific subjects (projects that create government positions or that alter the administrative structure of public institutions, for example). Members of Congress are not allowed to present bills of such a nature.

The model for preparing, voting, and executing the federal budget also gives great power to the president. It is the responsibility of the executive branch to prepare the annual budget proposal and present it to Congress. Congress may alter the revenue estimates as well as increase budgetary expenses. However, the budget law approved by the legislature is only an expenditure <u>authorization</u> and does not oblige the executive branch to incur the expense. As such, if it desires to incur fewer expenses than those approved by Congress, the executive has the right to do it.

Having in view the political pressure to create public expenditure that generates income in favor of social groups, federal government fiscal policy is conducted in such a way as to try to balance the expansion of these expenses with fiscal equilibrium. To this end, the executive branch uses its power to approve, in Congress, successive tax increases. Secondly, the President of the Republic detains the right to block part of the expenses contained in the budget. The main goal of these cuts has been investment in infrastructure. This is a type of expense that benefits the population in general, without representing a source of income for a specific social group. Therefore, there is not a powerful lobby in its favor and it loses out to other expenses, such as credit subsidies, civil servant salaries, or monetary transfers to poor families.

Another type of expenditure commonly restrained by the executive branch is increases to the budgetary expenses made by congressmen. These are called "parliamentary amendments to the budget," which are generally used for pork barrel politics. By releasing these resources in small amounts, the executive gains bargaining power to control the way senators and deputies vote. It is common for these resources to be released only after important votes are held in Congress in which the release of benefits is provided to those who voted in favor of the executive branch.

The President of the Republic is also able to control loans requested by states and municipalities. Most loans requested by these governments must be explicitly authorized by the federal executive power. Even though control was loose in the first years after democratization, which led to a debt crisis for the subnational entities, it was reinforced after 2000. With this, the federal government has the power to induce states and municipalities to balance their accounts and cooperate with the aggregate fiscal effort.

Even with ample powers at its disposal, the president cannot govern alone. Congress has the power to reject or alter bills and provisional measures proposed by the executive branch. The fact that these proposals must be approved both in the Chamber and the Senate increases the congressmen's bargaining power. There are also some issues that require a high quorum, such as amendments to the constitution, which increases the Congress' veto power.

Congress can form commissions of inquiry to investigate actions taken by the Executive Branch, and can overturn or veto presidential nominations for posts in regulatory agencies and other public institutions. It can also summon members of the executive to inquire regarding policy conduct. All these actions can create political hurdles for the executive branch.

To be able to approve their proposals in Congress, the President of the Republic needs to form a majority in both the Chamber and the Senate. The formation of this majority depends on providing incentives to the deputies and senators to stimulate them to vote in favor of the government. Such incentives are governed by electoral rules.

In the Chamber of Deputies elections, each state in the federation has a fixed number of chairs. The voter chooses a specific candidate. The candidate's vote is computed in favor of their party. The chairs in the Chamber of Deputies that belong to each state are proportionally divided between the parties according to the slice each association has received. The chairs obtained by each party are filled by the most voted candidates of that party (this is the so-called "open list system").

This voting system has several implications. First, it reduces party discipline because the candidate for deputy runs against his fellow party members. To be elected, it is necessary to be among the most voted in the party. The tendency is for each candidate to conduct their own campaign: individualism prevails. It does not make sense to campaign along with other candidates from the same party who could take one's vacancy.

Second, the candidate contends for votes in the entire state territory, being that the state territories are not divided into electoral districts. As Brazil is a country of continental proportions, most states have large territories. The combination of an individualized campaign with a large electoral district, which must be covered by the candidate, causes individual campaign costs to be quite high. (Samuels (2001a, 2001b) shows how Brazilian elections are expensive when compared to other democracies.) The candidates must find ways to finance their campaigns. One way to do this is to seek contributions from *lobbies,* which makes it easy to acquire a parliamentarian to support specific interests. This is a vehicle used by high economic power groups to derive public transfers and regulation that favor them.

Another common strategy is for the candidate to seek votes from a particular region of the state, which reduces campaign costs. In this case, during their campaign, they promise to obtain federal resources for municipalities in the target area. This is when *pork barrel politics* comes into play. In order to satisfy local interests, parliamentarians try to amend the federal budget. As has been stated above, the President of the Republic tends to hold back these disbursements, only authorizing them when interested parliamentarians vote according to government orientation. Moreover, parliamentary amendments to the budget may also be presented in favor of economic groups that financed the parliamentarian's campaign.

Minority representation in Congress is another feature of the electoral system, since it allows the election of representatives by different groups. In a voting system where the state is divided into various districts, and a representative is elected in each of them, a minority group scattered around the state territory will be unable to gain a majority in any district and be unable to elect a congressional representative. In the Brazilian system, where the state territory is not divided into smaller electoral districts, a minority group can add up its scattered votes and elect their representative.

Consequently, there is incentive for politicians to specialize in representing the interests of specific professional categories, or to sponsor the rights of ethnic or religious groups or economic sectors (farmers, industries, etc.). Frequently, they form informal representative groups in Congress, composed of parliamentarians from different parties, to represent specific interests (public health, public security, farming, etc.).

This dispersion of interests permits the many groups to organize themselves in Congress to pressure for public disbursement and regulation in their favor. Being that political responsibility and macroeconomic performance are in the hands of the Executive Branch, the deputies and senators are little interested in maintaining a balanced budget. To them, the more expenses they can insert into the budget, the better, because in this way they are able to fulfill their electoral promises. Therefore, the Executive is the only political power with incentives to control budgetary expenses, which shows the importance of the power of the president to control the pace and amount of public expenditure.

Whatever a candidate's electoral strategy, they must guarantee a great number of votes to be within the most voted in their party. Since a great majority of the voting public is poor, a natural bias arises in favor of policies directed toward the poor. Many of these policies are patronizing and shortsighted. Others have the effective ability to reduce poverty.

The poor are equally important in majority elections (president, senators, governors), by the simple fact that in this type of election, whoever receives the most votes, wins, with no consideration for party vote.

The electoral system also stimulates the creation of a large number of parties. First, because each party has the right to public funding and free TV time for electoral propaganda. Second, because it is possible to form party coalitions for elections to the Chamber. Many parties unite and their votes and chairs in the Chamber are counted as if they were one party. To be the leader of a party, even if the party is small, guarantees power, funds, and the flexibility to form coalitions.

The great dispersion of interests, the appetite of deputies to occasional disbursements to specific groups or to a poor majority, without concern regarding fiscal policy, and the large number of parties, forces the executive branch to form majorities in Congress by means of benefits distribution or the increase of welfare policies. It is rare that a party wins the presidential election and obtains, at the same time, the majority in the Chamber of Deputies. Therefore, it is necessary to form coalitions in Congress. Political analysts call it "coalition presidentialism" (Abranches, 1988).

Some political parties specialize in the function of offering support to the Executive power in Congress. Instead of seeking power by presenting a candidate for the presidential election, these parties concentrate their efforts on electing as many congressmen as possible, to form an ample support base in the Chamber and Senate. After the president is elected, those parties offer the necessary parliamentary majority in exchange for benefits financed by public resources (positions in government, funding for specific public programs, and regulatory measures demanded by lobby groups, etc.). Of course, there is much room for corruption and bribery.

A simple illustration shows how this need by the executive branch to form a majority coalition in Congress results in the expansion of the government apparatus. In the first government after democratization, the federal executive power had 25 ministries. Twenty-six years (or six presidential terms) later, the number had grown to 39! Not only have ministry positions increased, public employment ballooned, many positions being filled by political appointment.

There is, finally, the dimension of regional distribution of power. The military regime increased the number of chairs in the Chamber of Deputies that were due to the less developed states. The objective at the time was to guarantee political support from the regional leadership in regions most dependent on federal funds. Besides, the electorate of backward areas was under tight control by local patrons. By contrast, in the more developed states, with higher income and more informed voters, the power of command by local chiefs was less. The new constitution reinforced the disproportionate representation in favor of the less developed states situated in the North and Northeast of the country. First, several federal territories located in the North region, which had no legislative representation, were transformed into states and received the right to have deputies and senators to represent them. Second, a minimum of eight deputies per state was established, independent of the size of the population. Third, the number of senators for each state was increased from two to three.

As such, states in the less developed areas (North and Northeast) or more recently developed (Mid-West) are disproportionately represented in Congress, while the more developed South-Southwest states are underrepresented. The North, Northeast, and Mid-West combined have 74% of the chairs in the Senate and 50% of the votes in the Chamber, even though they represent only 46% of the population. This gives room to bargain for federal transfers to less developed states or regions. Regional bias in the Brazilian parliament is prominent with a long tradition of deputies and senators from those regions specializing in extracting federal resources to be transferred to their regions.

This state or regional pressure also restricts the ability of the executive branch to control state and municipal indebtedness. Pressure in parliament is common, especially in the Senate, for the federal government to exert less control over the debt limit of the subnational governments.

Summarizing, political institutions from the military regime were adapted and customized, in the new constitution, to allow public administration to function based on the distribution of public funds and regulatory advantages in favor of different groups, grouped according to social class, profession, geographic region, or any other feature that represents a common interest in a specific issue. The interests of these groups echo in a Congress that is elected by rules that favor individualism, minority representation, high influence by campaign contributors, no political responsibility for fiscal equilibrium, and regional imbalance. The result is political pressure to expand public expenditure and to create regulations that favor special interests.

At the same time, it was possible to do this with some degree of freedom so that the executive branch could control the overall fiscal balance, even if in a precarious manner. Permanent raises in tax revenue and the repression of infrastructure investment are used to finance ever increasing current expenses. The control of budgetary amendments that interest parliament members serves the double purpose of maintaining the government coalition in Congress and reducing the rhythm of public expense growth.

It is not the intent to argue that the political institutions, which were briefly described, are the <u>cause</u> of the Brazilian model of low growth with dissipative redistribution. This causal relationship would allow us to conclude that reforms in the political system would be a necessary condition, or even sufficient, to change the economic model. However, political institutions were not created in a vacuum. They are the result of choices made along the years in a country's history. They are mechanisms created to efficiently mediate the interests of different social groups. To change the rules in an attempt to change political behaviors considered inadequate could generate adverse collateral effects, which would result in a worsening in the quality of the decision making process and governability.

Take, for example the imposition of limits for the private financing of political campaigns. In 2014, the Supreme Court (*Supremo Tribunal Federal*) is reviewing a case that petitions the prohibition of this type of financing. The objective is to prevent large economic groups from holding influence over elected politicians. It should be questioned, however, if the prohibition of such financing will, effectively, eliminate it. It is possible that it will only increase non-declared (illegal) campaign financing, reducing transparency in the elections. In the current system, it is possible to clearly identify what company donated to which candidate. With no registers, it will be difficult to request an explanation from elected officials about why they showed preference to a particular company in public procurement or when enacting regulation. Another possible outcome is for politicians to become more dependent on public funds to finance their campaigns, which would stimulate corruption, the political exploration of state owned companies and, above all, would give an unfair competitive advantage to candidates who are members of the governing party, which would have greater access to public funds.

Rivers flow toward the sea. Trying to block their course with inefficient dykes would generate floods and adverse effects, without stopping the river from reaching its destination.

It may be possible to conduct reforms in the political-electoral system to reduce the effects of this system on fiscal policy and the quality of public administration. However, each alternative to the electoral and representation rules has its advantages and disadvantages. It is not easy to reach an agreement on which rules would generate a positive result for society as a whole. As such, contrary to what many Brazilian political leaders and analysts argue, political reform, regardless of what it is, is a long way from being the Holy Grail that would reestablish virtue and reasonableness to Brazilian public administration.

What is relevant to highlight is that the current politico-party system shows itself to be compatible and functional in a context where different heterogeneous social groups contend for benefits and regulation in their favor.

REFERENCES

Abranches, S., 1988. Presidencialismo de Coalizão: O Dilema Institucional Brasileiro. Dados 31 (1), 5–32.

Afonso, J.R., Araujo, E.A., 2005. Contribuições Sociais, mas Antieconômicas. In: Biderman, C., Arvate, P.R. (Eds.), Economia do Setor Público no Brasil. Elsevier-Campus.

Amadeo, E., Camargo, J.M., 1993. Labour legislation and institutional aspects of the Brazilian labour market. Labour 7 (1), 157–180, Spring.

Arida, P., Resende, A.L., 1985. Inertial inflation and monetary reform. In: Williamson, J. (Ed.), Inflation and Indexation: Argentina, Brasil and Israel. Institute for International Economics.

Bacha, E.L., 1974. O Rei da Belíndia: uma Fábula para Tecnocratas. J. Opinião. Available from, http://iepecdg.com.br/Arquivos/ArtigosBacha/Bel%EDndia.pdf.

Barbosa Filho, F.H., Pessôa, S.A., 2013. Educação e Desenvolvimento no Brasil. In: Veloso, F., et al. (Eds.), Desenvolvimento Econômico: Uma Perspectiva Brasileira. Elsevier-Campus.

Barro, R.J., Lee, J.W., 2010. A New Dataset of Educational Attainment in the World: 1950–2010. Database available from, www.barroandlee.com.

Barros, R.P., Corseuil, C.H., 2001. The Impact of Regulations on Brazilian Labor Market Performance. Inter-American Development Bank, Research Network Working Paper # R-427.

Biderman, C., Arvate, P.R. (Eds.), 2005. Economia do Setor Público no Brasil. Elsevier-Campus.

Brazil Central Bank, 2011. Relatório de Inflação: Junho. Available from, www.bcb.gov.br.

Brazil Central Bank, 2013. Relatório de Inflação: Março. Available from, www.bcb.gov.br.

Brazil Ministry of Finance, 2008. Reforma Tributária. Available from, http://www.fazenda.gov.br/divulgacao/publicacoes/reforma-tributaria/cartilha.reforma.tributaria.pdf.

Brazil Ministry of Finance, 2011. Carga Tributária 2011. Receita Federal – Estudos Tributários. Available from, www.receita.fazenda.gov.br.

Busso, M., Madrigal, L., Pagés, C., 2012. Productivity and Resource Misallocation in Latin America. IADB Working Paper Series No. IDB-WP-306.

Calderón, C., Servén, L., 2010. Infrastructure in Latin-America. The World Bank, Policy Research Working Paper n 5317.

Caselli, F., 2005. Accounting for cross-country income differences. In: Aghion, P., Durlauf, S. (Eds.), Handbook of Economic Growth. North-Holland Press.

Cintra, A.O., 2004. O Sistema de Governo no Brasil. In: Avelar, L., Cintra, A.C. (Eds.), Sistema Político Brasileiro: Uma Introdução. Konrad Adenauer Stiftung / Unesp.

Corseuil, C.H., Kume, H. (Eds.), 2003. A Abertura Comercial Brasileira nos Anos 1990: Impactos sobre Emprego e Salários. MTE and IPEA.

De Vries, G., 2009. Productivity in a Distorted Market: The Case of Brazil's Retail Sector. University of Groningen. Available from, https://workspace.imperial.ac.uk/businessschool/Public/CAED/D-de%20Vries-%20MicroProductivityBrazil_gjdevries.pdf.

Easterly, W., 2001. The middle class consensus and economic development. J. Econ. Growth 4 (6), 317–335.

Feldstein, M., Horioka, C., 1980. Domestic saving and international capital flows. Econ. J. 90 (358), 314–329.

Ferraz, C., Monteiro, J., 2009. Misallocation and manufacturing TFP in Brazil. Pontifícia Universidade Católica do Rio de Janeiro.

Ferreira, P.C., Rossi, J.L., 2003. New evidence from Brazil on trade liberalization and productivity growth. Int. Econ. Rev. 44 (4), 1383–1405.

Franco, G.H.B., 1995. O Plano Real e Outros Ensaios. Francisco Alves.

Friedmann, R., 2011. O que é Guerra Fiscal? Brasil, Economia e Governo. [Online] 28th July. Available from, http://www.brasil-economia-governo.org.br/2011/07/28/o-que-e-guerra-fiscal/.

Frischtak, C., 2008. O Investimento em Infraestrutura no Brasil: Histórico Recente e Perspectivas. Pesquisa e Planejamento Econômico 38 (2), 307–348.

Frischtak, 2013. Infraestrutura e Desenvolvimento no Brasil. In: Veloso, F., et al. (Eds.), Desenvolvimento Econômico: Uma Perspectiva Brasileira. Elsevier-Campus.

Giambiagi, F., 2008. 18 anos de política fiscal no Brasil: 1991/2008. Economia Aplicada 12 (4), 535–580.

Gomes, V., Pessôa, S.A., Veloso, F., 2003. Evolução da Produtividade Total dos Fatores na Economia Brasileira: Uma Análise Comparativa. Pesquisa e Planejamento Econômico 33 (3), 389–434.

Gonzaga, G., 2003. Labor Turnover and Labor Legislation in Brazil. Economia 4 (1), 165–222.

Hausmann, R., Rodrik, D., Velasco, A., 2005. Growth Diagnostics. Harvard Kennedy School. Available from, http://www.hks.harvard.edu/fs/drodrik/Research%20papers/barcelonafinalmarch2005.pdf.

Jones, C.I., 2002. Introduction to Economic Growth, second ed. Norton.

Lagakos, D., 2009. Superstores or Mom and Pops? Technology Adoption and Productivity Differences in Retail Trade. Federal Reserve Bank of Minneapolis, Research Department Staff Report 428.

Levi, P.M., Giambiagi, F., 2013. Poupança e Investimento: o Caso Brasileiro. In: Veloso, F., et al. (Eds.), Desenvolvimento Econômico: Uma Perspectiva Brasileira. Elsevier-Campus.

Menezes Filho, N., 2011. Pré-Escola, Horas-Aula, Ensino Médio e Avaliação. In: Bacha, E.L., Schwartzman, S. (Eds.), Brasil: A Nova Agenda Social. Gen/LTC.

Menezes Filho, N., Kannebley Jr., S., 2013. Abertura Comercial, Exportações e Inovações no Brasil. In: Veloso, F., et al. (Eds.), Desenvolvimento Econômico: Uma Perspectiva Brasileira. Elsevier-Campus.

Mesquita, M.M., Volpe, C., Blyde, J.S., 2008. Unclogging the Arteries: The Impact of Transport Costs on Latin American and Caribbean Trade. Inter-American Development Bank, Harvard University Press.

Nascimento, E.R., Debus, I., 2002. Lei complementar 101/2000: Entendendo a Lei de Responsabilidade Fiscal. ESAF.

Neri, M., Gonzaga, G., Camargo, J.M., 2001. Salário Mínimo, "Efeito-Farol" e Pobreza. Revista de Economia Política 21 (2 (82)), 78–90.

Pagés, C. (Ed.), 2010. The Age of Productivity: Transforming Economies from the Bottom Up. Inter-American Development Bank.

Pastore, J., 2005. O Custo do Trabalho na Microempresa. O Estado de S. Paulo, B2, 13th December. Economia e Negócios.

Pastore, A.C., 2013. O Fim da Bonança Externa. O Estado de S. Paulo, B5, 14th July. Economia e Negócios.

Pellegrini, J.A., 2012. Dívida Estadual. Núcleo de Estudos e Pesquisas do Senado Federal. Texto para Discussão n. 110,. Available from, http://www12.senado.gov.br/publicacoes/estudos-legislativos/tipos-de-estudos/textos-para-discussao/td-110-divida-estadual.

Pinheiro, A.C., 2005. Magistrados, Judiciário e Economia no Brasil. In: Zylbersztajn, D., Sztajn, R. (Eds.), Direito e Economia: Análise Econômica do Direito e das Organizações. Elsevier-Campus.

Pinheiro, A.C., Giambiagi, F., 2006. Rompendo o marasmo: A retomada do desenvolvimento no Brasil. Elsevier-Campus.

Rajan, R., 2006. Competitive Rent Preservation, Reform Paralysis, and the Persistence of Underdevelopment, NBER Working Paper 12093.

Rajaram, A., et al., 2008. Framework for Reviewing Public Investment Efficiency. Policy Research Working Paper n. 5397, The World Bank. Available from, http://elibrary.worldbank.org/doi/pdf/10.1596/1813-9450-5397.

Robinson, J.A., 2008. The Political Economy of Redistributive Policies. UNDP – Research for Public Policy Inclusive Development. ID-09-2009,. Available from, http://www.rrojasdatabank.info/09_RPPLAC_ID.pdf.

Salviano Jr., C., 2004. Bancos Estaduais: Dos Problemas Crônicos ao PROES. Banco Central do Brasil. Available from, http://www.bcb.gov.br/htms/public/BancosEstaduais/livro_bancos_estaduais.pdf.

Samuels, D., 2001a. Money, Elections and Democracy in Brazil. Lat. Am. Polit. Soc. 43 (2), 27–48.

Samuels, D., 2001b. Does money matter? Campaign finance in newly democratic countries: theory and evidence from Brazil. Comp. Polit. 34, 23–42.

Soto, H., 2003. The Mystery of Capital: Why Capitalism Triumphs in the West and Fails Everywhere else. Basic Books.

Stiglitz, J.E., 2000. Economics of the Public Sector. Ed: Norton, third ed.

Távora, F.L., 2008. Developments in the Soybean World Market: A Partial Equilibrium Trade Model. Available from: http://www12.senado.gov.br/senado/institucional/conleg/seminarios-workshops/seminario-desenvolvimento-no-mercado-mundial-de-soja-um-modelo-de-comercio-usando-equilibrio-parcial-texto-base-fernando-lagares-tavora-29-9-2008.

The World Bank, 2009. Brasil: Avaliação da Eficiência da Gestão do Investimento Público. The World Bank. Available from, http://siteresources.worldbank.org/BRAZILINPOREXTN/Resources/Avaliacao_Eficiencia_gesta pdf.

The World Bank, 2013a. Doing Business 2013. The World Bank/IFC.

Ubiergo, A.S., 2012. The Puzzle of Brazil's High Interest Rates. International Monetary Fund, IMF Working Paper WP/12/62.

Varsano, R., 1997. A Guerra Fiscal do ICMS: Quem Ganha e Quem Perde. Planejamento e Políticas Públicas. 15, 3–17.

Varsano, R., Afonso, J.R., 2004. Reforma Tributária: Sonhos e Frustrações. In: Giambiagi, F., Reis, J., Urani, A. (Eds.), Reformas no Brasil: Balanço e Agenda. Nova Fronteira.

Varsano, R., et al., 2001. Substituindo o PIS e a COFINS – e Porque não a CPMF – por uma Contribuição Não-Cumulativa. IPEA. Texto para Discussão n. 832. Available from, http://www.ipea.gov.br/portal/index.php?option=com_content&view=article&id=4395.

Veloso, F., 2011. A Evolução Recente e Propostas para a Melhoria da Educação. In: Bacha, E.L., Schwartzman, S. (Eds.), Brasil: A Nova Agenda Social. Gen/LTC.

World Bank, 2002. Brazil: The New Growth Agenda. The World Bank, Brazil Country Management Unit. Vol.I: policy briefing. Report n. 22950-BR.

Zouvi, A., et al., 2008. Reforma Tributária: a PEC n. 233, de 2008. Núcleo de Estudos e Pesquisas da Consultoria Legislativa. Texto para Discussão n. 44, Available from, http://www12.senado.gov.br/publicacoes/estudos-legislativos/tipos-de-estudos/textos-para-discussao/td-44-reforma-tributaria-a-pec-no-233-de-2008.

Chapter 2

Inequality

2.1 INTRODUCTION

In Brazil, an engineer earns seven times more than a carpenter. In the United Kingdom, this difference is 2.1 times, in the United States, no more than 1.8 and in Canada, 1.7. The curious thing is that high-income employment in Brazil has about the same remuneration as developed countries. The Brazilian engineer earns, on average, US$3700 per month, more than the Canadian (US$3000), almost equal to the British (US$3800) and a little less than the American (US$4700) (http://www.worldsalaries.org). Values expressed in US$ from 2005, corrected by purchasing power parity.

The Brazilian engineer can lead a standard of life similar to their colleagues in other countries. The situation for the carpenter, however, is much different. While they earn US$512 per month, their colleagues north of the equator receive about US$1800 in the United Kingdom and Canada and US$2500 in the United States. The Brazilian carpenter probably has a quality of life well below his foreign colleagues. This great difference in incomes between white- and blue-collar workers is a portrait of Brazilian inequality.

In the other three countries, for example, engineers and carpenters, and their respective families, often study at the same schools, use the same health services and drive the same kinds of cars. In Brazil, the engineer's son will be born in a private hospital, paid for by a private health plan, go to a private school and, most of the time, travel by car. The carpenter's son will probably be born in a public hospital, attend public school and use public transportation, all of lesser quality than his private counterpart. They live and grow up in parallel worlds. They may live in the same city, but usually go to different places in their leisure time. The engineer's son will probably do better in his studies and get a higher

paying job than the carpenter's son. This inequality carries on from one generation to the next.

The central argument of this book is that this inequality in income, assets,
and human capital is an important causal factor in the recent history of low economic growth in Brazil. Before exploring this idea in more detail, it is important
to take a closer look at inequality around the world, the degree of inequality in
Brazil and its tendency over the last few years.

The first relevant fact is that inequality persists over time. Countries that
were unequal in the past tend to perpetuate inequality over time. The causes for
this fact will be analyzed in Chapter 3. Figure 2.1 presents the Gini Index of
income inequality for several countries, comparing inequality in the past (using
the oldest available data) with current inequality (most recent available data).[1]
The main message of this figure is that, for this group of countries, inequality
in the past "explains" 80% of current inequality. The figure also highlights the
fact that Latin American and Caribbean countries (represented by spheres) are,

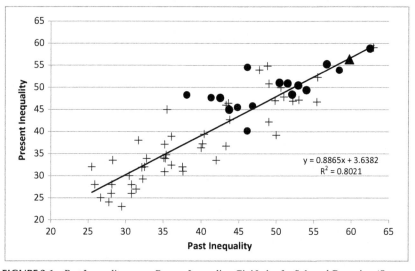

FIGURE 2.1   Past Inequality versus Present Inequality: Gini Index for Selected Countries. *(Source:
Brazil Presidency of the Republic, 2012. (http://www.wider.unu.edu/research/database/en_gb/
database/). Prepared by author. Note: Brazil is represented by a triangle, other Latin American
countries by a sphere and all other countries by a cross.)*

1. The Gini Index is one of the most commonly used standards to measure inequality. It varies
between 0 and 100 (or from 0 to 1, according to the scale), with greater values representing higher
inequality. For a description and analysis of different inequality indexes, see Ray 1998. The figure
includes only those countries that: (a) were not under a communist regime in the past; (b) whose
statistics are considered to be of good (quality classification level 1 or 2); and (c) where there is a
span of at least 5 years between the oldest available and most recent available data on inequality.
The average interval between the first (past) and last (present) observation is 23 years. The standard
deviation is 12.5.

in general, more unequal than other nations. Brazil (triangle) is among the most unequal in the world, both past and the present.

The news is that Brazilian inequality has fallen consistently since 1995, with acceleration of this trend from 2001 on, as presented in Figure 2.2. For reasons analyzed in this chapter, the inertia shown in Figure 2.1 has been partially broken in recent years. However, the reduction in the Gini Index may be fading out: in 2012, for the first time since 2001, it did not decrease in relation to the previous year, signaling that inequality could be stabilizing at a still high level.

The process of inequality reduction is not only Brazilian, having occurred in most Latin American countries. Figure 2.3 shows that 9 of the 14 regional countries had a reduction of inequality between 1995 and 2009. On average, this index fell 0.55% per year. The Brazilian reduction was a little more intense than the regional average and only came in behind Peru and Paraguay.

Despite the recent reduction, Brazil remains a very unequal country. Figure 2.4 compares the Gini Index for Brazil with the 27 other countries used in Chapter 1 as a comparison group. One notes that, even with the recent improvement, Brazilian inequality (and that of Latin America) continues well above the average and among the higher rates in the group.

The recent reduction in Brazilian inequality was translated into significant income growth by the poorest. In Figure 2.5, it can be seen that, between 2001 and 2011, the *per capita* income of the poorest 10% grew at an average of 6.7% per year, while the richest 10% was only 1.5% per year: on average, the poorer the household, the greater the income growth.

This is certainly one of the factors that created a sense of well-being and progress in the first decade of the 21st century. In these years, a large

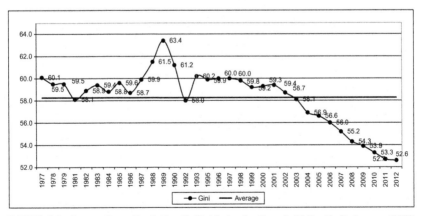

FIGURE 2.2   Income Inequality in Brazil: Gini Index for Household Per Capita Income (1977-2012). *(Source: Barros et al., 2009. Brazil IPEA, 2012 and Brazil, Instituto de Pesquisa Econômica Aplicada (IPEA), 2013. Primary Source: Pesquisa Nacional por Amostra de Domicílios – PNAD (National Research by Sample Households) 1977-2012. Prepared by the author.)*

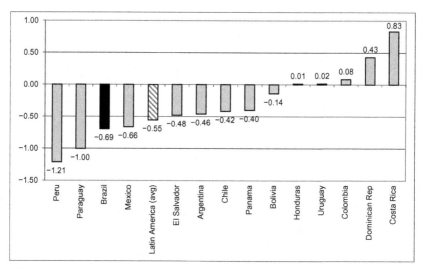

FIGURE 2.3   Yearly Average Rate of Variation of the Gini Index in Latin American Countries: 1995-2009 (% PY). *(Source: World Bank, 2011. Prepared by the author. Note: Data used is from time periods nearest to 1995 and 2009. The years vary from between 1995 and 1997 with the final year between 2007 and 2009.)*

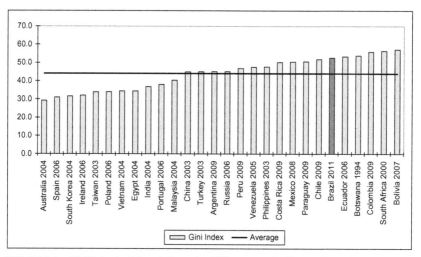

FIGURE 2.4   Gini Index in Selected Countries (different years). *(Source: Brazil IPEA, 2012 for Brazil, World Bank, 2011 for other Latin American countries and, for the remaining countries, World Inequality Database (WIID2C). Prepared by the author.)*

number of people escaped poverty. As seen in Figure 2.6, in 2003, 24.4% of the population lived below the poverty line (in the concept adopted by Millennium Development Goals of US$2 per day) and, in 2011, this percentage had fallen to 10.2%. According to estimates presented by a Brazilian public think tank (IPEA), the reduction in inequality was the main source of

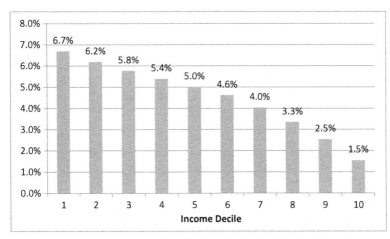

FIGURE 2.5   Yearly Average Real Growth Rate of Household *Per Capita* Income Between 2001 and 2011 in Brazil by Income Decile (% PY). *(Source: Brazil IPEA, 2012.)*

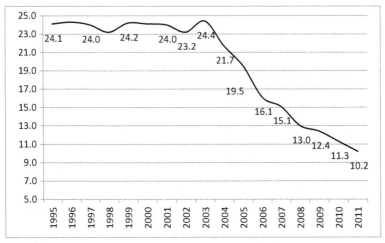

FIGURE 2.6   Population with *Per Capita* Household Income Below the Poverty Line in Brazil (Millennium Development Goals Criteria) (%). *(Source: Brazil IPEA, 2012. Prepared by the author.)*

poverty reduction: "about 52% [of this decrease in poverty] was caused by changes in income inequality, and the remainder explained by the effects of growth"(Brazil IPEA, 2012, p. 10).

According to the same study, if it had not been for the redistribution of income, the income growth necessary to produce such reduction would have to be 6.6% per year between 2001 and 2011, instead of 2.8% per year (the average rate of growth for the period). This data shows the great power of income redistribution as a mechanism to reduce poverty in a very unequal country.

Total household income is composed of different income sources: wages, retirement paid by the public sector, benefits received from governmental social assistance programs, dividends received from investments, unemployment compensation, etc. Each of these components of total household income can be more/less concentrated in the hands of the rich than others. Therefore, it is interesting to analyze how much each income component contributes to inequality and how this contribution changes over time.

It is important to ask:

- If income is so concentrated in Brazil, which sources of income are more concentrated than the others, and how does each of them contribute to such a high Gini Index?
- What would be the causes for the recent reduction in inequality? If it is so time resistant (as is shown in Figure 2.1 above), what broke the historical inertia and produced this uncommon tendency to fall?

According to what was highlighted in the previous chapter, one hypothesis analyzed in this book is that the coexistence of a democratic regime with a large population of poor living in an unequal society would have induced politicians to seek votes of the poor using redistributive policies. It is therefore important to evaluate if these policies had an important role in the reduction of inequality (and poverty). Moreover, it is relevant to evaluate future prospects. Will inequality continue to fall in the coming years?

2.2 THE COMPOSITION OF INEQUALITY

This section evaluates how each component of household income affects total income inequality. Before presenting the main results found in the literature, it is worthwhile to describe some Brazilian social welfare programs that represent relevant shares of the total household income.

Every Brazilian working in the formal sector of the economy has the right to retirement, after which they receive a pension paid by the Social Security system. Employers and employees are required by law to contribute to this system, in order for the employee to be eligible for a retirement pension after some years of work. (The amount of years depends on gender, profession, and age, which is usually 30 years of work for men and 25 for women.) Social Security also provides insurance in case of job related accidents, disease, maternity, or death as well as other benefits.

Social Security is financed by a pay-as-you-go system: those at work today finance pensions and benefits currently being paid. As commented below, the system has a large and increasing actuarial deficit, which is covered, every year, by federal government funds, i.e., tax revenue.

After democratization, Social Security acquired some features of a non-contributive welfare policy. The most important branch of this policy is the payment of pensions to rural workers: these workers are eligible to receive one minimum wage per month, <u>without having contributed</u> to Social Security during their working life. All they must do to be eligible is prove they have worked in agriculture. The payment of this benefit is one of the major causes for the ever-rising Social Security deficit.

It is important to mention that the federal government civil servants have their own system, insulated from that used by workers in the private sector and rural workers. While this is managed by the National Institute of Social Security (*Instituto Nacional de Seguridade Social* – INSS), civil-servant pensions and benefits are managed directly by the federal government.

In general, the system for civil servants is more benevolent, paying much higher pensions and benefits. Although employee contributions are higher, such contributions are not enough to cover expenses: the actuarial deficit in the civil-servant system is higher than in that for private-sector workers. This deficit is covered by the federal government as well. Many state and municipal governments offer their civil servants social security systems similar to the one enjoyed by federal civil servants. Others use the general private-sector system.

Parallel to the social security schemes, there are other programs directed toward workers in the private sector and jointly funded by the government, employers, and employees. These programs, however, are not included in Social Security books: its revenue and expenditures are collected and spent directly by the federal government. Two important programs are unemployment compensation (similar to schemes adopted in many countries) and the wage bonus (*abono salarial*). This bonus is paid once a year to workers in the formal sector who earn up to two minimum wages. Its value is equal to one minimum wage.

Besides these programs, there are other public policies targeted to the poor and, therefore, not restricted to workers in the formal sector. They are totally funded by the federal government. The most important and famous is the *Bolsa Família* program (family allowance): a cash transfer to low-income families conditioned on the enrollment of their children in school, and compliance with certain healthcare procedures, such as vaccinations, prenatal examinations, pediatric exams, etc. The unitary value of *Bolsa Família* is defined and adjusted by the federal government. Different from other welfare programs, this value is not linked to minimum wage.

Another important program is called *Benefício de Prestação Continuada* (continued benefit) – BPC, which is a cash transfer to low-income elderly and low-income physically challenged citizens. The unitary value of the BPC benefit equals one minimum wage.

Having made this general description, we are able to show what the literature has found in relation to the impact of each of these sources of income on inequality.

The aforementioned public think tank, IPEA, regularly publishes studies on inequality and poverty in Brazil (Brazil IPEA, 2012). In its 2012 version, it uses the National Research by Sample Households (*Pesquisa Nacional por Amostra de Domicílios* – PNAD) to subdivide *per capita* household income into the following sub-items:

- Labor income (earned in the private and public sectors);
- Pensions and benefits paid by social security (private and public sector);
- Bolsa Família program;
- *Benefícios de Prestação Continuada* – BPC;
- Other income.

The study analyzes how each of these sub-items in total income contributes to income inequality.

Using data from 2011, the study shows that income obtained in the labor market was responsible for 79% of the inequality: the great difference between the smallest and largest wages in the job market is the main component for inequality in Brazil.

Next are the pensions and benefits paid by Social Security, which are responsible for 18% of income concentration (9.66 points in the total index of 52.7). Even though this is a government expense in the so-called "social services" area, Social Security pays more to high-income persons and, therefore, concentrates income. This comes mainly from the fact that civil servants – most of them at the peak of the income pyramid – have privileged pensions and benefits. Moreover, in the private sector, low-income informal workers are excluded from the system, which, as described above, comprises only those in formally registered jobs.

The *Bolsa Família* program redistributes income and, as such, reduces the Gini Index(–0.47 points in the total index of 52.7). The BPC program has zero impact on concentration, while "other income" raises the Gini Index by 3%.

Each of the household-income components affects the concentration/de-concentration of income based on two elements: (a) the intensity of bias in favor of the wealthier or the poorer that particular income component has and (b) how important that component is in the total household income.

The great importance of labor-market income in the formation of a high Gini Index is a result of the fact that this income represents more than three-quarters of household income, while the others represent the remaining quarter. Being unequally distributed and weighing heavily on total income, labor income becomes a decisive factor for the high Brazilian inequality.

The *Bolsa Família* program is focused mainly on the poor and, therefore, redistributes income. However, as income derived from the program represents, on average, only 0.9% of *per capita* household income, the impact on total income is small.

It is therefore relevant to call attention to the fact that, considered as a whole, income paid by the public sector has an overall concentrating effect on income, because the impact by Social Security in this concentration is much greater than the opposite impact by social assistance programs (*Bolsa Família* and BPC).

Two economists from the University of Brasilia, Pedro de Souza and Marcelo Medeiros (Souza and Medeiros, 2013), present similar conclusions to those discussed previously. They also investigate the contribution of sub-items in household income toward inequality. They used a different source of data than that used by IPEA: the *Pesquisa de Orçamento Familiar* – POF (Family Budget Research). Using 2009 as a reference year, they performed a more detailed partition of income, which is subdivided as:

- Labor income in the private market;
- Labor income in the public sector (civil servant remuneration);
- Other income received from the private market;
- Social Security benefits;
- *Bolsa Família* program;
- BPC program;
- Unemployment compensation; and
- Direct taxes paid by families (this item as a deduction of total income).

The important contribution made by Souza and Medeiros is the separation of labor income into that which is paid by the private sector and that paid to civil servants. With this they were able to gain a more ample view of the impact of the public sector on income distribution. Besides income received from Social Security, *Bolsa Família* and BPC, the authors analyze the impact of income paid to civil servants as well as that of unemployment compensation and taxes.

Concurring with the previously cited IPEA study (Brazil IPEA, 2012) Souza and Medeiros show that inequality in labor income earned in the private market is the main source of income inequality in the country, representing 60% of the total Gini Index. Next are incomes originating from Social Security (22%), the remuneration of civil servants (21%) and other incomes in the private sector (11%). Unemployment compensation, another payment made by the government, also concentrates income, representing 1% of the total Gini Index. The effects of the *Bolsa Família* and BPC are similar to IPEA estimates: small redistributive impact and zero, respectively. Direct taxes, which are mainly paid by rich households, reduce the Gini Index by 14%.[2]

In short, this study presents a similar conclusion to the previous: the Brazilian public sector contributes to income concentration. Souza and Medeiros show that this is due not only to the regressive impact of Social Security pensions and benefits, but also to income concentration caused by remuneration paid to civil servants: They receive salaries that are higher than those paid in the private sector and, at the same time, are more concentrated at the top of the income pyramid.

---

2. This does not mean that taxation as a whole (direct and indirect taxes) redistributes income. There is no way to establish an amount paid in indirect taxes by means of family budget research, since these taxes are embedded in the prices of merchandise. Further ahead in this chapter, considerations are made regarding the general impact of taxation on inequality.

The income sub-items paid by the public sector (civil servant wages, Social Security payments, *Bolsa Família* program, BPC program, and unemployment compensation), together, are responsible for no less than 44% of income inequality. If one adds the redistributive effect of direct taxation, the concentration impact of the public sector still remains at a high level, representing 30% of the total Gini Index. Therefore, governmental expense decisions weigh greatly on the Brazilian level of inequality.

2.3   THE FALL OF INEQUALITY SINCE THE MID-1990S

The previous section sought to show what household-income components cause the concentration of income in Brazil. Another relevant question is to evaluate how the contribution of each of these sub-items <u>varied over time</u>.

As seen above, the Gini Index has fallen since 1998, and more intensely between 2001 and 2011 (Figure 2.2). What caused this fall? In general, the literature shows that labor income and Social Security had their concentration effect mitigated during this period, while *the Bolsa Família* program intensified its redistributive effect.

It is important to notice that declaring that a specific source of income became less regressive than in the past, is different from saying that this source of income redistributes income. Labor income and Social Security payments continue to have a regressive effect. However, their impact on income concentration is smaller now than it was in the past. On the other hand, *Bolsa Família* is more progressive now than in the past.

According to calculations from the previously mentioned IPEA study, labor income has become less concentrated along the first and second decades of the 21st century. The difference between low and high wages has become less in the job market. The conditions of supply and demand have raised wages for low-skilled jobs when compared to salaries at the top. This has resulted in a reduction of labor-income inequality, which was responsible for 58% of the total drop in the Gini Index between 2001 and 2011.

Social Security payments made to families also concentrate income less. This is because low-value pensions, especially those paid to rural pensioners, have been readjusted above inflation, following the same rule used to readjust minimum wage (see Chapter 1, Stylized Fact 6), while benefits whose values were superior to minimum wage were readjusted by the inflation rate. In other words, there was a narrowing between minimum and maximum pension values and other Social Security benefits. According to IPEA, this was responsible for 19% of the total fall in the Gini Index between 2001 and 2011 (Brazil IPEA, 2012, p. 28)

On the other hand, the *Bolsa Família* program has not only become more progressive (more focused on the poorest), but has also increased its participation in household income. In 2001, this program was responsible for 0.1% of household income. In 2011 it had grown to 0.6%. The cumulative effect of greater progressivity, with greater weight on total income, allowed the *Bolsa Família* program to be responsible for 13% of the total reduction in the Gini Index between 2001 and 2011. The BPC program contributed to 4% of the total fall in the inequality index.

As such, public programs as a whole (Social Security payments, *Bolsa Família*, and BPC) were responsible for 36% of the total fall in the Gini Index $(19 + 13 + 4)$, be it by the reduction in regressivity (Social Security), by the increase of progressivity (*Bolsa Família*) or by the increase in the weight on total income (*Bolsa Família* and BPC).

In the cited study by Pedro de Souza and Marcelo Medeiros, (Souza and Medeiros, 2013) a more detailed subdivision of incomes was used, as was described in the previous section. In their analysis of the reduction of inequality between 2003 and 2009, they present results similar to those in the IPEA study. They decompose the contribution to the reduction in the Gini Index as: 66% resulted from the narrowing of the wage differential in the private job market; 10% from the reduction in regressivity of Social Security benefits; 20% from *Bolsa Família* and BPC together (12% and 8%, respectively); and 8% from unemployment compensation, becoming less regressive and less important in the total income. As such, Social Security benefits, *Bolsa Família*, BPC, and unemployment compensation were responsible for a joint effect of 38%.

The most interesting point in the Souza and Medeiros analysis is that they showed that wages paid by the public sector acted <u>against</u> the reduction of inequality: salaries paid by the public sector are not only regressive (as previously shown), but have become even more regressive over the last few years. It could be said that almost all the income redistribution produced by the *Bolsa Família* program (12% of the Gini Index reduction) was offset by the concentration promoted by civil-servant remuneration (a negative contribution of 10%).

These numbers portray the distributive conflict process in an unequal society, which this text intends to highlight. On one hand, the desire for the votes of the poor stimulates the expansion of social programs such as *Bolsa Família*. On the other, there is an upper middle-income group (civil servants) with good connections to government authorities and that is well organized in strong unions, which makes it possible to promote income redistribution in its favor. The next chapters will analyze in detail the redistribution processes for the poor, the rich, and the well-organized and politically connected intermediate segments.

Souza and Medeiros show that the net contribution of the public sector to the reduction of inequality is about 34% of the total reduction of the Gini index between 2003 and 2009, very near the 30% contribution estimated by IPEA. (It must be remembered that the two studies analyze distinct periods: 2001 to 2011, for Brazil IPEA, 2012, and 2003 to 2009 for Souza and Medeiros, 2013. Also, one must remember that they worked with different data sources: PNAD, in the first case, and POF in the second.)

In another study, Ricardo Paes e Barros and co-authors estimate that a change in labor-income distribution per employed adult was responsible for

40% to 50% of the total reduction in inequality during the 2001-2007 period. The other half would have come from changes in the profile of public transfers (Barros et al., 2009).

Therefore, according to the studies mentioned above, a <u>reduction in the difference between high and low salaries in the private-labor market</u> seems to be the main factor in inequality reduction.

The second most important factor was the reduction of regressivity in public-sector transfers to families. These transfers (Social Security pensions and benefits, *Bolsa Família*, BPC, and unemployment compensation) had a relevant impact on the reduction of inequality. Considered as a whole, they still are regressive. However, since 2001 they have become less regressive.

Therefore, there seems to be empirical support for the idea that democratization induces the expansion of public programs in favor of the poor. The creation and amplification of the *Bolsa Família* and BPC programs, as well as the introduction of pensions to rural workers and the impact of a higher minimum wage on Social Security pensions and benefits, have contributed significantly to the reduction in inequality.

The reduction in inequality in other South American countries seems to follow the same pattern as Brazil. Lustig and co-authors argue that, in at least four countries (Argentina, Brazil, Peru, and Mexico), the two main causes were the reduction in the difference between the lower and higher wages and the expansion of governmental transfers to families by means of programs similar to *Bolsa Família*.

The techniques to separate the factors that affect inequality, used by the cited studies, are capable of detecting only the <u>immediate</u> causes for such changes. They do not detect indirect changes generated by market dynamics or the secondary effects of governmental policies.

For example, the importance of government policies is measured by observing the degree of regressivity/progressivity and the increase/reduction of government transfers in family income. The government policy of increasing the real value of minimum wage, however, can indirectly affect the reduction of inequality by changing salaries paid in the private sector. If minimum wage affects salaries paid in the informal sector of the economy and/or acts as a basis for salary negotiations for occupations that pay wages near the minimum, there will be a tendency to narrow the difference in remuneration (explaining the reduction in the wage gap). The smaller salaries will rise along with the minimum, while the others will be subject to market forces.

As discussed in Chapter 1 (Stylized Fact 6), this appears to happen in the Brazilian job market. Thus, a reduction in inequality that would appear to come from the private-labor market dynamic may be due, in part, to government economic regulation. In other words, the exercises in the separation of causes for inequality reduction would underestimate the impact of government policies (which is already significant, about 30% of total inequality reduction, as seen above) and overestimate the impact of the private job market dynamic. This does not invalidate the methods used in the literature, which extract as much information as possible from the available databases and give a reasonable estimate for the causes of the reduction in inequality.

Although the real increase in minimum wage may be a powerful tool to reduce inequality (by means of the labor market and by means of reducing the regressive effect of Social Security benefits), it is worth calling attention to the fact that this is not a benefit without cost. As has been argued in Chapter 1 (Stylized Fact 6), there is, on one hand, the negative impact of higher public expenditure on economic growth and, on the other, the discouragement of investment due to increased labor costs.

Since the reduction in wage differentials in the labor market cannot be fully credited to increases in minimum wage, the literature explores other potential sources for this phenomenon. The aforementioned study by Paes e Barros and co-authors, as well as a World Bank study by Azevedo and co-authors, (Azevedo et al., 2013) argues that there was a reduction in salary differences by level of education in Brazil and other Latin American countries. The difference in remuneration between an illiterate worker and one with primary education, shrunk. The same occurred between other levels of education. Workers with a primary education came to receive a salary closer to those with a secondary education, which came to receive compensation nearer to those with a college education. Or rather, there was a generalized reduction in the skill premium.

There are different possible causes for it. (For a discussion regarding the possible causes of the wage-gap reduction in Latin America, see Lustig et al., 2013.) The first possibility is that the reduction in wage differentials is a benign result of the increase in education: the educational advances in the country increased the average years of schooling for Brazilian workers (see Chapter 1, Figure 1.20) therefore raising the supply of more qualified workers and reducing the supply of low-skilled ones. This change in supply, all else remaining the same, would cause a reduction in the "price" of more qualified labor in relation to less qualified labor. The final result would be the reduction in wage differentials.

Another possibility, this one not so benign, is that there could have been a reduction in the demand for more qualified workers. In this hypothesis, the Brazilian economy (and that of Latin America) was not able to advance in the more sophisticated sectors that demanded more specialized labor. Consequently, the demand for labor grew more intensely in businesses that employ low-skilled workers. As a consequence, wages for those workers with less education grew faster than the wages for the less demanded high-skilled workers.

A World Bank study considers this a concrete possibility:

> A demand factor that is specific to the region [Latin America] and that appears to have played an important role is the commodity bonanza. It has promoted the expansion of the non-tradable sectors relative to (non-commodity) tradable ones in the commodity exporting LAC countries. And, at least in present-day LAC, the non-tradable sectors (such as services and construction) tend to be on average

less skill intensive that the (non-commodity) tradable ones (such as manufacturing). Hence, what appears as a fundamentally positive trend, the decline in household income and wage inequality, may hide a worrisome phenomenon, namely, the tendency in the region's commodity exporting countries to specialize in sectors that are relatively less intensive in skills (World Bank, 2012, p. 8).

In fact, Bonelli and Fontes (2013) show that the services sector gained importance in the total GDP between 2000 and 2012. Productivity in this sector is very low, both when compared with other sectors of the Brazilian economy as well as to the services sectors in other economies (as seen in Chapter 1, Stylized Fact 9). As such, the services sector, on average, hires less qualified workers. Growing faster than the industrial sector, the services sector would have increased the <u>demand</u> for less qualified labor. This greater demand would raise wages for less qualified labor when compared to the more qualified.

A third explanation for the reduction in the wage gap between lower and more educated labor would be in the <u>deterioration</u> in the <u>quality</u> of high-school and college education. This decrease in quality would cause that those with a university diploma have, practically, a capacity or ability that is expected from those who only finished high school. High-school graduates, in turn, would have knowledge that is expected from those who left school after finishing grade school. As such, wage differentials between the groups would be relatively smaller because, in practice, employers would not see much difference among workers with different years of schooling.

It is not easy to isolate which of the different causes is relevant to the reduction in wage differences in Brazil and Latin America, since the estimates depend on many hypotheses and vary according to the methods and parameters used. Literature has not been able to clearly establish the importance of each of the factors described above (Lustig et al., 2013).

It is clear, however, that the reduction in income inequality is not necessarily the bearer of only good news. It could be that the inability of the economy to create highly technical and well-paying jobs, in dynamic and more productive sectors, has led to a smaller difference in wages. Lower inequality could also be a symptom that the educational system is not capable of adequately preparing students for the labor market.

2.4 WILL INEQUALITY CONTINUE TO FALL?

The fact that inequality has fallen in the two first decades of the 21st century does not guarantee that this tendency will continue in the future. For this trend to continue, it is necessary that the factors generating the reduction in inequality continue to exist. In other words, it would be necessary for programs such as *Bolsa Família* and BPC to continue to expand their number of beneficiaries at the same rate as in previous years. Furthermore, the existing inequality among Social Security recipients needs to be squeezed (which means to maintain the trend of the real appreciation of minimum wage). The same should happen to the wage gap in the labor market. However, all these sources of inequality reduction are threatened to lose momentum.

Real increases in minimum wage represent high fiscal costs. As seen in Chapter 1, Figure 1.16, about 51% of the increase in current federal expenditure between 1998 and 2012 can be attributed exclusively to real increases in minimum wage due to its impact on Social Security benefits, BPC allowances and other social aid expenditures that are indirectly affected by minimum wage (wage bonus and unemployment compensation).

An IPEA study that evaluated these so-called "federal social expenditures"[3] through 2010 shows that these expenditures grew at a rate of 6.6% per year above inflation between 1995 and 2010. This resulted in a real accumulated growth of 161% in 15 years. The Ministry of Social Security alone is responsible for 53% of this expense, which shows the great weight of Social Security in total expenditure and the importance of minimum wage as a source of expenses increase (Brazil IPEA, 2011).

On one side, tax revenues have already reached a high percentage of GDP (Chapter 1, Figures 1.8 and 1.9). It won't be easy to increase the tax burden even more in order to finance additional increases in expenditure caused by raises in minimum wage. On the other hand, the Brazilian population is aging quickly, which puts pressure on Social Security expenses. Restrictions on tax revenues, together with spending pressures, show that there are clear limits on the current welfare model based on an ever-increasing minimum wage. Maintaining increases of this wage similar to those observed between 1996 and 2011 (Chapter 1, Figure 1.14) do not appear to be sustainable in the long term. Therefore, this source of inequality reduction tends to fade out.

Maintaining the rate of inequality reduction in Social Security without real increases in minimum wage (and, as a consequence, in pensions and benefits indexed to this minimum) would require a real reduction in the value of higher pensions, instead of an increase in the lower ones. However, this is quite difficult in political and even judicial terms.

The current fiscal restrictions, and the fact that the tax burden cannot continue to grow, imposes limits on the budgetary expansion of social-assistance programs such as *Bolsa Família*. Even if there was enough public money to fund expansion of these programs, there would not be an unattended target public large enough to justify additional social program coverage, since one quarter of the Brazilian population is already covered by redistributive governmental

---

3. The study defines as "federal social expenditures" those related to the following ministries and secretariats: Health, Education, Work and Labor, Social Development and Hunger Alleviation, Social Security, Agrarian Development, Cities, Culture, National Archives, Special Secretariat for Racial Equality, Special Secretariat for Women's Policies, Special Secretariat for Human Rights and the National Foundation for Children and Adolescents. In addition, considering budget appropriation by these public offices, it also includes money borrowed by the Ministry of Finance whose funds were used in programs related to small-scale agriculture, education and health" (Brazil IPEA, 2011).

programs. Therefore, the potential for inequality reduction by means of expansion of social assistance is limited.

With regard to the narrowing of the wage gap, it is important to notice that the increase in worker education is reaching a stage at which additional advances will face considerable resistance. In the first years of the 21st century, gains in education were made by including students who were not in school. With almost all children up to 14 effectively enrolled, however, increases in education depend on them continuing into high school, which is more difficult due to the rivalry imposed by the job market, which attracts young people and reduces their desire to study.

In fact, the previously mentioned studies by Souza and Medeiros and IPEA show that there has been, in recent years, a reduction in the narrowing of the wage gap, which means a weaker impact by the labor market on inequality reduction. In the IPEA text, for example, one reads that "the causes for the fall in inequality for the 2009/2011 period are quite different from other periods (...). Labor income, which until that time had been the main factor in the reduction, came in second place at 28% (...) 55% of the fall in the Gini Index between 2009 and 2011 came as result of a better distribution of Social Security benefits" (Brazil IPEA, 2012, pp. 28-29).

In other words, all sources of inequality reduction seem to be in check. This is what Souza and Medeiros conclude:

> *There are already signs that the decline in inequality in private sector wages is slowing down (systematic reductions in returns to schooling, for example) and that the expansion of social assistance will have less progressive effects (about a quarter of the entire population is already beneficiary of assistance policies). Pensions have also achieved high coverage and the pension floor, linked to the minimum wage, will hardly grow as fast as it did in an economy in recovery. Due to gradualism in the implementation of pension reforms, the control of the regressiveness of pensions for workers in the public sector will take more than a decade to be truly relevant to inequality. Most low hanging fruits were already picked and it is probable that Brazil slowly enters a new phase, in which the reduction of inequality will depend more on structural changes in the labor market and on the progressiveness of the tax system. If inequality keeps falling, it will hardly fall as fast as it did in the 2000s (Souza and Medeiros, 2013, p. 20).*

It is possible that the interruption in the fall of the Gini Index in 2012, shown in Figure 2.2, is a sign that the fall in inequality is losing strength. In this case, inequality would stabilize at a still high level.

In a detailed study by the World Bank by Ferreira and co-authors (Ferreira et al., 2013) regarding the increase in the Latin American middle class, attention is called to the fact that *inter-generational* social mobility is very low in Latin America, especially Brazil. There is high inter-generational mobility when the socio-economic *status* of the parents is not a good predictor of the future socio-economic *status* of the children. This is a concept that reflects equality of opportunities and, therefore, the possibility that a society offers poor children social programs (especially education) that allows them to remedy their initial disadvantages and open doors for social mobility.

The authors assess the extent to which the level of education of an individual is determined by the level of that of their parents. They show that, in a sample of 42 countries, Brazil has the fourth worse index of mobility in terms of years of study, only coming in before Peru, Ecuador, and Panama. In other words, in Brazil, the educational status of the parents strongly determines the limits of educational and social mobility of their children.

The result is not any better when international proficiency tests are taken into consideration. Performance by Brazilian students is not only low in comparison with the other countries, but is heavily correlated to their parents' degree of education. The authors explain this result, arguing that:

> In particular, it appears that sorting – the process whereby children from more-advantaged backgrounds concentrate in the same schools, from which those from less-privileged families are excluded – is a more important component of inter-generational immobility in Latin America than elsewhere. Sorting matters in Latin America because of the usual peer effects and because the schools attended by rich children are much better than those attended by the poor, in terms of their governance and accountability as well as their physical infrastructure and teaching quality. Of course, in addition, parental background also affects children's cognitive outcomes through better nutrition, exposure to richer vocabulary, differences in cognitive stimulation, material resources at home, and so on (Ferreira et al., 2013, p. 8).

According to the same study, the reduction in inequality in Latin America has been a typically *intra-generational* phenomenon. In other words, poorer individuals have been able to improve their income during their professional life more intensely than the richer, although this improvement is conditioned by family history. It is difficult to make large jumps, going from poverty to middle class in one generation. Considering the stratification of social groups into poor, vulnerable, middle class, and high class, what is observed most frequently is that the poor are typically able to advance only one step, rising to the condition of vulnerable. The vulnerable are able to rise one step, reaching middle class. Few make the great leap from poverty to middle class in one generation. This happens exactly because the level of education and opportunities for mobility are conditioned by the social environment and income level the person was born in.

The persistence of the inequality of opportunities makes it harder to keep the pace of inequality reduction in the future. The factors for the reduction of inequality analyzed in this chapter would have allowed for the "picking of low hanging fruit." Circumstantial movements in the labor market, increases in educational inclusion (without improvements in the quality of education) and expansion of unsustainable long-term fiscal social policies have improved the quality of life for the poorest. However, to maintain the reduction of inequality in motion demands equal opportunity and, consequently, the increase of *intergenerational* mobility. This requires policies that are more difficult to implement, especially advances in the quality of education, as is proposed by the World Bank:

> *The sustainability of the decline in inequality is tightly related to improvements in the quality of education in Latin American countries because the equalizing effect of an expansion in educational attainment is likely to reach a limit if the high disparities in quality of education persist (World Bank, 2011, p. 18).*

Additional challenges to the fall in inequality are the conditions for international trade to be faced by the Brazilian economy in the second decade of the 21st century. Chapter 1, Figure 1.1 shows that long-term economic growth in the country has been mediocre. It highlighted, however, that during the 2004-2012 period, there was a better performance with *per capita* GDP growth rising from the historical average of 1.4% per year to 2.8% per year. This improved performance seems to be associated with the strong increase in commodity prices on the international market due to the economic expansion of China. It certainly is easier to create jobs and redistribute income in the context of the improvement in terms of trade and its consequent impulse to growth. As of 2012, international market trends came to indicate a change in direction with the deceleration of the Chinese economy and, consequently, a fall in commodity prices. This lead Brazil back to the mediocre economic growth performance seen in the 1985-2003 period, making it more difficult to maintain the declining rate of poverty and inequality.

2.5   ARE SOCIAL POLICIES EFFECTIVE IN REDUCING INEQUALITY?

One may take the sizable reduction in inequality between 1998 and 2011 as an evidence of the effectiveness of governmental policies in favor of the poor. This, however, does not reflect reality.

Section 2.2 showed that the most expensive governmental program in the "social agenda" – Social Security – has a strong regressive bias. This fact is confirmed by estimates presented by Immervoll and co-authors. Using 2003 PNAD data, they show that 71.5% of income originating from retirement and pensions paid by the government go to the three highest income deciles. The richest 10% receive 43.7% of the total (Immervoll et al., 2009). Since expenditures with retirement and pensions represent more than half of the so-called federal government "social expense"(as shown in Brazil IPEA, 2011) we may conclude that most of the funds for the so-called "social programs" actually benefit the top of the income pyramid instead of being directed toward the poor.

The same study compares the distributive impact of Brazilian Social Security with similar systems in the OECD countries. Taking a concentration coefficient that varies between −1 (all resources go to the poorest individual in society) and +1 (all resources go to the richest individual), Brazilian Social Security expenses have a score of 0.566, which is far superior to Italy (0.212), the most regressive system among OECD countries. In 7 of the 15 countries considered in the study, the concentration coefficient is negative. In such countries, Social Security has a strong redistributive effect, a situation diametrically opposed to that in Brazil (Immervoll et al., 2009).

If on one side Brazilian Social Security is an income concentrator and consumes more than half of the federal government social funds, on the other, the *Bolsa Família* program has a large redistributive impact (concentration coefficient of − 0.525, in 2011; Brazil IPEA, 2012, p. 28) but consumes an insignificant portion of federal government social funds (only 2.7% of the total) (Brazil IPEA, 2011).

As commented above, the reduction in the degree of regressivity of Social Security funds was due to the increase in minimum wage. However, a reduction in inequality by means of minimum wage is expensive. According the aforementioned IPEA study regarding poverty and inequality in Brazil:

> (...) each percentage point in reduction of the Gini Index by means of Social Security costs 352% more than what was obtained by means of Bolsa Família (...) inequality may have fallen even more if we had given preference to the poor by giving preference to the Bolsa Família program (Brazil IPEA, 2012, p. 40).

Between these two extreme cases (Social Security and *Bolsa Família*), there are intermediate programs. The BPC program is also progressive, but more expensive than *Bolsa Família*, because its benefits are tied to minimum wage. Moreover, it is less focused on the poorest (it reaches only the poor elderly and poor physically challenged, leaving out young families and, above all, poor children). Programs associated with professional activity, such as unemployment compensation and wage bonuses, benefit mainly the intermediate income deciles, since they are restricted to those who are formally employed besides being directly or indirectly tied to minimum wage (Immervoll et al., 2009).

As a result, the previously cited study by Ricardo Paes e Barros and co-authors concludes that:

> The design of Brazilian social policy is still far from optimum. A very active minimum wage policy continues to be pursued, despite the fact that increases in the minimum wage are much less effective in reducing inequality than expansions in Bolsa Família benefits (...) optimizing social policy design gives Brazilian policymakers plenty of room to further reduce inequality, without the need of additional resources (Barros et al., 2009).

The above considerations are focused on government social <u>expense</u>. But what can be said regarding the tax system? Would it not be possible to seek greater progressivity by increasing taxation on the richer? This does not seem to be a promising path. A World Bank study produced by Lindert and co-authors (Lindert et al., 2006), for example, argues that there is little space for direct taxation in developing countries, meaning that a large part of activities are developed in the informal markets that escape this type of taxation. For this reason, taxation is more intensely pursued by means of indirect taxes on consumption.

Estimates regarding indirect tax regressivity or progressivity are strongly dependent on the hypotheses made regarding who pays the tax (which depends on how much of the tax cost is transferred from producers and retailers to final consumers by means of higher prices), and estimates vary greatly due to these hypotheses. Considering different hypotheses, Lindert and co-authors report that Latin American tax systems vary between lightly regressive and lightly progressive. There is not, however, much space to seek income redistribution by means of taxation. They conclude that:

> (...) the most important factor affecting the distributional impact of the tax system is how much revenue it generates – and how well these revenues are used as redistribution instruments by the public sector (Lindert et al., 2006).

Immervoll and co-authors come to a similar conclusion in the Brazilian case (Immervoll et al., 2009). They show that direct taxation is extremely progressive, while indirect taxation is regressive. Each opposing force cancels each other out, with the taxation system as a whole being approximately neutral in distributive terms.

Rozane Siqueira, who is a co-author in the previously cited Immervoll studies, shows, in co-authorship with other economists (Siqueira et al., 2012), that after correcting errors in income measurement, indirect taxation regressivity is quite weak, while direct taxation is progressive. The aggregate result is a tax system with near distributive neutrality.

With direct taxation strongly concentrated on the rich and representing a small portion of fiscal revenue (due to the prevalence of indirect taxation), there would be no room to increase the tax system progressivity anymore. As such, Immervoll and co-authors conclude that:

> (...) researchers and policy-makers in Brazil have frequently argued that the tax side of the budget should play a more significant redistributive role. However, the predominance of indirect taxes and the interaction of a progressive personal income tax interact with the highly unequal income distribution render the tax system a poor redistributive tool. Furthermore, there are indications that the most affluent groups have tended to benefit most from tax concessions and, more generally, tax avoidance opportunities and difficulties in enforcing tax compliance. (...) Our view is that the tax-benefit system should be as simple and transparent as possible, with the expenditure side of the budget as the fundamental redistributive instrument (...) (Immervoll et al., 2009, p. 298).

2.6   DID INEQUALITY ONLY BEGIN TO FALL MORE INTENSELY AS OF 2001?

If the democratization of the country is behind the recent fall in inequality, as argued in this book, one should question why the Gini Index only began to consistently fall as of 2001, even though democratization began in 1985. What seems to have happened is that fiscal disorganization and the hyperinflation of the 1980s, due to the redistributionist ecstasy that intended to please all demands at the same time, sacrificed, above all, the poorest, which had less protection against inflation.

Figure 2.7 shows two different measures of inequality: the already analyzed Gini Index and the income participation of the richest 1% of the population. The rich tend to increase their income participation during inflationary processes, since they have access to banking mechanisms to protect the real value of their income. Therefore, the participation of the top 1% in total income is more sensitive to variations in inflation than the Gini Index.

What the figure shows is that, between 1981 and 1989, there is an escalation in inequality measured by the two indicators, with the index for the richest 1% presenting, as one would expect, a more intense rate of concentration due to hyperinflation. Between 1989 and 1995, there is wide volatility, with no clear trend. This was the most intense period of hyperinflation, for which one cannot disregard errors in income measurement, since the real value of monthly income is lost when prices accelerated at rates of up to 80% per month.

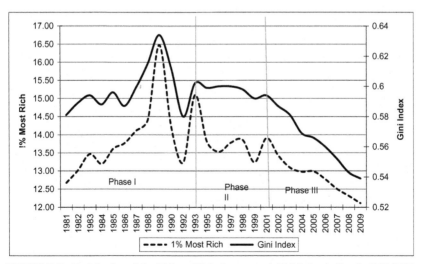

FIGURE 2.7   Participation of the Richest 1% in Income and Gini Index in Brazil: 1981-2009. *(Sources: Gini Index: Barros et al. (2009) and IPEA (2012). Primary source:* Pesquisa Nacional por Amostra de Domicílios – *PNAD (National Research by Sample Households) 1977-2011. Participation of 1% most rich on income: http://www.ipeadata.gov.br. Prepared by the author.)*

What is interesting to highlight is that, as of 1995, with the definite stabilization of hyperinflation after implementation of the Real Plan, participation by the richest 1% fell abruptly, while the Gini Index went down more slowly, presenting a clear tendency to fall only as of 2001.

The story that Figure 2.7 seems to tell can be divided into three phases. In the first decade of democratization (1985-1995), the redistributive impetus resulted in hyperinflation, which nullified redistributive attempts and concentrated income in the hands of the rich. Even though there was the political impulse for redistribution from the beginning of democratization, redistribution did not become a reality due to the inability of society to deal with the collateral effect of this redistribution, in other words, inflation.

Between 1995 and 2001, the main cause for income redistribution was price stability, which raised the real income for the poor, now protected against inflationary corrosion (the Gini Index falls slowly and participation by the richest 1% falls intensely). During this period, redistributive social policies (minimum-wage increases, welfare programs and expansion of rural retirement pensions) only had a secondary role. The fall of inflation had a strong enough effect to guarantee political popularity to those in power (re-electing the president in the first electoral round in 1998). As of 2001, when price stabilization had completed its effect of transferring income from the rich to the poor, redistribution by means of government policies came to gain importance. Added to these policies was the effect of the labor market on inequality, which has already been described.

It is possible (even though there is no consolidated evidence in this respect) that the job market could have also presented different tendencies during these three phases. The reduction of international trade barriers as of 1990 could have increased inequality in labor income due to job openings in sectors of greater technological sophistication, as has already been discussed. The demand for highly-skilled workers may have increased their wages relative to other jobs, reducing the pace of inequality reduction. Then, in the following two decades, things changed in the labor market. There was a gradual closure of the country to the external market, and industrial production lost space to the services sector. Both movements may have skewed the demand for labor in favor of less-skilled workers, which would have had the effect of reducing inequality.

As such, even though the impetus for redistribution had been present since the beginning of democratization, effective redistribution began with the stabilization of inflation (in 1995), the increase of broader public transfer programs in 2001, the intensification of policies to raise the real value of minimum wage and the emergence of a dynamic favorable to less inequality in the private-labor market.

2.7 SOCIAL STRATIFICATION AFTER TWO DECADES OF POVERTY AND INEQUALITY REDUCTION

Since there was an intense reduction of poverty and inequality as set forth in this chapter, one must ask how the Brazilian population is distributed among poor, middle and high classes after this remarkable social change. Is the number of poor still large enough to sustain demand for governmental social assistance and redistributive policies? Has the middle class expanded sufficiently to change voter demand in the direction of the public services most needed by this class?

It is not easy to divide a population into different social classes. Brazil does not have an official poverty line. The *Bolsa Família* program defines as "extremely poor" those families with a *per capita* monthly income of up to R$70.00 (about US$30.00, using an exchange rate of R$ 2.30 per dollar, as of May 2014) and as "poor" those families with a *per capita* monthly income of R$140.00 (about US$61.00) and that have members up to 17 years of age. Such monetary limits can be readjusted by the federal Executive Branch (http://www. mds.gov.br/bolsafamilia/beneficios/ingresso-de-familias).

On the other hand, the Social Assistance Organic Law (LOAS) (Law 8.742, of 1993, Article 20, § 3) considers an income inferior to one quarter of minimum wage *per capita* as a situation in which a family is unable to care for the elderly or physically challenged. Minimum wage is at times also used to establish the poverty line: the Brazilian Institute for Geography and Statistics (IBGE) usually adopts the amount of one-half minimum wage as a cutoff point.

It is also not easy to define who belongs to the middle class since an adequate definition depends on the context of the study. One can define the middle class in relative terms as being the group of individuals who are at the middle of income distribution: for example, the third distribution quintile. In this case, there would never be an increased participation of the middle class in the total population. By definition, it would be equal to one-fifth of the total population. In a context where there is strong income growth among the most poor, as has occurred in Brazil over the last few years, this definition of middle class only causes the rise of the monetary income that defines the limit between poverty and middle class (the separation between the second and third quintiles), and the same occurs between the middle and upper class (the limit between the third and fourth quintiles).

Alternatively, one could define a member of the middle class as a family or individual that has surpassed an <u>absolute</u> family *per capita* income limit (for example, R$140.00 per month as determined by the *Bolsa Família* program). In this case, the increase of income for the poorest would cause many to move from the poor to middle class, increasing the size of the latter.

The criteria could also include other variables, measuring, for example, the possession of household items (TV, refrigerator, etc.) and the degree of education;[4] or access to health services, quality of residence, and the oscillation in income over the years, among other things. As presented in the aforementioned

---

4. This criteria is used by the "Brazil Economic Classification Criteria" (*Critério de Classificação Econômica Brasil*), which divides the population into classes from A to E, and has as its objective the ability to calculate urban purchasing power. For details regarding this criteria, see: http://www. marketanalysis.com.br/arquivos-download/biblioteca/cceb-1.pdf.

World Bank study regarding the expansion of the middle class in Latin America, written by Ferreira and co-authors, "The middle class is a (…) slippery, or multifaceted, concept. Philosophers, political scientists, sociologists, and economists have meant different things by the same term"(Ferreira et al., 2013, p. 24).

For the purposes of this book, the most adequate concept to be used seems to be that of "vulnerability." Middle class would be the group that possesses economic security, that is, a low probability of returning to poverty. Feeling secure in its prospects of not returning to poverty, the middle-class family can make long-term plans and invest in its future, including the education of children.

This is the focus adopted by Ferreira and co-authors, for which a relevant criterion for classifying a household in the middle class is economic security, "and economic security is measured, in turn, as the converse of vulnerability to falling into poverty"(Ferreira et al., 2013, p. 32). This defined, the authors use the dividing line between security and vulnerability as a 10% chance the individual will return to poverty in the next five years. This fixes the *per capita* family income of US$10 per day as a dividing line between middle class and the population vulnerable to poverty in Latin America.

In Brazil the federal government created a "Commission to Define Middle Class in Brazil" (*Comissão para Definição da Classe Média no Brasil*), coordinated by economist Ricardo Paes e Barros. This commission opted to adopt a vulnerability criterion in the stratification of social classes, justifying their choice as follows:

> *Not only the poor, but also all those who perceive they have an increased probability of returning to poverty in the near future, adopt more immediate defensive strategies directed toward mitigating the effects of poverty and reduce the chances of becoming poor or aggravating their level of poverty. This type of attitude leads to preventive forms of action that involve few investments, with a low propensity to assume risks. For such reasons, a certain shortsightedness becomes apparent, a certain indifference in relation to events not too far into the future.*

However, whenever the possibility of becoming poor declines, families gain the ability to imagine and plan the future, as well as make investments and assume concrete attitudes towards the construction of this future. This difference in attitude in relation to the future is what makes, according to this approach, the middle class distant from the low class and poor, particularly.

According to this perspective, the low, middle, and high classes differ from each other by the differences in the probability of becoming poor in the immediate future, which we have come to designate as the degree of vulnerability. As such, the high class would be formed by those people with a low degree of vulnerability, that is, with a very low probability of becoming poor in the near future. In a similar way, the low class would be formed by people with a high degree of vulnerability, or rather, possibly high probability of becoming poor in the near future. The middle class, therefore, is formed by those with an intermediate level of vulnerability, sufficiently low, however, that they come to show a genuine interest in the long term (Brazil Presidency of the Republic, 2012, pp. 40-41).

To establish quantitative limits to separate classes in Brazil, using the vulnerability concept, the Commission to Define Middle Class in Brazil used the poverty line defined by the *Bolsa Família* program, readjusted to March 2012 values, which raised the *per capita* monthly family income to R$81.00 (about US$35) as the line for extreme poverty and R$162.00 (about US$70) as the poverty line. Using the 2009 PNAD results, the commission calculated the probability of a family becoming poor in some year during the next five years. Instead of defining a specific percentage for the probability of becoming poor, as was done by Ferreira et al., 2013, the commission used a statistical grouping method for individuals according to the similarity of their probability of becoming poor (polarization). They came to the stratification shown in Table 2.1.

According to this method, the middle class would begin with a *per capita* family income of R$291.00 (about US$126.50) per month. The authors recognize that the amount appears to be low and advise that the monthly income database gathered by PNAD tends to underestimate income, both because it did not do deeper research on the theme (the research had broader objectives, such as the evaluation of living, consumption, and labor conditions), and because it did not consider important remunerations, such as unemployment compensation, wage bonuses, 13th salary (an extra month's salary employers are obliged, by law, to pay to workers every December) or eventual overtime hours.

TABLE 2.1 Social Stratification in Brazil: Monthly Household Income (R$, April 2012)

Classes	R$/month		Frequency (%)	Range	
Extremely Poor	0	81	5	0	5
Poor	81	162	10	5	15
Vulnerable	162	291	19	15	34
Low Middle Class	291	441	16	34	50
Average Middle Class	441	641	17	50	67
Upper Middle Class	641	1019	15	67	82
Low Upper Class	1019	2480	14	82	96
High Upper Class	2480		4	96	100

Source: Brazil Presidency of the Republic, 2012, p. 61. Prepared by the author.

In a comparison with the data gathered by the POF research, which is more focused than PNAD on inquiring the population about their total income, authors point out that individuals in the 34th income percentile in the POF report an income 57% higher than in PNAD. This would raise minimum *per capita* monthly middle-class family income from R$291.00 (about US$126.50) as shown on Table 2.1 to R$458.00 (about US$200). The upper limit, which would divide the middle class from the upper class, would go up to R$1661.00 (about US$722) *per capita* (Brazil Presidency of the Republic, 2012, p. 59). A four-person family would be considered middle class if they had a monthly income of between R$1832.00 (about US$796.50) and R$6644.00 (about US$2889).[5]

Despite the underestimation of income by PNAD, the commission preferred to use this database in order to be able to frequently update the limits shown in Table 2.1, since POF research is done on a 5-year interval.

Supposing that the PNAD underestimate is equally true for all income percentiles, the data presented in Table 2.1 allows one to say that approximately 34% of the Brazilian population is poor or vulnerable. This is a significant number. As such, even though there was a large decrease in poverty in the recent past, the number of voters demanding redistributive and social assistance policies remains high. By this estimate, the middle class represents 48% of the population, making them an important power in the definition of public choices. The middle class is already large, able to feel economically secure to the point of planning long-term investments to improve their quality of life, and demand from the government things other than cash transfers and social assistance: good infrastructure, efficient public services and so on. At the top of the social pyramid, classified as upper class, is 18% of the population.

An alternate estimate, performed in the previously cited study by Ferreira and co-authors (Ferreira et al., 2013) establishes a stratification in which participation by poor and vulnerable households is much higher: about 30% and 35%, respectively. The middle class (as US$10 *per capita* per day) would represent only 30% of the total population and the upper class (as of US$50 *per capita* per day) would be no more than 5% of the population.

2.8 CONCLUSIONS

The main conclusions in this chapter can be summarized as follows:

1. Inequality is persistent over time. Countries that establish economic models that generate inequality at the onset of their economic organization tend to carry this inequality throughout their history. Considerations will be made in Chapter 3 regarding how this occurred in Brazil and Latin America.

---

5. This calculation, which is the *per capita* income by the number of family members, is approximate as it does not consider economies of scale derived from family life. In general, the unitary maintenance cost per individual living alone is greater than the same cost for individuals living in the same home.

2. The post-1985 political model, associated with favorable international economic conditions, led to the reduction of inequality in Brazil beginning in the mid-1990s. In spite of this, the country remains one of the most unequal in the world.

3. Income inequality in the job market is the main immediate cause for high-income inequality in Brazil, followed by the regressive effect of benefits paid by Social Security. High wages paid to civil servants also has a significant regressive impact on income distribution.

4. Government programs with the greatest redistributive effect are the *Bolsa Família* and the BPC, the first being more effective in reaching the most poor, besides costing less.

5. The fall in inequality seen between 2001 and 2011 was caused by a reduction in the wage gap in the job market and by the reduction of the regressive effect of government programs, especially that of Social Security pensions and benefits, which, due to real increases in minimum wage, benefited low-income retirees and pensioners.

6. It is not clear that the fall in inequality referred to previously is sustainable and will be maintained during the second decade of the 21st century. There is a fading out of factors that caused such redistribution. Moreover, the high fiscal cost of the political model adopted by the federal government, and the reversal of the favorable situation in the international commodities market, may play against inequality reduction as well.

7. The intense fall of inequality does not mean that government policies directed toward this end are efficient. Actually, the chapter shows that social expenditure by the federal government is highly concentrated in Social Security pensions and benefits, which has a regressive effect, and dedicates few resources to programs with a greater redistributive effect.

8. The path of inequality during the democratic regime that began in 1985 can be divided into three phases: (1) hyperinflation and increase in inequality (1985-1995); (2) the end of hyperinflation as the main factor in the fall of inequality (1995-2001); and (3) the intensification of this fall by means of government income transfers, real increases to minimum wage and a job market dynamic favorable to the reduction of the wage gap between the poor and rich.

9. In spite of the significant fall in poverty that accompanies the reduction in inequality, at least 34% of the Brazilian population remained in a situation of poverty or vulnerability at the end of the first ten years of the 21st century. The middle class came to represent a significant portion of the population, between 30% and 48%, depending on the criteria used in the stratification. On one side, this implies that there still remains a large contingent of poor and vulnerable that demands short-term social assistance directed toward relieving poverty. On the other, there also are a significant number of middle-class households able to feel economically secure to the point of planning long-term investments to improve their quality of life. This middle class

will have less interest in policies targeting the poor, and may intensify their demand for better public services, lower taxes and so on.

The next chapter will enter the core of the argument presented in the text – analyzing how the rich strata of society are able to obtain public expenditures and regulations that benefit them.

REFERENCES

Azevedo, J.P., et al., 2013. Fifteen Years of Inequality in Latin America: How Have Labor Markets Helped? The World Bank, Poverty Gender and Equity Unit. Policy Research Working Paper 6384.

Barros, R.P., et al., 2009. Markets, the State and the Dynamics of Inequality: Brazil's Case Study. UNDP, Research for Public Policy Inclusive Development, ID-14-2009.

Bonelli, R., Fontes, J., 2013. Desafios Brasileiros no Longo Prazo. Fundação Getúlio Vargas. Instituto Brasileiro de Economia. Texto para Discussão. May. Available from, http://iepecdg.com.br/uploads/artigos/Desafios%20Brasileiros%20no%20Longo%20Prazo%20-%2028_05_2013.pdf.

Brazil IPEA, 2011. Gasto Social Federal: uma Análise da Execução Orçamentária de 2010. Comunicados do IPEA n. 108. Available from, http://www.ipea.gov.br/agencia/images/stories/PDFs/comunicado/110825_comunicadoipea108.pdf.

Brazil. IPEA, 2012. A Década Inclusiva (2001 – 2011): Desigualdade, Pobreza e Políticas de Renda. Comunicados do IPEA n. 155. Available from, http://www.ipea.gov.br/portal/index.php?option=com_content&view=article&id=15611.

Brazil IPEA, 2013. Duas Décadas de Desigualdade e Pobreza no Brasil. *Comunicados do IPEA n.* 159, Available from: http://www.ipea.gov.br/portal/index.php?option=com_content&view=article&id=19995.

Brazil Presidency of the Republic, 2012. Relatório da Comissão para Definição da Classe Média no Brasil. Secretaria de Assuntos Estratégicos. Available from, http://www.sae.gov.br/vozesdaclassemedia/wp-content/uploads/Relat%C3%B3rio-Defini%C3%A7%C3%A3o-da-Classe-M%C3%A9dia-no-Brasil.pdf.

Ferreira, F.H.G., et al., 2013. Economic Mobility and the Rise of Latin American Middle Class. World Bank Latin American and Caribbean Studies,. The World Bank.

Immervoll, H., et al., 2009. The Impact of Brazil's Tax-Benefit System on Inequality and Poverty. In: Klasen, S., Lehmann, F. (Eds.), Poverty, Inequality, and Policy in Latin America. The MIT Press.

Lindert, K., Skoufias, E., Shapiro, J., 2006. Redistributing Income to the Poor and the Rich: Public Transfers in Latin American and the Caribbean. World Bank, Social Protection. SP Discussion Paper No 0605.

Lustig, N., et al., 2013. Deconstructing the Decline in Inequality in Latin America. The World Bank, Poverty, Gender and Equit Unit. Policy Research Working Paper 6552.

Ray, D., 1998. Development Economics. Princeton University Press.

Siqueira, R.B., Nogueira, J.R.B., Souza, E.S., 2012. O Sistema Tributário Brasileiro é Regressivo? Universidade Federal de Pernambuco, Departamento de Economia.

Souza, P.H.G.F., Medeiros, M., 2013. The Decline in Inequality in Brazil, 2003–2009: The role of the State. Universidade de Brasília. Economics and Politics Research Group, Working Paper 14/2013.

The World Bank, 2011. A Break with History: Fifteen Years of Inequality Reduction in Latin America.

The World Bank, 2012. The Labor Market Story Behind Latin America's Transformation.

Chapter 3

Redistribution to the Rich

Chapter Outline

3.1 INTRODUCTION

In March 2012, Eike Batista was the 18th richest person in the world with assets estimated at US$34.5 billion (http://www.bbc.co.uk/portuguese/noticias/2013/07/130705_eike_campeoes_nacionais_ru.shtml.) He was the featured cover article on one of the main weekly magazines in Brazil, which spoke of a businessman who would be the idol of the new Brazilian millionaires, a group that "works hard, competes honestly, is proud to generate employment and is not ashamed of being rich" (Veja, 2012).

His business complex consisted of a group of companies called EBX, which specialized in commodities. The main company, Oil Exploration (OGX), promised to rival the giant state oil company – Petrobras – in the amount of oil produced. To build ships capable of transporting this expected huge production, EBX set up the OSX shipyard. These ships would also be used to transport minerals mined by MMX. Since the OSX ships would need a port, Eike created LLX Logistics, of which the main project was the Açu "superport." There were also companies in the areas of power generation (MPX) and coal mining (CCX), among other smaller ones.

Between 2006 and 2010, the EBX group went public and offered shares on the *Bolsa de Valores de São Paulo* – BOVESPA (São Paulo Stock Exchange). OGX had the largest initial public offering in the history of Bovespa.

The son of an ex-Minister of Mines and Energy and ex-president of the state mining company Vale do Rio Doce during the military government, Eike had always rubbed shoulders with political leaders. In 2009, he donated R$10 million to the Rio de Janeiro campaign to host the 2016 Olympic Games. He was the single largest individual donor to the ex-president Luís Inácio Lula da Silva presidential campaign in 2006 and the largest private donor for the film *Lula, filho do Brasil* (Lula, Son of Brazil), which portrayed a heroic image of Mr. Lula da Silva (Lazzarini, 2011, p. 1). He lent his plane to a State of Rio de Janeiro governor for private trips. (http://www.bbc.co.uk/portuguese/noticias/2013/07/130704_eike_batista_ascensao_e_queda_lgb.shtml). For the board of directors of his main firm, he invited no less than an ex-Minister of Finance, ex-Minister of the Supreme Federal Court and an ex-Senator and ex-Minister of Mines and Energy.

On July 1, 2013, the Eike Batista Empire began to collapse, revealing a history based on the expropriation of minority shareholders, taking advantage of regulatory agency political and administrative weaknesses, subsidized credit provided by publicly owned banks and capitalizing based on pension funds controlled by state companies.

The starting point in the crisis was a declaration by the OGX oil company that their most promising field, Blue Shark *(Tubarão Azul),* was commercially unviable, which unleashed a crisis of confidence in the company and dropped its stock prices. Since the group of businesses was interconnected, the other companies were also damaged. After all, if there was no oil to be explored, what would one do with the ships that would transport it, and the port that would dock them? Also, problems in mineral production and in some LLX and OSX projects completed the negative prospect.

It is interesting to note that the wells in the field now considered unviable had been, a year earlier, declared viable by the company, which was officially registered with the regulatory agency, the *Agência Nacional do Petróleo* – ANP (National Petroleum Agency). Even though faced with the inconsistency of information and OGX actions, the ANP did not adopt any punitive measures, but only waited the period demanded by regulation while minority stakeholders saw their investments go up in smoke (*O Globo,* 2013).

The regulatory agency for the capital market, the *Comissão de Valores Mobiliários* – CVM (Securities Commission), and the stock exchange (Bovespa) also showed passive behavior regarding the episode.[1] The Eike Batista companies and the businessman himself did not operate by the rules imposed on open capital societies. Initial stock offers were made when the companies were still

---

1. The information to follow was based on an article published in the *Exame* magazine on 7 August 2013.

in a pre-operational stage, not generating income and with future profit based on optimistic projections. No restrictions were imposed on this type of offer either by Bovespa or CVM rules, as is normally done in other countries, such as by the Securities and Exchange Commission (SEC) in the United States.

Eike used the mandatory "disclosure of relevant information to the market" to make optimistic predictions regarding production, when the law states that such kinds of communication should be restricted to objective, proven facts in order to avoid the speculation and manipulation of stock prices. Similarly, the entrepreneur actively used his Twitter account to disclose optimistic projections regarding business production and profitability. This type of misleading propaganda went largely unnoticed by the Securities Commission, deceiving minority investors. Remuneration for company executives was based on stock market values, inducing them to publicize optimistic information, inflating stock prices and directly affecting their personal worth.

The businessman sold part of his OGX stock 20 days before announcing that Blue Shark field was not profitable. The regulatory agencies only began proceedings that could lead to punitive action 2 years after this maneuver. In the midst of the crisis, Eike decided to transfer R$50 million (about US$22 million) of OGX capital to OSX. This action harmed stakeholders in the first company and favored those in the second, again with no apparent reaction by the Securities Commission (*O Globo,* 2013).

Exasperated with what was considered Securities Commission indolence, an investor published an open letter to the president on the Internet, suggesting possible maneuvers Eike could make to bypass rules and exploit legal loopholes:

Dear Mr. President:

Even though I publicly predicted that OGX controller Mr. Eike Batista would sell OGXP3 stock between the end of August and the first of September (…), the Security Commission did nothing. According to Article 118[1] of Security Commission Instruction 461, this regulatory agency should have cancelled all deals made by Eike Batista in the last exchanges, being that the sales were made using insider information (…). After realizing at the beginning of this year that the greater part of the oil fields explored was unprofitable, Mr. Eike Batista transferred 123 million shares of company stock. And, as everyone knows, he did this before disclosing to the market that OGX would cease exploration of a major part of what had originally been projected (http://www.infomoney.com.br/ogxpetroleo/noticia/2951706/ investidor-que-alertou-sobre-vendas-eike-explica-truque-put-ogx).

This is a clear example of regulatory agency sluggishness – the Securities Commission (CVM) and ANP. They were unable to protect minority shareholder property rights and exposed the stock market to a crisis of confidence.

Public banks lent a lot of money (with subsidized interest rates) to the EBX group. At the time the crisis came into the open, The National Bank for Economic and Social Development (BNDES), a Brazilian development bank that is 100% state owned, had lent R$10.4 billion (about US$4.5 billion) and the *Caixa*

Economica Federal, R$1.4 billion (about US$600 million). (http://www.bbc. co.uk/portuguese/noticias/2013/07/130704_eike_batista_ascensao_e_queda_lgb. shtml). The BNDES subsidiary company (BNDESpar) also participated by investing another R$500 million (about US$220 million) in EBX stock. (http://www.bbc. co.uk/portuguese/noticias/2013/07/130705_eike_campeoes_nacionais_ru.shtml).

According to a very common standard in the Brazilian financial and capital markets, in addition to public banks, state-employee pension funds are also used to finance projects that have received government blessing. The Bank of Brazil and *Correios* (the postal service, which is 100% state owned) employee funds also hold credit in the EBX group, with the *Correios* having invested 20% of its total stock portfolio in Eike's shares (*O Globo,* 2013). Commenting on the EBX case, *The New York Times* observed that "governing structures subject to corruption in Brazil remained largely the same throughout the long economic boom, as authorities channeled huge resources of the state to projects controlled by tycoons" (*The New York Times,* 2013).

At the time of writing, the fall of Mr. Batista's Empire was still under way, with new developments unfolding: minority shareholders filing law suits, the Securities Commission beginning investigations and the entrepreneur taking steps to sell companies and restructure the group.

The facts that had occurred up to this time, however, are a vivid illustration of how economic power and political influence can be used to bypass laws and allow very rich individuals to expropriate taxpayers, minority shareholders and public pension fund account holders. Weak and slow judicial and regulatory institutions that allow for such behavior are, according to theories described in the next section, the historic result of nations with a high level of inequality. Such fragile institutions biased in favor of the very rich have had a harmful effect on long-term economic growth.

3.2   WHAT DOES ECONOMIC THEORY HAVE TO SAY?

Glaeser and co-authors (Glaeser et al., 2003) discuss the effect of inequality on the function of legal, political and regulatory institutions. They argue that the very rich and politically powerful are able to subvert such institutions to their own benefit, with a negative impact on the potential for economic development. They call attention to the fact that an individual or social group that feels threatened by the risk of being dispossessed is less likely to invest in a new business. Only the rich, powerful and those with good connections feel safe enough to invest in a society where justice is slow, some judges accept bribes or the bureaucrats alter regulations in a casuistic way.

Going to court to complain about a right or using judicial maneuvers to delay sentences is usually expensive. Individuals and companies with limited resources do not only have to pay court costs, but also must cope with the opportunity costs of waiting years for a final ruling.

With a slow, unreliable, and unpredictable court system, economic inequality allows the rich to retain good (expensive) lawyers that help them to expropriate those unable to afford legal disputes. Protecting one's property from aggression is also easier for the rich. Private security is expensive, which impedes small business from using it as much as the rich.

As proposed by Mark Gradstein: in unequal societies, there is a high probability that the court, political and regulatory systems are unable to restrain the ability of the rich to take advantage of activities such as forming cartels, disrespecting commercial rules or trafficking influence. In unequal societies, property rights, laws, and rules tend to be weak and do not offer protection to the poor, who are generally expropriated by the rich (Gradstein, 2007).

"In societies where the rich hold great influence over state decisions or where they have the ability to restrict access to property rights to those members of the oligarchy, there are few incentives to improve these rights so that they cover the economy as a whole. The beneficiaries prefer that things remain as they are. This constitutes a barrier to investment and growth"(Sonin, 2003).

Acemoglu and Robinson propose, as part of the central argument in their acclaimed book *Why Nations Fail*, the concepts of "extractive economic institutions," and "inclusive economic institutions":

Inclusive economic institutions, such as those in South Korea or in the United States, are those that allow and encourage participation by the great mass of people in economic activities that make best use of their talents and skills and that enable individuals to make the choices they wish. To be inclusive, economic institutions must feature secure private property, an unbiased system of law, and a provision of public services that provides a level playing field in which people can exchange and contract; it also must permit the entry of new businesses and allow people to choose their careers. (...) We call [institutions] which have opposite properties to those we call inclusive, extractive economic institutions – extractive because such institutions are designed to extract incomes and wealth from one subset of society to benefit a different subset (Acemoglu and Robinson, 2011, pp. 74-76).

In this context, growth can be hindered by means of at least five distinct mechanisms. World Bank (2006) offers an extensive review of these topics:

- Investment will be low because the underprivileged or unprotected portion of society is afraid to invest;
- There is a concentration of investment in the hands of those who are not necessarily the most capable or efficient. The comparative advantage is not based on technical knowledge or skill, but on political contacts and wealth, which tends to result in less productive companies;[2]

---

2. Claessens et al. (2008), for example, show that companies that make more election campaign donations in Brazil show inferior economic performance, which suggests that the quest for political connections is a way to keep businesses alive that should be eliminated from the market by more efficient competitors, or, rephrasing, they count on political connections to guarantee credit subsidies or preferential access to public contracts, which allows them to not be as efficient as necessary to contend in the market without the aid of political connections.

- People waste time and resources on rent-seeking activities: disputing existing wealth, instead of focussing on producing new wealth; using defensive activities (bribes, political bargaining, private security, etc.). Time and the financial and material resources employed in these activities could be alternately invested in the production of goods and services that are more beneficial to society;
- There is a tendency to protect markets controlled by influential groups or individuals, leading to low competition, which destimulates improvements in productivity;
- The government is used by wealthy individuals as an instrument to transfer income to privileged groups instead of providing public benefits essential to development, such as infrastructure and public education; instead of forming a civil service specialized in providing services that facilitate and stimulate growth, it specializes in conceding subsidies and benefits, which generates a web of rules and exceptions for access or exclusion, resulting in high corporate administrative costs.

Therefore, unequal societies tend to have less competition and insufficient incentives to increase productivity, accumulate physical and human capital and use their natural resources in an efficient way. In the long term, this translates into less growth.

The result may not only be a lower growth rate, but also a vicious cycle where inequality produces institutions that are not only weak, but biased toward the rich, as well. It reinforces inequality by concentrating investments, human capital, credit, wealth and power (Chong and Gradstein, 2007). Only those capable of protecting themselves against expropriation become rich. The probability is low that a strong middle class makes itself into such a society.

This dual causal relationship (inequality generating extractive institutions, which in turn perpetuate inequality) may explain why inequality and institutional quality are persistent and do not change over time (Chapter 2, Figure 2.1). Existing social and economic conditions at the time of colonization can define a trajectory of inequality and low institutional quality for many centuries (Acemoglu and Robinson, 2011).

Engerman and Sokoloff published an influential study where they sought to explain why the United States and Canada are currently more developed than Latin American and Caribbean countries. First, they argue that different sets of natural endowments (soil, climate, size or density of native populations) created different degrees of inequality in wealth, human capital and political power in the different colonies. These differences, in turn, formed disparate institutions:

(…) the colonies established in the Caribbean or Brazil, enjoyed a climate and soil conditions that were extremely well suited for growing crops, such as sugar, that were highly valued on world markets and most efficiently produced on large slave plantations. Their populations came to be dominated by large numbers of slaves

*obtained through the international slave market, and quickly generated vastly un-
equal distributions of wealth, human capital, and political power. (...)*

*In contrast, small, family-sized farms were the rule in the northern colonies
of the North American mainland, where climatic conditions favored a regime of
mixed farming centered on grains and livestock that exhibited quite limited economies of scale in production and used few slaves. (...)*

*These initial differences in the degree of inequality — which can be attributed
largely to factor endowments, broadly conceived — had profound and enduring
effects on the paths of development of the respective economies
(...) The logic is that great equality or homogeneity among the population led,
over time, to more democratic political institutions, to more investment in public
goods and infrastructure, and to institutions that offered relatively broad access to
economic opportunities.*

*(...) [On the other hand, in Latin America] colonists of European descent
could enjoy the high incomes that come from a strong comparative advantage in
producing highly valued commodities as well as relatively elite status (relying on
slaves and Indians to provide the bulk of the manual labor)*

*(...)The principal areas of exception, namely, the northern United States and
Canada, were correspondingly less attractive to Europeans at first.*

*(...) Efforts to implant a European-style organization of agriculture based
on concentrated ownership of land combined with labor provided by tenant
farmers or indentured servants, as when Pennsylvania and New York were established, invariably failed: the large landholdings unraveled because even
men of rather ordinary means could set up independent farms when land was
cheap and scale economies were absent (Engerman and Sokoloff, 2002, pp. 3,
4, 9 and 14).*

After emphasizing the difference between the two types of colonization and its
effects on the formation of institutions, the authors argue that institutions dis-
similar at their inception, perpetuate over time:

*(...) in societies that began with extreme inequality, the elites were both inclined
and able to establish a basic legal framework that ensured them a disproportionate share of political power and to use that influence to establish rules, laws, and
other government policies that gave them greater access to economic opportunities than the rest of the population, thereby contributing to the persistence of the
high degree of inequality. In societies that began with greater equality in wealth
and human capital or homogeneity among the population, the elites were either
less able or less inclined to institutionalize rules, laws, and other government policies that grossly advantaged them, and thus the institutions that evolved tended
to provide more equal treatment and opportunities, thereby contributing to the
persistence of the relatively high degree of equality (Engerman and Sokoloff, 2002,
pp. 17-18).*

The cycle comes full circle when inequality generates extractive institutions,
which nurtures inequality.

3.3 INEQUALITY, EXTRACTIVE INSTITUTIONS, AND RENT SEEKING IN BRAZIL

Naritomi and co-authors explored historic microeconomic data from Brazilian municipalities and discovered evidence that initial conditions in Brazilian colonization generated institutions that continue to be prejudicial to present economic growth (Naritomi et al., 2012). The authors analyzed two types of economic activity from colonial Brazil based on slave labor and with extractive profile: sugar production (1570-1670) and gold mining (1700-1770). They showed that municipalities that produced sugar had greater inequality in land ownership at the end of the 20th century (more than 400 years later). The municipalities located in gold-mining regions had, over 200 years after the gold rush, inferior governing practices and offered their population less access to judicial institutions.

The concept of rent seeking in favor of some and in disadvantage to others seems central to the legal and institutional design and regulatory bias in favor of the more wealthy, as expressed in the concept of "extractive economic institutions." In the Brazilian case, the first great beneficiary of rents was the Portuguese royal family and its associates that used colonial economic activities to fill their coffers.

Typical income extractive regulation policies, used by Portugal and other colonizing countries, were to: prohibit the colony from trading with countries other than the metropolis; restrict cultivating products that were not of the metropolis interest; demand permits for colonists to open new businesses; concede service monopolies (shipping, for example) to companies and persons connected to the royal family; and excessive taxation.

The consequence of the extractive colonial model was the rise of a class revolving around the center of metropolitan power (royal court, state bureaucracy) that came to live from the income extracted by means of the listed procedures. Another consequence was the stimulus to influence peddling, in which high-income individuals that exploited colonial economic activity came to seek means to have access to the king in order to obtain favors, concessions, monopolies and the reduction of regulations applying to them.

The efficacy of the extractive model depended on the operational ability of the metropolitan government to impose restrictions on colonial economic activity. Between the 16th and 18th centuries, when travel and communication were restricted, it was expected that Portugal should be able to maintain more strict control over economic activities exercised on Brazilian lands closest to the metropolis. At the same time, transportation costs induced a concentration of production in areas near the metropolis and consumer market. In fact, Naritomi and co-authors showed that the negative effects of the sugar and gold cycles were more intense in municipalities located nearer to Portugal (i.e., in the northeast region of Brazil).

Consistent with this evidence, Zanella and co-authors show how Brazilian institutions were harmed more than those in North America due to the intensity of extractivist control exercised by the respective metropolis (Zanella et al., 2003). The territories that would result in the United States were free of English extractivism until the end of the 17th century, since was no large-scale economic activity to generate profit, therefore attracting metropolis attention. Only when the force of the colonial economy came to compete with metropolis activities did the English take an interest in imposing restrictions; for example, importing and exporting only on ships flying the English flag (1650) or restrictions on the production of hats in order to protect metropolis industry (1732).

Brazil, however, since the beginning of its colonization, was of strategic interest to the small metropolis since it was there that Portugal obtained a higher income than that generated within its borders. According to Lisboa and Latif more than half of Portuguese income came from the Brazilian colony during most of the colonial era (Lisboa and Latif, 2013, p. 8). Due to this, the metropolis perfected itself in the creation of a bureaucratic apparatus in order to maximize the extraction of income.

Furthermore, according to Zanella and co-authors, the process of Portuguese institutional centralization and control was increased when the Royal family moved to Brazil in 1808 to escape the Napoleonic invasion of Portugal. The presence of the Portuguese crown on Brazilian territory practically eliminated the barrier to effective royal control over the territory imposed by distance. A system of government, economic regulation and distribution of privileges was created on Brazilian soil that concentrated power in the hands of the king:

> The executive branch of the government was highly centralized and controlled practically all commercial activity, even at the provincial and city levels. An important tool for regulating mercantile activity was the Conselho do Estado (Council of State). The Council (...) had twelve ordinary members and several extraordinary members. Thus, at this level the benefits from rent seeking were highly concentrated. (...) The members were lifetime appointees, but could be dismissed by the king. In addition, the Council reported directly to the king.
>
> The Council of State was the pinnacle of a highly centralized bureaucratic structure that dealt with economic issues. For example, the founding of any society or company, in any province, required a license and the approval of its statutes by the government. Further, the society or company was required to receive the approval of the Council of State. The regulatory authority and reach of the Council was extensive; the deleterious effects on commerce obvious.
>
> [There was a] de facto Crown control over most governmental positions, whether elected or not. The king appointed all major positions in the Brazilian bureaucracy, directly or indirectly.
>
> The provincial legislatures had far less autonomy than state legislatures in the U.S. and practically none on economic issues, thus were not a source of competition against the crown with respect to commercial regulation (Zanella et al., 2003, pp. 386-389).

Such concentration resulted in intense influence peddling, where access to the king or the State Council was strategic for local capitalists to obtain privileges and monopolies or to reduce the burden of state regulation on their activities:

> *The court of nobles who fled en masse from Portugal to Brazil [after the French invasion of Portugal in 1808] had no financial resources. As one means of raising money, Dom João sold 119 non-hereditary titles of nobility to local merchants (...). While the titles undoubtedly provided a measure of personal satisfaction and prestige, they also provided entree to the crown's rent-seeking market.*

In Brazil, the central government (crown) was the primary vehicle for redistributing wealth – i.e., to bestow privileges to those close to the power. To participate in the competition for special favors, rent seekers had to give the appearance of wealth. The appearance of wealth, in turn, was one way of securing invitations to parties and other social events at which crown officials were present and at which the payoff to personal promotion could be greater than the payoff from manual labor. These social events provided opportunities to develop and maintain contacts with influential persons and to secure jobs, favors and economic privileges. Nobility provided entrance to the social scene; for this reason a title of nobility was a *sine qua non* for entering the rent-seeking market (Zanella et al., 2003, p. 386).

Therefore, institutions were structured toward the control and rent extraction by the government, along with mechanisms for privileged access to this income by the wealthier social groups, which fed the high degree of social inequality. This structure survived the country's independence and is reproduced until today.

As the previously mentioned article by Lisboa and Latif describes, throughout post-colonial history, the Brazilian government has been a central part of economic functions, providing funding for public and private investments, coordinating investment decisions, distributing incentives to selected sectors and regulating prices of important goods, such as energy or food.

During the so-called "Old Republic" (*República Velha*, 1889-1930), there was a government system controlled by alternating agrarian groups. It was characterized by the exclusion of a large part of the population to the right of voting and the access to education. The rise of Getúlio Vargas to power (1930-1945) opened the country to greater urbanization and industrialization, which was done, however, in the same extractive mold.

National developmentism was consolidated and continues to be a strong ideology in the country (for a description of national developmentism, see, for example, Bresser-Pereira, 2011). National developmentism is characterized by the idea that development is the result of industrialization. It then becomes necessary to protect the "infant national industry," which includes not only stimulating national industry, but also attracting foreign industry to produce on national soil.

This proposal is useful to social groups that possess capital and can invest in protected national industry. In an unequal society, this is an instrument to generate high profits for businessmen by means of protection against imported products. This profit accelerates the accumulation of wealth by the rich and perpetuates inequality. Even in the case of foreign companies producing within the country, high-level management and leadership positions are occupied by the national elite.

There are many opportunities for rent seeking within this type of policy. The degree of protection for each sector depends on the influence in government exercised by the group of firms that want to be protected. The protection of national companies against competition from imported products is also provided by means of credit subsidies, preferential exchange rates, import tariffs, and other benefits, which concession is affected by the political and economic power of the one requesting.

The idea that government intervention was necessary to stimulate investments led to the creation and expansion of public banks (BNDES, Bank of Brazil, Caixa Econômica Federal, Bank of the Northeast, Bank of Amazônia), a forced savings mechanism (Time of Service Guarantee Fund – FGTS[3] and public funds or public entities devoted to the allocation, by means of political decision, of public money to finance investment in private companies, such as The Amazon Development Superintendence (Sudam) and The Northeast Development Superintendence (Sudene). Loans from these sources are almost always at a subsidized rate. Access to it was, and continues to be, dependent on political intermediation.

The government also placed itself in the position of investment coordinator, creating state companies in the areas of electric generation and steel production, which supplied consumer goods industries with subsidized raw materials. Price, purchasing and investment policies for these state-owned companies, as well as well-paid employment opportunities, created additional opportunities for rent seeking by the well-connected.

Private agents found two ways to operate within the model of strong state regulation and intervention in price and economic decisions. The first was to form lobby groups to represent their *collective* interests. The great dynamism of sectorial associations and unions, such as the São Paulo State Industrial Federation (*Federação das Indústrias de São Paulo* – FIESP), the National Motor Vehicle

---

3. Time of Service Guarantee Fund is (FGTS) is a kind of saving account that every worker with a regular job contract is obliged to maintain. Every month the employee and his employer make deposits equivalent to a percentage of the total employee salary. This savings account pays interest below the market rate (most of the time, below inflation). Workers may withdraw their funds in certain special cases, such as dismissal, purchase of real estate, or terminal disease. Funds raised by means of FGTS are used by the government to offer subsidized credit to public investment in sanitation, housing and other infrastructure issue. In sum, it is a mechanism of forced saving, in which the government uses the funds to finance public and private investment. Employers and employees that are obliged to make deposits in FGTS subsidize the government and those who are financed by funds collected by this instrument.

Manufacturers Association (*Associação Nacional de Fabricantes de Veículos Automotores* – ANFAVEA) and National Banking Federation (*Federação Nacional de Bancos* – FEBRABAN), among others, is a mere reflection of the environment where it is fundamental to demand favors and defend against benefits conceded to other groups that can affect the interests of the associated members.

The second is *individual* connections. To care for specific interests, which are not unanimously demanded by a group of companies or sectors, or to seek individual advantages that go against the interests of other companies represented by the same association, it may be necessary to appeal to individual channels to access government. In as much as the purchase of titles of nobility opened access by businessmen to the royal court, financing an electoral campaign can open important doors in government offices and public banks. It is the old practice of *clientelism.*

Sérgio Lazarinni, in his book *Capitalismo de Laços,* which analyzes crony capitalism in Brazil, defines clientelism as:

> ...*reciprocal contacts that permit actors to obtain unequal influence. If the point of contact is the state, it is easy to see how one private actor can become more influential than another due to their personal relationships. Even if a specific sector has a relatively strong representative association, with great power of influence in government, the benefits brought by this initiative will fall to all companies in the sector. (...) specific ties, and not collective ones, are what allow private competitive advantages (Lazzarini, 2011, pp. 42-43).*

Clientelism spreads, coming to be a rational means of individual action in a society based on exclusion and rent seeking. Just as a businessman needs government contacts to obtain competitive advantages, a citizen needs intermediation by a politician to obtain employment or a medical appointment at a public hospital. Politicians negotiate access to this kind of benefit in exchange for votes. Exclusion creates a market for trading of influence.

Therefore, one notices that the rent-seeking behavior and extractive economic regulation have been an integral part of the Brazilian institutional DNA since the beginning of colonization. This created a vicious cycle of inequality, exclusion and low, long-term economic growth. In this scenario, the richer social groups have found fertile soil to harvest income from their relations with the state.

3.4 EVIDENCE OF REDISTRIBUTION TO THE RICH IN BRAZIL

3.4.1 Slow and Inefficient Judicial System

Section 3.2 argues that the weakness of the courts and other institutions could be the consequence of a historically unequal society, where groups of elite shape institutions to their interests. Up to what point does the Brazilian court system fit this mold?

Chapter 1, Stylized Fact 8 gives evidence that the Brazilian court system has little power to enforce the fulfillment of contracts, provide solutions for commercial bankruptcy, impose property rights and protect the rights of minority stakeholders. That section showed that judicial sluggishness was an important cause for this low performance, in addition to the demand for innumerous legal procedures and a low rate of credit recovery in bankruptcy cases.

This is the ideal setting for those who wish to benefit from illegal procedures or unfair competition, while trusting in the legal slowness to escape punishment for their opportunist behavior. All that is needed is enough money to finance the court proceedings, making use of a wide range of possible appeals every time a court delivers a contrary decision, all of which allow a guilty defendant to postpone his sentence for many years.

Literature dealing with problems in the Brazilian judicial system has increased significantly over the last few years, allowing one to develop a more detailed picture of its flaws. In a synthesis of the literature, André Gambier Campos says that:

> *Access to judicial institutions is difficult and costly for a significant portion of society, which is unable to obtain a final ruling for cases in which its rights are violated. Even when they do gain access to these institutions, an important portion of society perceives a morose, partial and uncertain court that does not effectively indemnify those violations (Campos, 2008, p. 9).*

What seems to distinguish the Brazilian court from the theoretical considerations made in Section 3.2 is that it is not only the "very rich" who benefit from the loopholes, imperfections, and slowness of the judicial system. Actually, as will be seen in greater detail in Chapter 5 (Section 5.3), the 1988 Constitution not only increased access to the courts, but the set of cases on which the court can rule, increasing the number of cases to be judged. This expanded access, however, did not horizontally benefit population as a whole. Those who did benefit were residents in urban centers, who had greater access to information and were organized into associations or unions. Also, the expansion in the role of the courts gave way to abuse, where some groups file cases where there is an opportunity for economic gain. Once again quoting Campos:

> *Regarding access, what stands out is that it has grown significantly in the last years (...) the total number lawsuits initially filed/distributed in court increased three times over between 1990 and 2003 (...) Nevertheless, these numbers conceal distinct dynamics. While a great portion of the Brazilian population simply does not file suit in the legal system, seeking their rights, a small portion uses the system in an ample and unrestricted way that is repetitive and abusive. In other words, on one side there is insufficient access, many times for reasons already mentioned, such as the lack of financial resources or ignorance of violated rights, as well as lack of confidence regarding the ability of the state system to indemnify. On the other, there is too much access, many times to take advantage of the difficult, costly, morose, partial and complicated nature of the judicial system (Campos, 2008, p. 11).*

Even though they are not the only beneficiaries of a slow, uncertain judicial system, members of the economically and politically elite have ample room to benefit from the system sluggishness and distortions. This can be done by retaining expensive law firms that use their considerable financial attributes to maintain long legal disputes and exploit loopholes and the excess appeals allowed by law to delay conviction until the crimes have reached their statute of limitations. They can also delay payment of indemnities or fines, obtaining financial and inflationary gain while the sentence execution is delayed.

According to Armando Castelar Pinheiro, in his work "Magistrates, Courts and Economy in Brazil" (Magistrados, Judiciário e economia no Brasil):

> *The big problem with the judicial ordering and legal procedure in the country today is in procedural legislation, both in relation to the many means of delaying decisions and in respect to the opportunity for an excessive number of appeals to higher courts, considered by almost 80% of the judges as a crucial cause of the slowness of justice in Brazil (Pinheiro, 2005, p. 256).*

The inability of the judicial system to quickly and predictably resolve conflicts stimulates economic agents to adopt defensive or opportunistic behavior, exploiting judicial sluggishness according to their interests. Sérgio Lazzarini, in his already mentioned book *Capitalismo de Laços* (Crony Capitalism), calls attention to the fact that in countries with weak legal protection for minority stakeholders, as in Brazil, investors try to organize in such a way as to form majority groups, uniting with others who share the same interests. Those who lose their majority position become vulnerable to be expropriated by third parties. International investors that don't know the "rules of the game" in Brazil become easy prey for national groups that know how to use their government connections, get shareholders controlled by the state on their side and put the other group in the minority. The author gives an example:

> *[In the privatization of Telebras – a state-owned communication holding] the Canadian company TIW decided to form a consortium with domestic actors: Opportunity Bank, controlled by Daniel Dantas, and a group of pension funds (PREVI, PETROS, SISTEL and TELOS). The consortium competed for and won the bid for cellular telephone operations in the state of Minas Gerais (Telemig) and in several states in the north of the country (Tele Norte). A new company was formed,* Telepart Participações, *to seal the consortium. In this corporation, TIW retained 49% of the capital, with Opportunity and the pension funds, 27% and 24%, respectively. Therefore, none of the partners held majority control. Canadian expectations were that decisions would be shared, according to what was provided for in the agreement originally proposed.*

Soon after the auction, however, Daniel Dantas made a move that went unnoticed by the Canadians. Somehow, he was able to convince the pension funds to form a new entity, Newtel, which would shelter Opportunity and fund shares (a total of 51%). With this, Newtel came to be the majority shareholder in

Telepart. What's more, given that Opportunity detained a small amount of shares more than the pension funds, the bank was able to establish control of Newtel, which controlled Telepart. Dantas took over the telephone companies due the complexity of the societal pyramid.

Alleging that they had been aggrieved by the change, TIW and the pension funds fought innumerable legal battles with Dantas to restore their voice in the group. At the end of the proceedings, the TIW shareholders opted to leave the country, selling their holdings to Opportunity for only 18% of what they, allegedly, had invested in the deal (Lazzarini, 2011, pp. 81-83).

Resorting to the courts was not enough to render the Canadians from TIW the shareholder rights that had been taken by a local businessman who took advantage of his government connections (especially with people in control of state pension funds). Forsaking their quest for victory in court (which would certainly represent a high opportunity cost), TIW took their losses and left the Brazilian market. Regulatory uncertainty drove an international investor away.

In spite of the problems seen in the Brazilian judicial system, attention should be given to the importance of democracy and freedom of speech (especially in the press) in the perfection of judicial institutions. During the new democratic era, society has pressured to improve the system. Accusations of crimes (especially corruption) by the press against politicians, businessmen and civil servants have been investigated by the Public Prosecutor's Office with a high degree of independence. The Federal Police, although subordinate to the Executive Branch, has shown a reasonable degree of independence and investigative ability.

The country is certainly far from a high degree of corruption and white-collar crime prevention. Furthermore, many times the Public Prosecutor's Office exceeds its limits, opens investigations motivated by the political preferences of prosecutors and prematurely "condemns" individuals who are later proven innocent. The press usually echoes those accusations, which also undermines the reputation of innocent people. Open and free debate, however, has allowed advances.

An example of this advance was a reform of the judicial system by means of Constitutional Amendment 45 in 2004. Among its main objectives, the reform sought to reduce the sluggishness of the system and institute external control over the legislators and court management. (Regarding this judicial reform, see Renault and Bottini, 2005.)

There were, in fact, improvements after such reform. An example is the creation of the National Justice Council (*Conselho Nacional de Justiça*), an independent body with judicial, correctional, punitive and planning powers, which has been able to identify problems and induce increases in the productivity of the courts.

These advances, however, have not been sufficient for the Brazilian court system to be considered agile and immune to delay tactics. A clear example of this duality between perfections in process and the historic lethargy and malleability of the court can be seen in the famous *mensalão* (large-scale bribery case). In it, part of the political elite, with ties to the governing party, was taken to court for judgment by the Supreme Federal Court, being accused of many crimes, such as corruption, money laundering, organized crime, and racketeering.

On one hand, one could say that the court was quick in ruling in a case with so many powerful defendants. The population, used to hearing stories of powerful people being absolved or never being taken to court, was stupefied to see so many important politicians and businessmen condemned.

There was reason for such incredulity. After condemnation, lawyers for the defense began to file an innumerable amount of appeals (almost never questioning the verdict in and of itself, but dealing with formal procedures) with the objective of delaying imprisonment, converting the sentence from complete imprisonment to a half-way house or to shorten the term. After such appeals, the sentences and terms of imprisonment were substantially mitigated.

In summary, the Brazilian judicial system mixes features from the elitist, non-democratic past (difficult to access courts, high cost, numerous appeals) with the present democratic system (which allows broader access). The richer, however, still have room to take advantage of the resources and delays in order to avoid punishment and to take commercial advantage of court lethargy.

Chapter 5 (Section 5.3) extends the analysis of the Brazilian court system in order to show how organized middle-income groups have exploited the expansion in access to the court to extract government benefits in their favor. It will be shown how after democratization mechanisms were created that distort judicial action and reduce economic efficiency.

3.4.2 Regulatory Agency Weakness

In Chapter 1 (Stylized Fact 5) it was argued that there are natural hindrances for private companies to invest in infrastructure. As mentioned, such investments involve many sunk costs. In other words, the company must put a lot of money into the deal before beginning to operate. Imagine, for example, the telecommunications infrastructure needed to operate a mobile telephone company; the investments in building a new highway; or the research, logistics and equipment necessary to extract oil from beneath the seabed.

This money, once invested, is very difficult to recover if the company ceases operations or is prohibited from operating due to government decision. If a company has its railroad concession canceled by the government, it cannot pull up the track and install this equipment in another country. The investment will be lost. Knowing this weakness facing the private partner, governments have incentives to change the game rules during the term of contract, expropriate private investors and obtain short-term gains. Investors, seeing this weakness, resist entering this type of deal. Especially because contracts in the infrastructure sector are long-term, a company is left exposed to "government risk" for many years. Private firms may sign a contract today with a government led by one party, without knowing if an opposing party will win the next election and undo all that was done by their predecessors.

On the other hand, there is the risk of putting too much into the hands of the private investor. Many types of infrastructure services have monopolistic or oligopolistic features. For example, it does not make sense to have more than one residential gas distribution network in a city. Whoever wins the concession will be the only company on the market, with no competition forcing it to moderate prices and improve service quality.

Some private groups can ally themselves to government officials in power, receiving excessively advantageous contract conditions, earning a great amount of profit, and be assured that no potential competition will enter the market. In this case, instead of there being a confrontation between the private sector and government, there is collusion between the government and a specific business group, to the detriment of other companies and consumers in general.

There also could be an agreement between several private groups operating in the infrastructure market to, with government approval, establish an infrastructure regulation policy biased in favor of the companies, with high prices and weak quality requirements, with obvious consumer disadvantage.

A common solution found to avoid collusion and conflict and to create conditions to attract private investment in infrastructure while preventing companies and governors from adopting abusive behavior was to create autonomous regulatory agencies. These agencies should be independent, not only of the government but also the companies that offer infrastructure services.

The government would be responsible for defining the public policies to be followed in the infrastructure sector. The agencies should have the power to follow these long-term policy goals. Eventual changes in the direction or design of such public policies should not be sudden. The agencies would have the power and responsibility to safeguard contracts and limit the ability of the government to change policies, without infringing on current contracts.

The authority of such agencies would transcend government desire. This would guarantee rule stability and reassure all parts involved (government, companies and consumers) to sign long-term contracts that involve sunk costs and the many uncertainties of future market developments.

After the privatization of state infrastructure companies in the 1990s, Brazil created several regulatory agencies. Among the main ones are the National Agency of Petroleum, Natural Gas and Biofuels (*Agência Nacional do Petróleo, Gás Natural e Biocombustíveis* – ANP), the National Electricity Regulatory Agency (*Agência Nacional de Energia Elétrica* – ANEEL) and the National Agency of Telecommunications (*Agência Nacional de Telecomunicações* – ANATEL).

Theoretically, these and other agencies were created with all the prerequisites necessary for their administrative and financial autonomy in relation to government. As per the letter of the law, they are not subordinate to the ministries within their area of competence. They have ample normative power, to inspect, impose sanctions and settle conflicts between regulated companies and the government. The directors have fixed terms and cannot be dismissed at any time by the government.

In practice, however, Brazilian regulatory agencies have many restrictions to their autonomy and decision-making power. The first of these is due to the fact that positions on their main governing board often remain empty for extended periods of time. It is the responsibility of the President of the Republic to nominate, and the Senate to approve after examination, those nominated as agency directors. It has been common, since the creation of these agencies, for the President to delay nominations. The lack of quorum in the agency board of directors causes delays in management and decision making, reducing their efficacy and ability to fulfill their mission.

Figure 3.1 shows the percentage of time in which some agencies have had their complete administration (five directors) and incomplete (three or four directors) since their creation until 2009. In addition to those already referred to, ANP, ANEEL and ANATEL, the figure also shows data for the National Civil Aviation Agency (*Agência Nacional de Aviação Civil* – ANAC), National Ground Transportation Agency (*Agência Nacional de Transportes Terrestres* – ANTT) and the National Water Agency (*Agência Nacional de Águas* – ANA).

According to an audit report by the Brazilian Federal Court of Audits (TCU):

"meetings of the board of directors can only be held if 3 directors are exercising their mandate. The law requires an absolute majority of votes by members to make board decisions. In the case of the need for an absolute majority, if only 3 directors are exercising their mandate, it is required that all be present in the meeting and that all votes be unanimous for any approvals to be viable" (Brazil TCU, 2009, pp. 18-19).

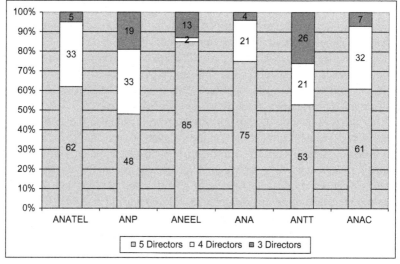

FIGURE 3.1   Percentage of Time Regulatory Agencies had 3, 4 or 5 Directors since Their Creation in 2009. *(Source: Brazil TCU (2009).)*

It can be seen that the agencies spent long periods with reduced governing boards. The ANP, for example, only had a complete board 48% of the time. The ANTT had only three directors 26% of the time.

Another problem is regarding financial autonomy. The agencies are forced to contend for funds with other areas of public administration. Year after year, their budget endowments suffer from cuts made by the Ministry of Planning. The simple ability to make these cuts gives the Executive branch bargaining power over agency directors, who may feel pressured to adopt some procedure desired by the President or her Ministers in exchange for less cuts in the agency budget.

Table 3.1 compares expenses the national budget authorizes agencies to make and expenses they effectively make. This difference shows the cuts the federal Executive Branch unilaterally promotes in agency expenses. In addition to the agencies previously identified, this table also includes the National Waterway Transportation Agency (*Agência Nacional de Transportes Aquaviários* – ANTAQ).

Notice that agency expenses are heavily cut by the government. During 2004-2012 there was an average agency budgetary cut of 30%.

Table 3.2 shows the evolution of agency expenses between 2002 and 2012. On average, in 2012 expenses were 35% greater than in 2002. This growth is not large since those agencies are new administrative bodies, which naturally should grow, be structured, increase their personnel and invest in physical installations in order to fulfill their proposal. As a comparison, take the Chamber of Deputies, an old institution whose functions have been well defined for many

TABLE 3.1 Effective Expenditure by Regulatory Agencies as a Proportion of Authorized Expenditure (%)

	2002 (%)	2004 (%)	2006 (%)	2008 (%)	2010 (%)	2012 (%)	2004-2012 Average (%)
ANA	40	54	65	76	58	60	62
ANEEL	76	64	76	81	76	89	77
ANATEL	36	80	93	72	79	78	80
ANTAQ	41	57	65	86	85	69	72
ANTT	33	65	63	73	61	68	66
ANP	50	85	69	77	58	74	73
TOTAL	45	72	74	76	67	73	72

Source: *Siafi/Sistema Siga-Brasil* (Siga Brasil System). Notes: effective expense = expense paid plus expenses from previous years paid during the current year. Expenses considered were personnel and associated expenses, investments, financial inversions, and other current expenses. Contingency reserves and interest payments were not considered. ANAC is not included in the table since it was only created in 2005. Prepared by the author.

TABLE 3.2 Effective Primary Expense Made by Regulatory Agencies: 2002 vs. 2012 (R$millions in 2012)

	2002	2012	Variation 2002-2012
ANA	141	219	54%
ANEEL	240	217	-10%
ANATEL	379	388	2%
ANTAQ	18	95	437%
ANTT	62	309	399%
ANP	340	372	9%
TOTAL	1,181	1,599	35%
Health Min.	40,900	74,080	81%
Chamber of Deputies	3,186	4,246	33%

Source: *Siafi/Sistema Siga-Brasil* (Siga Brasil System). Deflator: IPCA. Note: expenses paid plus expenses from previous years paid during the current year. Expenses considered were personnel and associated expenses, investments, financial inversions and other current expenses. Contingency reserves and interest payments were not considered. Prepared by the author.

years and which was fully structured in the first year shown in Table 3.2 (2002). Growth in Chamber of Deputies expenses was similar to the average of regulatory agencies, despite the fact that agencies were beginning and demanded large increases in their budgets in the first years.

For a second comparison, one may take the Ministry of Health, where there is always an alleged budget restriction and shortage of funds. Expenses for this ministry grew 81% in real terms during the same period, a much greater rate than the regulatory agencies.

It can also be noted that agencies operating in sectors involving large volumes of private investment (ANP, ANEEL and ANATEL) have lived with real decreases or paltry increases to their budgets.

A report prepared by the TCU on the ANTT in 2013 states that the agency lacks the basic means to monitor fulfillment of highway concession contracts. ANTT does not have enough vehicles, notebook computers with Internet access, or security equipment to be used in everyday inspection activities. Consequently, inspection, most of the time, was based on data sent by the regulated firms. ANTT agents have no means to verify the legitimacy of such data. This may explain why more than 80% of the investments private operators were obliged to make, as stipulated in contract, were behind schedule (*Valor Econômico*, 2013).

In summary, the private company that wins the bid for concession has the right to charge a toll. In compensation, they should invest in road improvement and maintenance. Given that the inspection agency does not possess the technical ability to verify if investments were duly made, the private operator can either postpone or not make them at all, but continue charging a toll as normal, not being fined and, as such, earning extraordinary profits.

Another means government has to influence agency decisions is by nominating as agency directors with strong political connections to the governing party, but who may not be technically qualified to work with the complex topics associated with infrastructure services regulation. Actually, it should be up to the federal senate to not accept the nomination of candidates who do not have the proper technical training or experience for the position they are being nominated for. However, political negotiations easily bypass this filter.

Table 3.3 summarizes a survey done based on résumés presented to the Federal Senate by 67 candidates nominated to director positions in ANEEL, ANP, ANTT, ANTAQ, ANA, ANAC and ANATEL during the period of 2005-2011. It classifies candidates based on the principle that, to adequately exercise the position of director in these regulatory agencies, the candidate should fulfill four basic requirements:

- Not be a political party militant;
- Not have served in elected positions in the executive or legislative branches in the federal, state or local governments;
- Have at least 10 years professional or academic experience in the sector to be regulated by the agency to which they are being nominated;
- Have a graduate-level education: master's, doctorate or graduate specialization course related to the regulatory area to which they were appointed.

Although some nominees are technically highly qualified and have proven experience in their areas, one can see from Table 3.3 that almost half of them

TABLE 3.3 Characteristics of Nominated Candidates for Director Positions in Federal Infrastructure Regulatory Agencies (2005 to 2013)

Political party militant	10%
Served at least one elected term in the Executive or Legislative branch of the federal, state or local governments.	6%
Less than 10 years professional or academic activity in an area related to the regulatory agency to which they were appointed	36%
Does not have a Master's, Doctorate or graduate specialization course related to the regulatory area to which they were appointed.	34%
Does not meet at least 1 of 4 requisites	46%
Does not meet at least 2 of 4 requisites	25%

Source: Federal Senate – Messages by the President of the Republic. Note: Agencies under consideration: ANEEL, ANP, ANTT, ANTAQ, ANA, ANAC, and ANATEL. Prepared by the author.

(46%) did not meet at least one of the four requirements listed above, and one fourth did not meet at least two requisites.

One case worth noting is that of ex-congressman, Haroldo Lima, who was General Director of the ANP from 2003-2011. He did not meet any of the four requirements. A historically militant communist and member of that party, he had defended state ownership of the petroleum industry since the beginning of his political career. Such a model is obviously contrary to private participation with state regulation. In other words, it was his responsibility to direct, as the maximum ANP authority, a model to which he was opposed.

Another interesting case is that of Milton Zuanazzi, ex-alderman for the PT (Workers Party) in the city of Porto Alegre. He graduated as a sociologist and specialized in tourism. Without fulfilling any of the four requirements proposed above, Zuanazzi was one of the ANAC directors during the episode of a plane crash in the city of São Paulo where 199 people died. Zuanazzi and Denise Abreu (ANAC director who did not fulfill two of the four above requirements) were indicted in the process of verifying responsibility for the accident.

Permeability of the regulatory agencies to regulated companies, and by government itself, also emerges due to rules relating to agency director mandates. One of these rules is the imposition of a 4-month quarantine period to which ex-directors are subject. This is to avoid them from being hired by companies in the regulated sector that seek to use ex-director's political contacts and access to the agency to lobby in favor of the companies. The previously cited TCU report on regulatory agencies states that this period of 4 months is too short (Law 9.986, of 2000, Article 8). According to a recommendation given by a study done by the OECD, which proposes regulatory reform for Brazil (OECD, 2008), this period should be at least 1 year. The TCU audit report is emphatic in relation to this point:

> *The short quarantine period for Brazilian regulatory agency directors increases the capture of these professionals by the regulated sector. The greater the time the ex-director is away from the regulated sector, the less the flow of privileged information from the regulator to the regulated, which makes this security mechanism more effective (Brazil TCU, 2009, p. 16).*

Another issue is the possibility of a director being re-nominated for a position. He could become receptive to government and regulated company demands in order to make his re-nomination politically feasible. The previously mentioned study by the OECD strongly recommends the end of re-nominations, with each director serving a single term.

In 2004, the federal Executive Branch sent Bill 3.337 to the National Congress. Its objective was to create general rules for regulatory agencies. The project did not receive priority treatment by the Chamber of Deputies and the Executive Branch leaders in the Chamber did not make an effort to approve it. In 2013, the Bill was officially shelved.

The low priority given to the project is a symptom of the secondary role to which regulatory agencies have been relegated. Even though much progress has been made in areas such as consumer protection and improvement in the technical quality of legislation in the area of infrastructure, the agencies are still far from being autonomous state bodies able to act impartially.

Such fragility has allowed regulated companies to lobby against rules that interfere in their interests. There have been times when the government and some regulated companies have worked together to pressure agencies and harm other market competitors. The government almost always uses credit from public banks (BNDES, BB and Caixa) and its influence over state-employee pension-fund managers (PREVI, PETROS, FUNCEF and others) as means to this end.

One example was the sale of Brasil Telecom to another telecommunications company, Telemar. When it was decided to privatize Brazilian telecommunications services, a design was adopted to divide the country into regions in such a way that the service in each would be provided by different companies. The purchase of Brasil Telecom by Telemar in 2007 represented nothing more than the control of two regions by one telecommunications company, concentrating market power. All this happened in disrespect to ANATEL regulation, which adjusted its rules *after* the deal between the companies was closed, in which the government actively participated. The economist Mansueto Almeida, in his influential *blog*, clearly described this episode:

> (...) when the sale [of Brasil Telecom to Telemar] was approved in 2007, there was great government interference, with BNDES loan guarantees, even before legislation at the time permitted such concentration (...)
>
> One of the partners in Brasil Telecom at the time, Telecom Italia, showed interest several times in increasing its participation in the company. In an interview published in the Folha de São Paulo on July 13, 2005, the president of Telecom Italia in Brazil, Paolo Dal Pino, gave the following statement regarding the possible sale of Brasil Telecom to Telemar:
>
> Yes, we were sought after by Telemar and were very surprised, because this company could not even begin to think of participating in another telephone company. It is an obvious violation of the law and all the most basic principles that inspired the privatization of the Brazilian telecommunications system, in which international investors placed their confidence. Or Telemar is affronting legislation, or the proposal that we received is already part of a company plan, along with pension funds and Citigroup, to change the General Telecommunications Law. (...) By the information we have, it seems that this will be done, supported by Telemar itself, by means of *lobbying* Congress to drastically change the law (...)(Folha de São Paulo, July 13, 2005).
>
> (...) [There was] the sale of the 19% Telecom Italia held in Brasil Telecom to the pension funds on July 18, 2007. The next year, the Opportunity group sold their shares in Brasil Telecom to Telemar. This gave origins to the Oi Company, which came to have the same majority shareholders as Telemar: the businessmen Carlos Jereisatti, of the Grupo La Fonte, and Sérgio Andrade, of the Grupo Andrade Gutierrez – both national.

*Only after the operation had been totally structured and the financing of R$2.6
billion [about US$1.6 billion] from BNDES and R$4.3 billion [about US$2.7 bil-
lion] from the Bank of Brazil secured, did ANATEL approve, on October 16, 2008,
by 3 votes to 2, the new General Concession Plan (Plano Geral de Outorgas) of
the telecommunication sector, that eased the sector rules in Brazil and allowed the
sale of Brasil Telecom to Telemar/Oi.*

*Besides the R$6.9 billion [about US$4.3 billion] loan from public banks to
allow the sale of Brasil Telecom to Telemar, state pension funds (Previ, Petros and
Funcef) actively participated and came to own 34% of the new telecommunications company (Almeida, 2013b).*

The intense participation of the government in this sale was vested in the ideological argument of the importance of creating a large telecommunications
company able to expand abroad and compete with large, international companies. Actually, it meant the capture of a market by business groups with good
government connections. Just in passing, Telemar (and the government) failed
in their attempt to create a super company. In 2013, undergoing a financial crisis, Oi (the company created after the purchase of Brasil Telecom by Telemar)
sold its control to Portugal Telecom.

This story is similar to the case discussed in the chapter introduction, where
the Eike Batista businesses bypassed ANP and CVM regulations, with compla-
cency by those in authority, and were able to accumulate gains and expropriate
minority stakeholders.

It is therefore clear that the fragility of regulatory agencies leaves ample
room for the private interests of large groups to mold regulations in their favor.
Mechanisms are created to transfer income to some groups at the pinnacle of
the social pyramid, in detriment of the consumers, taxpayers and the country as
a whole. Those companies that did not previously invest in creating politically
powerful connections lose as well.

3.4.3   Privileged Access to Public Credit

Stylized Fact 3, in Chapter 1, showed that Brazil has low aggregate savings.
This means that the amount of resources available in the country to finance
investment is scarce. As in any capitalist economy, scarce goods are expensive.
The "price" for financial resources is interest, which, as shown in Chapter 1
(Stylized Fact 4), is very high in Brazil.

If access to capital to finance investments is expensive, it should be
expected that companies would compete fiercely for access to this capital. One way to compete is to establish political connections for privileged access to credit offered by public banks and other similar sources,
which are almost always subsidized by taxpayers. A business that is able
to acquire financing with subsidized interest, in a country where market
interest (non-subsidized) is expensive, has an obvious advantage over its
competitors.

TABLE 3.4 Balance of Credit Provided by Public and Private Financial Institutions – September 2013 (%)

	% of GDP	Share (%)
Private	27.41	49.3
Public	28.14	51.7
TOTAL	55.55	100.0

Source: Brazil Central Bank – Time Series System (*Sistema de Séries Temporais*). Prepared by the author.

The Brazilian financial market is prone to political bargaining for subsidized public credit since public financial institutions have great market share. Table 3.4 shows that in September 2013, public institutions held 51% of the total credit provided by financial institutions.

In addition to this, there is a great deal of credit-market regulation, with the government controlling or restricting interest for credit offered to some segments of the economy. The credit market is divided between "earmarked credit" (directed to some economic activities privileged by the government) and "free credit" (where market rules apply). (For a detailed analysis of earmarked credit in Brazil, see Lundberg, 2011.)

The main sectors that benefit from earmarked credit are agriculture, real-estate financing and business investments. Three public financial institutions are leaders in each of these three markets: the Bank of Brazil, in agriculture, the Caixa Econômica Federal in real estate financing and BNDES in business finance. Private banks also offer lines of earmarked credit, with funding below market cost, such as savings accounts, compulsory banking resources or public resources passed on to them. The leadership of public institutions in the allocation of directed credit, however, is ample.

Table 3.5 presents average rates charged in the free and earmarked credit markets. The difference is huge. The average rate for all operations performed in the earmarked segment, between 2011 and 2013, was 8.5% per year, while on the free market, it was 29.5% per year. The advantage obtained by those who have access to earmarked (and subsidized) credit, usually provided by public banks or funds, is substantial.

BNDES

Within the earmarked credit segment, it is worth drawing attention to the role of the BNDES. This development bank (100% owned by the federal government) was created in 1952 with the objective of offering long-term credit to industry in an effort to help the country develop. Later, the bank extended its lines of credit to agriculture and services, but the industrial sector continued to be its main

TABLE 3.5 Average Interest Rates in the Earmarked and Free Markets – Average from March 2011 to September 2013 (% PY)

Earmarked	% PY
Average	8.54
Legal Entity	8.98
Legal Entity - Total Rural Credit	8.68
Legal Entity - Working Capital with BNDES Resources	9.82
Legal Entity - Financial Investments with BNDES Resources	8.82
Natural Persons - Real Estate Financing	15.16
Market Rates	**% PY**
Average	29.54
Legal Entity - Total	21.89
Legal Entity - Promissory Note Discount	31.13
Legal Entity - Total Working Capital	19.04
Natural Persons - Total	38.07
Natural Persons - Non-Consigned Personal Credit	73.45

Source: Brazil Central Bank – Times Series Systems (*Sistema de Séries Temporais*). Prepared by the author.

business. Since its creation, the BNDES has become practically monopolistic in long-term credit for investment in the country. To have access to its low-cost credit is the dream of every Brazilian entrepreneur. The demand, however, is much greater than the supply and to get one's hands on this cheap money requires some "special" abilities.

The first thing that calls attention to the BNDES is its size. The bank, which operates basically in Brazil, has a larger amount of disbursements than the World Bank, which operates in over 100 countries. In 2012, the BNDES lent US$68 billion, compared with US$35.3 billion by the World Bank in its 2012 fiscal year (http://www.oeco.org.br/bndes-na-amazonia/27808-bndes-se-internacionaliza-e-ultrapassa-banco-mundial).

Who gets all this BNDES financing? Table 3.6 shows that credit concession by the bank is highly concentrated in large business. Nothing less than 63% of its disbursements in 2012 (equal to 2.2% of GDP) went to large companies.

It is then proper to ask where the BNDES gets this huge amount of money to lend to big companies at reduced interest rates. It comes in large part from taxpayers. Table 3.7 shows that no less than 80% of the resources used by the

TABLE 3.6 BNDES Disbursements by Company Size (2012)

	R$ billions	% GDP	Share (%)
Micro	23.9	0.5	15
Small	12.5	0.3	8
Medium	13.7	0.3	9
Medium-Large	8.2	0.2	5
Large	97.7	2.2	63
TOTAL	156.0	3.5	100

Source: BNDES. Prepared by the author.

TABLE 3.7 Sources of BNDES Funding (2007 to 2012)

	Treasury	FAT	Treasury + FAT	Other	Total
2007	7	66	73	27	100
2008	16	53	68	32	100
2009	37	39	77	23	100
2010	46	30	76	24	100
2011	50	28	78	22	100
2012	53	27	80	20	100

Source: OECD, 2013, p. 67. Primary source: BNDES. Prepared by the author.

BNDES come from direct transfers made by the Treasury from the Worker Support Fund (*Fundo de Amparo ao Trabalhador* – FAT) account.

The FAT is a public fund financed by company taxes (PIS – Social Integration Program and PASEP – Civil Servant Asset Formation Program) used to pay for the unemployment insurance and wage bonus (*Abono Salarial*) programs. Its cash balance is lent to the BNDES to be used as a source of financing. Summarizing, the government imposes a tax on all companies in the country in order to raise money to pay for labor benefits and credit subsidies for (large) BNDES clients.

The National Treasury allocations to BNDES have been made more intensely as of 2009 and take the form of loans from the Treasury to the bank. These loans are financially expensive for the taxpayer since the Treasury lends to the BNDES at rates below those the Treasury pays to finance itself. (Regarding this point, see Almeida, 2013a.) As the Treasury does not have a surplus in its accounts, it must go into debt to lend to the BNDES. Or, as in the words of Sérgio Lazzarini, "public debt is used to finance private projects" (Lazzarini, 2011, p. 50). It should be added: private projects of large companies.

The BNDES preference to finance large companies is intriguing. As presented in the report "OECD Economic Surveys: Brazil 2013" (OECD, 2013) if the government objective is to use its public bank to stimulate economic development, it should focus on small- and medium-sized companies with promising projects. These are the businesses that face market-credit restrictions. Being they are new or have few assets, they do not have many guarantees to offer banks, or they may be in new technology areas where the entrepreneurial risk is greater. On the other hand, large companies have sufficient resources and market tradition to obtain credit in the private market. If the BNDES did not exist, they certainly would obtain credit on the free market.

Since 2005-2006, the BNDES broadened its policy to focus on large groups, in what the institution president, Luciano Coutinho, called the "promotion of the competitiveness of large, international quality businesses" (*The Estado de São Paulo* 2013) and that economic analysts nicknamed as the policy of "choosing national champions." It deals with conceding financing and buying stock in businesses the BNDES considers having the ability to become Brazilian multinational corporations.

Even though it has invested large amounts in a few big companies chosen to become "large, international quality businesses," the BNDES has not concerned itself with making official documents public that explain its strategy and justify why each specific business was chosen to be the lucky recipient of cheap credit.

It is possible to find on the bank's website an article published by BNDES economists that, without referencing the bank's practical activity, propose the advantages of such a strategy. In this text, Além and Cavalcanti argue that the internationalization of companies is an important means to increase their productivity in an environment where international competition is fierce. By setting up abroad, large national companies would not only have access to more advanced production methods, but also create new jobs within the country by increasing demand for the national raw materials and supplies used in their installations abroad. Another advantage would be the increase in international reserves held by the country, be it due to the increase of exports made by the internationalized company or by the remittance of profits and dividends they would make to the home office on Brazilian soil.

Comparing the flow of direct investment made by Brazilian companies abroad, with data from other emerging countries, the authors argue that Brazil is behind in this process. They conclude that there is a lot of productivity gain and external market expansion to be conquered by means of the internationalization of national companies. They also argue that, at the time the article was published (2005), the Brazilian government was not aware of the importance of creating explicit policies to stimulate such internationalization.

In spite of the clear evidence of the growing importance of transnational companies in the world economy, public policies to stimulate the internationalization of national companies are still very new in Latin America.

In the case of Brazil, for example, until recently, successful cases of internationalization have occurred due to company initiative, and not the result of a deliberate government policy to support the creation of Brazilian multinational companies (Além and Cavalcanti, 2005, p. 54).

This seems to be the type of diagnostic used by the bank, and embraced by government policy as a whole: to adopt the "national champions" policy. A few companies were selected to spearhead Brazil's entrance into the large multinational company club. However, studies were not published to justify the choice of such companies. With no clear criteria, a large void was opened for political meddling to influence the choice of who would receive subsidized loans and the injection of capital by means of BNDES shareholding. Lazzarini describes what seems to be the typical case:

> *Consider, for example, the case of the meat packing group JBS-Friboi (one of the largest presidential campaign contributors in 2006). The BNDES participated with 1.4 billion reais [about US$720 million] in opening capital for the company in 2007, and later, at the beginning of 2010, acquired another 3.4 billion reais [about US$1.8 billion] in debentures. The justification, according to the bank, was to support the group's aggressive international expansion strategy, which needed funds to make gigantic acquisitions, such as Swift and Pilgrim's Pride (North American meat packing industries) (Lazzarini, 2011, p. 50).*

Pinheiro, in a news article, lists other cases, among which is the previously cited purchase of Brasil Telecom by Telamar, and the adverse effects of the "national champions" policy:

> *(...) the classification of Oi as a national champion arose in 2008, when Telemar bought Brasil Telecom with BNDES funding and came to dominate the Brazilian land line telephone market, except in São Paulo. The justification at the time was that this would give the country a telecommunications company that could fight on equal ground for the international market, raising the Brazilian flag in other countries. As we know, this did not happen. Oi only operates in Brazil.*
>
> *What did happen was a great market concentration that did not afflict the consumer more thanks to intense competition in the mobile and Internet market.*
>
> *(...) The first case in which the national champion argument was used to justify official approval of an operation that went contrary to consumer interest was the fusion of beer producers Brahma (owner of Skol) and Antártica (which did not have BNDES support). The new company (Ambev) came to control 72% of the beer market, with market presence in some areas of over 90%. In trade for enormous market power, the company promised to make Brazilian guaraná an internationally consumed soft drink, globally rivaling Coca Cola. After more than a decade, there is no news that this has happened.*

> *(...) The creation of these national champions was clearly a success for their controlling shareholders. Ambev, for example, became the largest Brazilian company in market value. But the consumer, and especially, the Brazilian taxpayer who pays the subsidies for these operations, what do they gain by this? (Pinheiro, 2013).*

Even though the internationalization of a company is justified in order to expand markets, attract new technology and reduce balance of payment vulnerability, such argument is insufficient to justify a policy of subsidized credit and use of public capital for large private enterprises. It is necessary to show that such policies would be the best and least expensive instruments to attain the desired objectives. As such, one must ask:

- In a country with such infrastructure bottlenecks, would it not be best to use such enormous BNDES resources to finance infrastructure investments, both public and private, which would benefit all companies in the country, instead of a few that are handpicked?
- Why not invest such resources in public policies that could generate large productivity gains, like education, which has other positive effects on the economy?
- Would productivity gains resulting from internationalization (such internationalization that, in many cases, did not occur, as in the Telemar/Oi episode) not be lost due to the concentration of market power, which allows companies to raise prices and be less efficient?

If the objective is to stimulate productivity, why concentrate BNDES support on large companies, in sectors with well-known technology and far from the cutting edge (meat packers and beverages, for example), instead of focussing in innovative projects?

In a country with high inequality, does it make sense to adopt policies whose main effects are to generate asset gains for large groups, with benefits to the population coming only as a secondary effect of these policies? After all, productivity, employment and currency gains will come if, and only if, the companies are successful, while shareholder gains are immediate.

Even if the BNDES had used a large technical filter to choose the "national champions," it is obvious that in a country with high inequality (in income and political power) and scarcity of credit (which makes such resources even more desired), political connections would play a role in that choice. Add to this the fact that, being a bank, the BNDES has the details of its operations protected by banking secrecy legislation, which reduces transparency and opens room for undisclosed negotiations.

Constitutional Funds

Preferential access by large companies to public credit is not restricted to the BNDES case. It is also possible to see it in the operations of the North, Northeast and Mid-West Constitutional Funds. The Federal Constitution

(Article 159, Subsection I, Point C) earmarks 3% of the Income Tax and the Tax on Industrialized Products (IPI) revenue for "application in the North, Northeast and Mid-West productive sectors by means of its regional finance institutions, according to regional development plans (…)." It is, therefore, a subsidized credit for private investment in areas considered less developed. As in the case of credit offered by the BNDES, it would be expected that this would be to support small businesses in those regions, certainly those most affected by restricted access to credit due to insufficient collateral to back loans. These would be the most affected by the imperfections of the credit market, which would demand the attention of a corrective public policy. However, it is once more the large companies that absorb the large part of credit, as is shown in Table 3.8.

Even though the concentration of credit on big companies is not as large as in the BNDES case, large companies receive no less than one-third of the total credit offered by those funds. On the other hand, contrary to the BNDES, which has a reasonable control policy for client default, the constitutional funds suffer heavy losses. In a study done in partnership with Miranda and Cosio, the author describes the financial mechanics of these funds as follows:

> (…) the rates of return for the funds are highly negative, indicating that they lose resources during each period. In the case of the FNO, for example, there is a loss of more than 70% of the capital employed, which practically represents a donation of financial resources to private companies that receive credit. This means that, by the way in which the fund is managed, resources would simply run out if it were not for their permanent replenishment by the treasury (Mendes et al., 2008, p. 103).

TABLE 3.8 Disbursements by FNO (North Constitutional Financing Fund), FCO (Mid-West Constitutional Financing Fund) and FNE (Northeast Constitutional Financing Fund) by Company Size (2012)

	R$ billions	% GDP	Share (%)
Informal, mini & micro	4.8	0.11	22
Small	5.0	0.11	23
Small-Medium	2.2	0.05	10
Medium	2.9	0.07	13
Large	7.2	0.16	33
Total	22.1	0.50	100

Source: Valor Econômico. Primary source: *Balanço do desempenho dos fundos constitucionais em 2012* (Evaluation of constitutional fund performance in 2012) – Ministry of National Integration.

In other words, the companies financed by these funds do not only receive subsidies, they receive "semi-donations." Another factor that affects constitutional-fund cash flows are the high administrative costs charged by public banks that manage them, which represents a type of capture of public funds by the bureaucracy of these institutions, a topic to be covered in Chapter 5, Section 5.10.

State-Company-Sponsored Pension Funds

Besides the mandatory participation by all formally registered private sector workers in the federal government social security system, there are complementary retirement funds. Workers pay into an investment institution that will in turn pay them a sum to complement the benefit received by social security upon retirement. These complementary retirement entities, better known as pension funds, administer contributions made by workers and their employing companies, also known as "sponsors." A relevant group of pension funds is that sponsored by state companies.

Table 3.9 shows that state-company-sponsored funds have assets equivalent to almost 10% of GDP. It is a mountain of money that needs long-term investment to generate sufficient income to pay member retirements.

Since these sponsors are state companies and their directors are politically appointed, there is opportunity to use political connections to obtain access to pension-fund loans and stock acquisitions. Add to this the fact that employee representative on the pension-fund board is, frequently, a union leader with political aspirations (Silva (2007). This creates incentives for forging ties with companies that offer large-election-campaign financing and tends to affect the way representatives vote when deciding on fund investments.

Table 3.10 describes the types of investments made by state pension funds in 2013. They not only invested in (low-risk) government bonds, but also in stock, real estate, loans and buying shares in investment funds. There is plenty of money available to invest in private companies. Having access to this large amount of money, in an economy where savings to finance investments is scarce, is essential for companies that want to have the competitive edge and scale in large investments.

There are many cases involving corruption with state pension-fund investments (and those supported by private companies as well). Two reports by Parliamentary Investigation Committees (CPI) held in the National Congress offer abundant examples of racketeering among public agents, pension fund managers and companies.[4]

---

4. There was the pension fund CPI, in 1992, that investigated cases of corruption in the Collor administration and that brought about the impeachment of the president; and the postal service CPI that investigated the payment of bribes by the executive to parliamentarians (the *mensalão* scandal), which had a sub-commission exclusively designated to investigate crimes involving pension funds. Reports available at http://www.senado.gov.br/atividade/materia/getPDF.asp?t=56653&tp=1 and http://www.senado.leg.br/comissoes/CPI/RelatorioFinalVol3.pdf.

TABLE 3.9 Pension Fund Sponsored by State Entities and their Total Assets (June 2013)

	Sponsoring State Company	R$ Billions	% GDP
PREVI	Banco do Brasil	165.5	3.8
PETROS	Petrobras	72.7	1.7
FUNCEF	Caixa Econômica Federal	52.0	1.2
FORLUZ	Cia Energética de Minas Gerais - CEMIG	12.4	0.3
REAL GRANDEZA	Furnas Centrais Elétricas	11.4	0.3
FAPES	BNDES	9.3	0.2
CENTRUS	Banco Central	8.4	0.2
POSTALIS	Correios	8.1	0.2
FUNDAÇÃO COPEL	COPEL - Cia Paranaense de Energia	6.8	0.2
FACHESF	Cia Hidrelétrica do São Francisco	5.4	0.1
Total 10 Largest (A)		352.0	8.0
Other Funds Sponsored by State Companies (B)		76.0	1.7
General Total (A)+(B)		428.0	9.7

Source: Previc – quarterly statistic. Prepared by the author.

Even though cases of corruption receive a lot of attention and generate headlines, what is interesting to highlight in this section is another point: the use of pension funds to channel financing and capital to enterprises undertaken by large groups with political connections to government. There is a natural attraction between large investment projects (made by large economic groups) and large volumes of capital (generated by pension funds). When the government has the power to interfere in fund decisions, this attraction becomes even greater. This does not necessarily have to do with corruption, but it does create advantages and gains for large groups.

Take the case of the privatization of state companies in the 1990s. Facing strong ideological resistance and the opposition of state-company unions, the Fernando Henrique Cardoso government (1995-2002) needed to charge high prices for the state companies up for sale in order to reduce political pressure against privatization. One means found to increase the sale price for public

TABLE 3.10 Composition of Investments Made by State-Entity-Sponsored Pension Funds (June 2013)

	R$ Billions	% GDP	% Participation
Investment Funds	218.20	5.0	54
Shares	73.80	1.7	18
Government Bonds	60.80	1.4	15
Real Estate Investments	21.60	0.5	5
Private Credit and Deposits	18.60	0.4	5
Loans and Financing	14.30	0.3	4
Other Receivables	0.20	0.0	0
Judicial/Appeal Deposits	0.10	0.0	0
TOTAL	407.60	9.3	100

Source: Previc – quarterly statistic. Prepared by the author.

companies being privatized was to offer state-controlled pension funds as partners to private companies interested in buying the state companies. The participation of pension funds in the groups bidding for state companies on sale would increase the financial capacity of interested buyers, who would make larger bids. As a result, the government would sell its companies at higher prices, reducing criticism by the opposition. When all was said and done, part of the money paid to the government had come from the government itself: state companies sponsor pension funds and those funds by other state companies!

There was not necessarily any corruption in this process. The pension funds are investors with long-range goals and the privatizations really were great business opportunities. In fact, they came to be lucrative deals for the funds. This, however, does not dismiss the fact that the formation of consortiums between private firms and state pension funds depend on political connections, access to government offices and lobbying.

Instead of supporting a direct connection between large groups and pension funds, the government could have adopted, for example, a model of selling stock on the market. In this case, the pension funds could have made the deal by buying stock without forming alliances with large private groups. However, the government opted for the formation of a direct coalition between the funds and large companies, since, as has already been highlighted, due to judicial uncertainty, no company or pension fund wants to assume a minority position and run the risk of being expropriated by the majority shareholders.

Some large companies use pension funds as an instrument to acquire control of other companies without using their own capital, employing maneuvers within the rules of society control. A typical action is the dispossession of minority stakeholders, as in the related case where the Opportunity Group used the PREVI pension fund as an instrument to dispossess the Canadian TIW.

Another interesting case is the Sadia bankruptcy, which at one time was the largest and most traditional producer of canned goods, chicken and other processed foods. In 2008, on the vestiges of the international crisis, Sadia went bankrupt due to making bad investments in the derivatives market. The company belonged to the Furlan family. Luiz Fernando Furlan was president of the Corporate Administrative Council from 1993 to 2003, when he took leave to become Minister of Development in the first year of the Lula da Silva administration. Leaving the Ministry in 2007, he returned to Sadia. With the company bankruptcy the following year, a merger was engineered with the second largest company in the market, and main competitor, Perdigão, creating Brasil Foods. Once more, the merger was presented to the public as the creation of a large Brazilian multinational company, able to compete internationally. Once again there was intense participation by the government in engineering the merger, pension funds (PREVI and PETROS) and the BNDES were summoned to buy stock participation in the new company.

Company bailouts were common in the 1970s and 1980s, a time when the BNDES was dubbed the "hospital for ailing companies." The Sadia case brought back that practice, which many thought had been overcome.

The model of making state pension funds available to private groups allows the advance of projects with no financial viability, but that are of interest to the government due to their political-electoral appeal. Private companies would not invest their own capital in a project with little chance of making a profit. But if capital is provided by pension funds, the deal can be attractive. Private companies can partner with pension funds without compromising their own capital and there is leeway to push future losses onto the partners that provided the public capital (the government ends up being called to rescue the state pension funds, be it by funding the sponsor or capitalizing the funds.[5]

This was the case with the defunct high-speed train project. The Federal Government made three attempts to hold an auction for the concession of a high-speed train between Rio de Janeiro and São Paulo. Due to the fragility of viability studies, private companies were cautious about entering the deal.

---

5. Even though in the last few years the state companies and their pension funds did a large amount of work to migrate participants and beneficiaries from defined benefit plans (which could demand the eventual transfer of additional resources from supporters) to defined contribution plans, such movement was not sufficient to eliminate the risk of the flow of public resources due to the eventual pension actuary deficits.

Most of the ones that showed interest in the project were, in fact, equipment manufacturers interested in selling trains and track to the country, but that were shy of the risky activity of train operation. The clearer the financial infeasibility of the project became, the more the government emphasized the "availability" of pension funds to cooperate in the financing. (See, for example, *O Estado de São Paulo*, 2013.) It came to promise the formation of a "bride fund": the pension funds would be "the bride" waiting for a "groom". Pension funds would be awaiting the decision of which company would win the bid (the groom), and then form an association with the winner. The project, however, had so many uncertainties and involved such large amounts of money that it was canceled.

It is interesting to observe that, even though responsible for more than 15% of GDP, and being subject to intense political pressure, state pension funds are regulated by an autarchy, PREVIC, whose directors have limited autonomy in relation to the government. Contrary to what was seen in Section 3.4.2, the mandates of PREVIC directors are not fixed, and are at risk of dismissal at any time. If the autonomy of the agencies for which mandates are fixed is precarious, the situation in PREVIC is even worse.

Political Connections and Access to Credit

There is statistical evidence that political connections increase access to public credit. Claessens and co-authors show that companies that had made campaign contributions to federal deputy candidates in the 1998 and 2002 elections had greater access to credit in the 4 years following each election (Claessens et al., 2008). The estimated effect is quite large: companies that contributed with a value equal to 1 standard deviation above the contribution average received bank credit 9.4% above the average.

The authors show that companies that contributed to elected candidates had a greater increase in credit: the effect described above rises to 12.1%, which shows the importance of contributing to the right candidates.

This idea is reinforced by the fact that effects of campaign contributions on credit access is statistically more robust when the deputy is a member of the winning coalition in the presidential election (effect of 9.3% for one standard deviation of contributions made to deputies that are part of the presidential coalition against a statistical effect equal to zero for those of the opposition). The same is true for deputies who are reelected and, therefore, were already part of the political circuit before the elections (effect of 10.7% for re-elected and zero for deputies in their first mandate).

Another very relevant observation made by the authors is that companies that had more access to credit, in spite of this competitive advantage, had lower profit than others:

> (...) *the performance of firms during the post election period is significantly lower, the more contributions they provide.* (...) *[suggesting that] contributing firms perform worse and that the additional investment generated by improved*

financing has not been efficient. The results so far suggest that political favors (...)
come in the form of improved access to finance for often poorly performing firms
(Claessens et al., 2008).

This is a typical case of poor resource allocation: if bank financing had gone to more productive companies, the economy would have grown more. The authors calculate a 0.2% loss in GDP per year, but argue that this number, even though representing a significant loss, is a "low" estimate since it takes into account only companies listed on the Brazilian stock market (BOVESPA), the data was used in the calculations. An extrapolation including the remaining companies that supported campaigns, but that did not have stock on the exchange, would take the loss to 1.4% of GDP.

3.4.4   Protection of National Industry

Since at least the 1940s, Brazil has intensely protected its industry. There may be no other characteristic that has been so immutable over the different phases of Brazilian history. The idea that development is created through industrialization and that the agricultural and services industries represent a setback is deeply imbedded in the national mindset.[6]

In Brazil, and in Latin America in general, industrialization by means of "import substitution" is not merely one among many economic policy options. It has been the central idea sponsored over many decades by an international organization belonging to the United Nations: the United Nations Economic Commission for Latin America and the Caribbean (ECLAC). It is an international organism that, with all its political influence and financial capacity, over the decades has supported the formation of economists that have assimilated, since the beginning of their intellectual formation, the ideology that it is fundamental to protect industry, preferentially that from national capital.

Add to this that fact that the two "golden eras" in terms of Brazilian economic growth were under the political "developmentalist" sign that included intense industrial protection and subsidies: the years of the Juscelino Kubitschek presidency (1956-1961) and the so-called "economic miracle years" (1968-1973). It seems of little importance that the macroenomic imbalance generated by these periods of intense growth put the country into crises with considerable economic, social and political costs. The high inflation brought by Kubitschek preceded the economic crisis that led to the military coup in 1964. The economic miracle ended with a serious crisis in the balance of payments that imposed the long years of stagnation of the 1980s.

These atrocious consequences do not seem to be associated, in the minds of Brazilian politicians and citizens, with their causes, which are the inconsistent economic models adopted by Kubitschek and the military. These policies were

---

6. Thanks to Samuel Pessôa and Marcos Lisboa for calling my attention to the power of ideology in sustaining industrial protection policies.

based on protected and subsidized industrialization, associated with a high level of state participation in the economy, coupled with unsustainable fiscal deficits. What is left, for historical interpretation and basis for political discourse, is the memory of the happy days of strong growth and optimism in relation to the future. The lack of temporal coincidence between cause and effect allows the survival, over time, of a political discourse favorable to inconsistent economic policies.

In the thesis proposed by Raúl Prebisch, one of the main founders of the ECLAC school of economic thought, the terms of trade between agricultural and industrialized products would present a historical tendency in favor of the latter, condemning nations that depend on agriculture to underdevelopment. This proposition was easily associated with socialist ideology, which states that poor nations were exploited by international capital. According to this way of thinking, it would be necessary to have a national industrial base that would remove the peripheral nation from the trap of international trade, considered unjust, and, by nature, harmful to exporters of basic goods.

Strong nationalism was also stimulated by two world wars. During these conflicts, there were interruptions in international trade, which left Latin American countries (as well as the rest of the world) without the supply of imported basic goods. This reinforced the idea that each country needed a local production base, not associated with foreign interests.

In fact, the experience of a forced interruption in trade during the two world wars stimulated the rise of national manufactures, giving practical support to the idea that creating trade barriers to the import of foreign goods would be a way to make the national industry bloom. Initially unable to compete with companies operating on a large scale on the international market, the national "infant industry" needed to be temporarily protected to grow and to compete as equals with industry from other countries.

Add to this the fact that some economies that "got it right" used industrial protection policies. Countries such as Japan, South Korea and more recently, China, are usually cited as examples that protecting the internal market and subsidizing the installation of industry on national soil would be a viable path in the direction of economic development.

However, there is not necessarily a causal relationship between the fact that these countries adopted such policies and their long growth cycles. Growth could have come from other factors and could have occurred "in spite of" the industrial policies adopted and not "because of" these policies, as will be discussed below.

The ideological power of protecting Brazilian national industry is illustrated in Chapter 1, Stylized Fact 7, which shows that the Brazilian economy is among the most closed to international trade in the world.

It is evident that the main beneficiaries from industrial protection are the owners of protected businesses and their employees. An industry that is protected from international competition can charge higher prices because the consumer does not have the right to choose products offered by other companies.

As such, protected businesses earn higher profits and can transfer part of it to their laborers, be it in the form of higher salaries or by means of hiring more employees than necessary for efficient production.

There is an immediate cost to consumers, and not just by paying higher prices, but by consuming products of lower quality as well. The costs don't stop there. The more closed a production market to imports, the greater chances a cartel will form, which leads to even higher prices and greater consumer losses (Carrasco and Mello, 2013).

There are also systemic costs to the economy. As argued in Chapter 1, Stylized Fact 7, in an economy that is open to international competition, the less efficient companies cannot survive competition. This means that, by failing, they release labor and capital to be used in more efficient companies, which raises average economic productivity. Also, opening to trade allows the entrance of high-technology goods, which permits greater productivity in all sectors that employ them. The gains from open trade also come through external sales: exporting companies need to be more efficient and productive in order to attend the high standards demanded by international clients, which forces them to seek improvements in their production process.

Industrial protection is not only done by means of blocking international trade. There are many different means. Besides subsidized credit, as considered in the previous section, there are bureaucratic restrictions (non-tariff barriers), preference for national products in government purchases, subsidies given directly to industry (for example, accelerated depreciation of assets in order to reduce taxes) and the creation of state companies to produce raw materials and supplies to be sold at low cost to industries. At the same time, these policies generate increased public expenditure (paid by taxpayers) and additional losses in economic efficiency.

The immediate winners and losers are clearly defined: industry owners and their employees. The losers are the consumers, taxpayers and the current and future generations (that cannot take advantage of faster economic growth).

For this type of policy to have such longevity, and survive such different political cycles (ebbing and flowing), it is necessary that a large part of society be convinced that its benefits surpass its costs. Or, in other words, the winners (industry and its labor force) need to convince the rest of society that it gains with this type of policy and that the gains surpass the immediate losses. This seems to be the ideological power of industrial protection: even the losers seem to be convinced that they are benefited by such a policy.

In fact, there are arguments in the sense that industrial protection generates social gains that outweigh its costs. These arguments will be analyzed next.

Arguments in Favor of Industrial Protection

The main idea seems to be that proposed by Rosenstein-Rodan, which associates industrialization with an **increase in general economic productivity** (Rosenstein-Rodan, 1943). Industry, with its assembly-line production and the urbanization it causes, tends to be more productive than agriculture, especially traditional agriculture. This means that more industrialization is a sign of more intense growth, increases in scale due to the formation of urban conglomerations, more trade activity due to people living in urban centers and the expansion of infrastructure service, which becomes viable in urban agglomerations. In addition to this, innovations in industry can be used by other segments, generating collective gains.

As such, the cost that a part of society would pay in the short term, to finance the installation of industry, would be compensated in the long term, when industry would drive the whole economy and stimulate the formation of urban centers. The "externalities" would be sufficiently large to compensate the losses.

Canêdo-Pinheiro presents a summary of the arguments that explain why industry did not spontaneously arise in more backward countries, becoming dependent on government stimulus policies instead (Canedo-Pinheiro, 2013). The first has already been referred to in the idea of "infant industry": if production costs for a pioneer company in a specific economic sector are high, then no entrepreneur will be interested in being the pioneer in this sector, because they will not be able to compete against imported goods that are produced (abroad) and sold by larger and more efficient international companies. Therefore, initial protection should be used to block the entrance of imported goods into the market, allowing the creation of a local business that could sell its products at higher prices.

In time, new businesses would be formed, attracted by the profits obtained by the pioneer. The scale of production would grow and productivity would increase as new companies gained experience in a "learn by doing" process. In the long term, it would be possible to foster an efficient industry. Society would pay the costs of forced industrialization during the initial years, but later, industry could fly on its own, no longer requiring subsidies, and the country would have acquired more economic dynamism, counting on a (more) productive sector that previously did not exist. This reinforces the idea that short-term costs would be compensated by long-term, generalized gains for society in general.

Another relevant argument is the **need for coordination.** It is possible that the country has the income and population necessary to generate a market for a given industrial product, but national production of this good does not occur due to lack of coordination in the installation of the different sectors necessary for its production. Take the automobile industry as an example. The production of vehicles depends on a steel industry to offer raw materials. The production of steel and cars depends on the supply of energy. The government would then enter as a coordinator, offering incentives to the different industries with complementary functions so that all were installed at the same time, therefore resolving the problem of coordination.

Also cited by those that defend industrial protection is the idea of the "linkage" of the productive activity. Industry requires raw materials or supplies from other sectors. The installation of a specific manufacturing activity would stimulate the creation of other industries that would arise as suppliers. The production of appliances and vehicles is usually cited as an example of sectors capable of generating great dynamism by stimulating the production of plastics, rubber, steel, parts, etc.

Industry would also be a center to **generate and spread new technologies**. Technological advances would be stronger in this sector than in agriculture or services. The technological gains promoted by one industrial sector would be useful to others, creating a process of social gains.

Furthermore, the successive balance of payment crises experienced by Brazil during its history reinforces the idea that it is important to develop a diversified production base that reduces the **volatility of economic cycles**. Having an economy based on agricultural exports seems risky in a world of volatile commodity market prices. A diversified industrial base would be necessary to provide more economic stability.

Up to what point do these arguments sustain themselves and effectively guarantee that those who pay the cost of industrial protection (consumer, taxpayers and the general population) are adequately compensated for the positive externalities resulting from industrialization?

Critiques of Industrial Protection

There is no doubt that industrialization stimulates **increases in productivity**, be it by innovative production methods or by urban growth. It is also reasonable to admit that protecting the **infant industry** can kick off industrialization that, left to its own, would never happen.

These two arguments, however, lead to the conclusion that protection, if adopted, should be for a *limited time*. After industry and urbanization have been installed, and the infant industry has grown and increased its productivity to international levels, there would be no more reason to continue protection or subsidies. Industry, at some point in time, must walk on its own two feet. Urbanization, once consolidated, no longer needs to be supported as it takes on a life of its own.

This is in contrast to the long life of Brazilian protection policies. The industries and labor unions permanently cry the threat of industrial destruction (and their respective jobs) by international competition and demand indefinite protection. The "infant" Brazilian industry is already over 70 years old! The costs, instead of being short-term, incurred at onset of industrialization, have perpetuated over the long term.

This permanent need for protection comes, in part, from the fact that it does not necessarily cause industry to seek better technology. It will only do this when there is a credible threat that, at some point in the future, national industry will be faced with the hard facts of international competition. If industrialists and their workers believe they are protected for a long time, industry will tend to use cheaper, less efficient technology, producing inferior quality goods and selling them for higher prices, thanks to the protection available. The ghost of de-industrialization feeds a permanent lobby for the renewal and expansion of protection (Bacha and Bolle, 2013 compile several articles on the theme).

In fact, as shown in the already mentioned Canêdo-Pinheiro study, a fundamental difference between Brazilian industrial policy and that of Asian countries is that in those countries, incentives had a definite expiration date and, in fact, ended. In Brazil however, protection seems to have an infinite time limit, floating from one political cycle to the next.

If it is true that industrialization and the consequent urbanization raise economic productivity, then it is also true that excessively protected companies become unproductive. The gain in productivity that results from the migration of rural workers to the industrial sector can be offset by the low evolution of productivity in the protected industry. As shown in Chapter 1, Stylized Fact 7, there is evidence that a temporary opening to trade in the 1990s caused significant gains in productivity.

Furthermore, as highlighted in the already mentioned IADB study coordinated by Pagés (2010) urbanization causes the services sector to expand a great deal. This is a broad segment that goes from the small, retail business to large financial conglomerates, from the dentist's office to telecommunications companies. According to IBGE data, services represent 60% of Brazilian GDP. If the final goal is gains in economic productivity, why should it be done by protecting industry instead of adopting policies that provide gains in productivity in the (larger) services sector?

Policies to improve education, investment in infrastructure and public security in the urban centers, for example, would promote gains in all sectors. Such policies would have the advantage of immediately benefiting the general population and not only specific protected industries and their labor force. Broad public policies guarantee positive externalities for the entire economy.

Speaking on the idea that industrial policy should promote the **coordination** of different distinct industry decisions, inducing them to install in the country at the same time, it should be observed that such an assertion loses strength when one considers the possibility of an industry importing its raw materials and supplies. Only in a closed economy is it necessary to coordinate installation of steel mills or auto-part companies at the same time as, say, a vehicle manufacturer. Being able to import materials and machines, the vehicle industry can install itself and import whatever is needed for production. Later and more slowly, other companies will see the opportunity and move to the country as suppliers to those already installed.

Only those goods and services not sold on the international market should not be imported, such as power generation, qualified labor and transportation to distribute the product within the country. In this case, however, the most important policy would be providing the public services of education and infrastructure, in a generalized way, to all sectors, and not by means of incentives directed toward some industries.

In fact, one should ask: If Brazil is a country with so many needs in education (Chapter 1, Stylized Fact 10) and infrastructure (Chapter 1, Stylized Fact 5), and having in view that such needs are an evident hindrance to long-term growth, why should growth be stimulated by means of subsidies directed toward a specific sector of the economy? It would be more rational and fair to stimulate growth by means of government policies that, being paid by all taxpayers, would benefit large segments of the population instead of adopting policies that concentrate gains on some groups (industries and their labor forces), promising a (uncertain) spreading of future gains over society.

The public funding that pays for infrastructure and education is the same that pays for industrial subsidies. There is a clear tension between the two types of policies. Historically, Brazil has opted to subsidize private industrial capital and put aside the formation of human capital and investments in infrastructure. In contrast, the Asian countries, usually pointed out as industrial policy success cases, not only have a national education level much higher than that in Brazil at the onset of industrialization, but also invested heavily in human capital, in addition to caring to provide the available infrastructure for all areas of the economy.

The argument for industrial **linkage**, which would create more jobs in an economy, loses strength when the empirical data is analyzed. According to Schymura and Canêdo-Pinheiro:

> *Recent research indicates that sectors with greater linking in terms of production are not always those that generate more jobs. In terms of creating new positions, if the direct and indirect effects are considered, the highlights would be in commerce, cattle farming, agro-industry, shoes, wood and real estate. But if consideration is made regarding the quality of the position, taking into account education, rotativity and average salary, the advantage from the linking point of view transfers to the services sector (...) in spite of the relevance of the structural character of industry, it does not distinguish itself from other sectors in this aspect (Schymura and Canêdo-Pinheiro, 2013, p. 87).*

Another advantage attributed to industry is that it is the source for the **generation and diffusion of new technology**. This should also be analyzed carefully. It is obvious that technological advances are at the heart of long-term economic growth, as seen in Chapter 1, Section 1.2. It is also a known fact that the production of new technology involves strong externalities: Microsoft and Apple profits, for example, resulting from manufacturing computers, are just a fraction of those that these machines allow for society as a whole. As such, it is worth subsidizing individuals and organizations involved in the research and development of new technology.

This, however, does not mean that one should subsidize industry based on the presupposition that they are, by nature, innovators. It is much more effective to directly subsidize research and development (R&D) activities, be they by universities, companies or public or private foundations. Nothing guarantees that subsidized industries will invest in R&D. Nothing justifies an indirect subsidy to R&D, by means of industry, instead of a direct subsidy conceded to research programs, even if some of them are developed in industry.

As Almeida observed, Australia is an economy where over 70% of its exports are commodities and, in spite of this, invests more in R&D than Brazil

(Almeida, 2013a). There is not necessarily a direct connection between the importance of industry in an economy and its level of investment in R&D.

Last, but not least, one must consider that industrialization reduces the **volatility of the economic cycles** by reducing the impact of unpredictable and oscillating international commodity prices on local economic activity. In fact, diversification of the productive structure tends to reduce such volatility, but this can also be attained by other means that cost less than subsidizing industry over decades.

One way to act directly on the problem is by means of rainy-day funds, where resources from financial surplus from times of economic boom are deposited. Such resources accumulate and are spent to stimulate the economy during recessions. Chile has applied this system with a great deal of success, accumulating resources from copper-mining operations, its main source of exports.

Summarizing, there are no absolute and irrefutable arguments in favor of the protection and subsidy of national industry, even less so when this protection extends for time interminable.

Why Is Industrial Protection so Resistant?

The existence of this type of policy over the last seven decades seems to have its roots in the great power of large industrial groups and the coalition of their interests and those of their employees, who are interested in maintaining their jobs and salaries. Behind the technical arguments in favor of industrial policies there is, actually, a type of rent-seeking interest to protect against competition, preserve extraordinary profits and wages above the market average. As such, potential benefits are exalted and costs disregarded.

As will be seen in more detail in Chapter 5, what guarantees the power of industrial policies is a typical collective-action issue, analyzed in a classic study by Mancur Olson: policy benefits are concentrated in specific groups, which have a lot to gain with their approval, with the costs being paid by society as a whole (Olson, 1965). Each individual in society pays a small portion of these costs (by means of taxes, inferior quality products, high prices, etc.), and does it without noticing, without clearly associating the costs with their causes. Moreover, the losers do not have the ability to mobilize themselves against the policy, while the winners have a great interest in its approval and, thus, intensify their lobby in its favor. Add to this the strong ideological and nationalistic appeal, described at the beginning of this section, used by the policy beneficiaries to derive support from the losers.

In recent Brazilian history, the brief episodes of commercial freedom and dismantling of industrial support mechanisms occurred during times when political balance was ruptured, making it possible to break the alliance between industrialist and government officials. As soon as political crises were overcome, and balance was again restored, protectionist policies gradually came back. Immediately after the military coup in 1964, which destroyed the power coalitions of the time, a policy of free trade was implanted within the scope of a liberal economic model. Then, in 1968, free trade began to be reduced due to the "deterioration of the balance of payments and pressure by the sectors most affected by tax reform"(Pinheiro and Almeida, 1995, p. 200).

A new episode of free trade came during the Collor government (1990-1992). The first government elected directly by the people, the President felt politically powerful enough to defy interest groups that supported industrial protection. He promoted the significant dismantling of the protective structure mentioned in Stylized Fact 7 (Chapter 1). After remarkable gains in productivity due to this freedom and the beneficial effects of long-term growth, there has been, since that time, a slow, progressive movement to close the economy and protect industry.

Marta Castilho and co-authors show that between 2000 and 2005 there was an increase in active protection of national production, especially due to changes in the import tariff system. According to the authors, the average effective tariff, which considers the effect of the tax system on the price of imports, jumped from 15.3% to 25.8% in only 5 years. The automotive industry was highly favored by protectionist policies and had its effective protection increased from 46% to 180%! (Castilho et al., 2009).

Two of the greatest experts in Brazilian commercial policy, Renato Bauman and Honório Kume, also wrote that there have been signs of a progressive closing of the Brazilian economy in the last years. According to the authors, in 2000, only 2.7% of imported products had import tariffs above 25%, with the group growing to 8.4% by 2012, which leads them to conclude that there has come to be "a more extensive use of the tariff policy to maintain domestic industrial protection, above all for consumption goods" (Baumann and Kume, 2013, p. 259).

The ascencion of the *Partido dos Trabalhadores* – PT (Worker's Party) to power in 2003 had much to do with the rebirth of industrial protectionism. From the point of view of political action, the PT has strong connections with the industrial unions, who are interested in such protection. From the ideological point of view, there is a great affinity of the party with the ECLAC school of thought and its incisive defense of the import substitution model. In addition, the long period of high international commodities prices induced an overvaluation of the national currency, which reduced national industrial protection against the highly productive Chinese and Korean industries, leading national industries to pressure for more protection.

The result was a progressive and generalized reintroduction of industrial policies. From 2004 to 2012, the Federal Government adopted several initiatives. In 2003, the *Política Industrial, Tecnológica e de Comércio Exterior* – PITCE (Industrial, Technology and Trade Policy) was adopted, and is probably the least aggressive policy adopted during this period. Its focus was on technological innovation, increase in external competitiveness and industrial modernization. It was not directed toward specific sectors of the economy, such as textiles, vehicles, etc., as Brazilian industrial policies tend to be. It sought to stimulate research in areas it considered promising, which could be useful to different industrial sectors, or even in areas outside of industry. In general, it was an attempt to stimulate technological research that could be applied in the production process, moving away from the traditional direct subsidy to industrial sectors.

This directive didn't last long. In 2008 the *Política de Desenvolvimento Produtivo* – PDP (Productive Development Policy) was launched in the traditional mold of nominating benefited sectors. It was actually an ample device including all old clients of this type of policy: motor vehicles, textiles and clothing, capital goods, furniture, plastics, petrochemicals and maritime industries. The instruments were the same as always: selective tax breaks for each sector, accelerated depreciation of assets for tax purposes and increases in specific tariffs. Broader language was used, indicating the search for productivity gains and internationalization of national companies. The policies that were eventually implemented, however, are the traditional instruments for sectorial protection.

The PDP also acted as a type of conceptual umbrella for the policy of choosing "national champions" described above, under the title of "promotion of the competetivity of large, international quality businesses."

The final transition to the traditional model of industrial protection policy came in the form of the *Plano Brasil Maior* (Greater Brazil Plan) launched in 2011. It focussed on 11 economic sectors (the ever present "clients") and heavily motivated the idea of protecting sectors affected by the international crisis and by the fierce competition by imported goods (see Mattos, 2013).

There was also intensification of the policy to impose a minimum amount of required inputs produced in the country into sectors regulated by the government. Since the opening of the petroleum sector to participation by private enterprises in 1997, there are rules governing the minimum amount of national equipment used in the exploration and commercialization of oil. Braga and Freitas cite a study by the *Organização Nacional de Indústria de Petróleo* – ONIP (National Petroleum Industry Organization) that contracted the Booz & Co. consultancy to measure the competitivity of national suppliers to the petroleum industry:

> *A Brazilian naval cauldron costs 48% more than one made in China and a national sea water lift costs 49% more than a North American equivalent. When taking quotes for jackets, deck modules and conveyors and conductors, it was noted that the national producer requested prices 80%, 20% and 200% greater than the foreign competitor! Also, while foreign quotes presented a dispersion of 8%, that of the national suppliers varied between 188% and 456% (Braga and Freitas, 2013, p. 3).*

Another powerful instrument for national industrial protection was the approval of Law 12.349 in 2010, which altered the public bidding law (Law 8.666, of 1993.) to permit the government to pay up to 25% more in auctions for the acquisition of "nationally manufactured products and services."

In all this trajectory of reconstructing industrial protection and subsidy, Almeida, (2013b) highlights many undesirable characteristics:

- High financial cost to be paid by the taxpayers;
- Protection of traditional sectors where there is little perspective of producing innovative technologies or gains in scale or productivity that could spread to the rest of the economy;
- Concentration of benefits to large companies;
- Contempt for the option to offer public goods that benefit the economy as a whole (infrastructure, human capital, diffusion of technology);
- Inexistence of goals to be achieved by the beneficiaries of the policy and of punishment for those who do not attain the targets stipulated in the incentive program.

One cannot, however, attribute the intensification of industrial protection exclusively to the three successive Worker's Party administrations during the period of 2003-2014. The National Congress, composed by members from different parties, has many times passed protectionist measures that were apparently not connected to the Executive Power. This was the case, for example, with the approval of Federal Senate Resolution 13, in 2012, which had as its objective to solve a tax dispute among state governments. Senators included a device in the resolution that penalized "merchandise or goods that have an imported content of over 40%," which was the insertion of a topic totally foreign to the essence of the issue under discussion, but of great interest to national industry.

Obviously, in intense situations of exchange-rate appreciation or currency-market imbalance, one cannot allow ample industrial segments to go broke. Conjectural imbalances can lead to intense periods of exchange overvaluation. After all, Brazil paid a high economic and social price to consolidate its industry and cannot allow it to be destroyed by temporary circumstances. However, temporary problems should be treated with topical measures that are revoked as soon as the problems dissipate. Protection and subsidies of an undetermined duration are not the answer for temporary situations.

Many times crises are ideal opportunities for pressure groups to cry for protection and increase their profits and privileges. In a long-term perspective, industrial protection policies seem to be a good example of institutions created to favor industrial groups commanded by part of the economic elite in the country.

REFERENCES

Acemoglu, D., Robinson, J.A., 2011. Why Nations Fail: The Origins of Power, Prosperity and Poverty. Princeton University Press.

Além, A.C., Cavalcanti, C.E., 2005. O BNDES e o Apoio à Internacionalização de Empresas Brasileiras: Algumas Reflexões. Revista do BNDES 12 (24), 43–76.

Almeida, M., 2013a. Estrutura do Gasto Público no Brasil: Evolução Histórica e Desafios. In: Rezende, F., Cunha, A. (Eds.), A Reforma Esquecida: Orçamento, Gestão Pública e Desenvolvimento. Fundação Getúlio Vargas.

Almeida, M., 2013b. Brasil Telecom/Oi mais um Campeão Nacional que Fugiu do Script. [Online] Available from, http://mansueto.wordpress.com/2013/10/02/brasil-telecomoi-mais-um-campeao-nacional-que-fugiu-do-script/ (accessed 01.07.14).

Bacha, E., Bolle, M.B. (Eds.), 2013. O Futuro da Indústria no Brasil: Desindustrialização em Debate. Civilização Brasileira.

Baumann, R., Kume, H., 2013. Novos Padrões de Comércio e Política Tarifária no Brasil. In: Bacha, E., Bolle, M.B. (Eds.), O Futuro da Indústria no Brasil: Desindustrialização em Debate. Civilização Brasileira.

Braga, J.A., Freitas, P.S., 2013. A Petrobras Conseguirá Explorar Plenamente o Pré-Sal? Brasil, Economia e Governo. [Online] 1st July. Available from, http://www.brasil-economia-governo.org.br/2013/07/01/a-petrobras-conseguira-explorar-plenamente-o-pre-sal/ (accessed 01.07.14).

Brazil TCU, 2009. Governança Regulatória no Âmbito das Agências Reguladoras de Infraestrutura. Relatório de Auditoria de Natureza Operacional, TC 012.693/2009-9.

Bresser-Pereira, L.C., 2011. Getúlio Vargas: o Estadista, a Nação e a democracia. In: Bastos, P., Fonseca, P. (Eds.), A Era Vargas: Desenvolvimento, Economia e Sociedade. Ed. Unesp, 93-120.

Campos, A.G., 2008. Sistemas de Justiça no Brasil: Problemas de Equidade e Efetividade. IPEA, Texto para Discussão n. 1328.

Canêdo-Pinheiro, M., 2013. Experiências Comparadas de Política Industrial no Pós-Guerra: Lições para o Brasil. In: Veloso, F., et al. (Eds.), Desenvolvimento Econômico: Uma Perspectiva Brasileira. Elsevier-Campus.

Carrasco, V., Mello, J.M.P., 2013. Um Conflito Distributivo Esquecido: Notas Sobre a Economia Política da Desindustrialização. In: Bacha, E., Bolle, M.B. (Eds.), O Futuro da Indústria no Brasil: Desindustrialização em Debate. Civilização Brasileira.

Castilho, M.R., Ruiz, A.U., Melo, M., 2009. Evolução da Proteção Efetiva no Brasil 2000-2005. ANPEC XXXVII National Annual Meeting, Available from, http://www.anpec.org.br/encontro2009/inscricao.on/arquivos/000-e604cef117775b4e016615ed3c92b7c6.pdf.

Chong, A., Gradstein, M., 2007. Inequality and institutions. Rev. Econ. Stat. 89 (3), 454–465.

Claessens, S., Feijen, E., Laeven, L., 2008. Political connections and preferential access to finance: the role of campaign contributions. J. Financ. Econ. 88, 554–580.

Engerman, S., Sokoloff, K., 2002. Factor Endowments, Inequality, and Paths of Development among New World Economies. NBER Working Paper 9259.

Glaeser, E., Scheinkman, J., Shleifer, A., 2003. The injustice of inequality. J. Monet. Econ. 50, 199–222.

Gradstein, M., 2007. Inequality, democracy and the protection of property rights. Econ. J. 117, Jan, 252–269.

Landim, R., Leopoldo, R., Tereza, I., 2013. BNDES Decide Abandonar a Política de Criação de Campeões Nacionais. O Estado de São Paulo [On Line]. Available from: http://economia.estadao.com.br/noticias/geral,bndes-decide-abandonar-a-politica-de-criacao-de-campeas-nacionais,151356e (accessed 03.02.14).

Lattman, P., Romero, S., 2013. Brazil, fortune and fate turn on Billionaire. N. Y. Times [On Line], 23 June. Available from: http://www.nytimes.com/2013/06/24/business/global/brazil-fortune-and-fate-turn-on-billionaire.html?pagewanted=all&_r=0 (accessed 21.01.14).

Lazzarini, S.G., 2011. Capitalismo de Laços: os Donos do Brasil e suas Conexões. Elsevier-Campus.

Leitão, M., 2013. Tubarões e peixinhos. O Globo (Newspaper) [On Line], 2 July 2013. Available from: http://oglobo.globo.com/economia/miriam/posts/2013/07/02/tubaroes-peixinhos-501972.asp (accessed 21.01.14).

Lisboa, M.B., Latif, Z.A., 2013. Democracy and Growth in Brazil. INSPER Working Papers, Available from, http://www.insper.edu.br/working-papers/working-papers-2013/democracy-and-growth-in-brazil/.

Lundberg, E.L., 2011. Bancos Oficiais e Crédito Direcionado: o que Diferencia o Mercado de Crédito Brasileiro? Banco Central do Brasil. Working Paper n. 258. Available from, http://www.bcb.gov.br/pec/wps/port/td258.pdf.

Mattos, C.C.A., 2013. O que é o Plano Brasil Maior? Brasil, Economia e Governo. [Online] 23rd October. Available from, http://www.brasil-economia-governo.org.br/2013/10/23/o-que-e-o-plano-brasil-maior/ (accessed 01.07.14).

Mendes, M.J., Miranda, R.B., Cosio, F.A.B., 2008. Transferências Intergovernamentais no Brasil: Diagnóstico e Proposta de Reforma. Núcleo de Estudos e Pesquisas da Consultoria Legislativa. Texto para Discussão n. 40. Available from, http://www12.senado.gov.br/publicacoes/estudos-legislativos/tipos-de-estudos/textos-para-discussao/td-40-transferencias-intergovernamentais-no-brasil-diagnostico-e-proposta-de-reforma.

Naritomi, J., Soares, R.R., Assunção, J.J., 2012. Institutional development and colonial heritage in Brazil. J. Econ. Hist. 72 (2), 393–422.

OECD, 2008. OECD Reviews of Regulatory Reform - Brazil: Strengthening Governance for Growth. OECD Publishing.

OECD, 2013. OECD Economic Surveys: Brazil 2013. OECD Publishing.

Olson, M., 1965. The Logic of Collective Action: Public Goods and the Theory of Groups. Harvard University Press.

Pagés, C. (Ed.), 2010. The Age of Productivity: Transforming Economies from the Bottom Up. Inter-American Development Bank.

Pinheiro, A.C., 2005. Magistrados, Judiciário e Economia no Brasil. In: Zylbersztajn, D., Sztajn, R. (Eds.), Direito e Economia: Análise Econômica do Direito e das Organizações. Elsevier-Campus.

Pinheiro, A.C., 2013. Os Empréstimos do BNDES para os "Campeões Nacionais". Valor Econômico, 12, 1st March.

Pinheiro, A.C., Almeida, G.B., 1995. O Que Mudou na Proteção à Indústria Brasileira nos Últimos 45 Anos? Pesquisa e Planejamento Econômico 25 (1), 199–222.

Renault, S.R.T., Bottini, P. (Eds.), 2005. Reforma do Judiciário. Saraiva.

Riter, R., 2013. TCU Aponta Falhas na Fiscalização de Concessões Valor Econômico. [On Line], 4 December. Available from, www.valoronline.com.br (accessed 05.02.14).

Rodrigues, L., 2013. Postalis tem R$ 127 milhões em ações das "X" O Globo. [On Line], 6 July. Available from, http://oglobo.globo.com/economia/postalis-tem-127-milhoes-em-acoes-das-x-8939844 (accessed 21.01.14).

Rosenstein-Rodan, P.N., 1943. Problems of industrialization of Eastern and South-Eastern Europe. Econ. J. 53 (210/211), 202–211.

Schymura, L., Canêdo-Pinheiro, M., 2013. Política Industrial Brasileira: Motivações e Diretrizes. In: Bacha, E., Bolle, M.B. (Eds.), O Futuro da Indústria no Brasil: Desindustrialização em Debate. Civilização Brasileira.

Silva, R.S., 2007. O desenho institucional do Estado sob uma perspectiva temporal: o caso da política regulatória dos fundos de pensão. Universidade de Brasília. Instituto de Ciência Política.

Sonin, K., 2003. Why the rich may favor poor protection of property rights. J. Comp. Econ. 31, 715–731.

The World bank, 2006. Equity and Development. World Development Report 2006.

VEJA, (2012). Brasil: dezenove novos milionários a cada dia. Veja 45, 3 Jan 2012, 78-89. Veja - weekly magazine.

Zanella, F.C., et al., 2003. Monarchy, monopoly and mercantilism: Brazil vs. United States in the 1800s. Publ. Choice 116, 381–398.

Chapter 4

Redistribution to the Poor

Chapter Outline

4.1 INTRODUCTION

Hired housekeepers are common in Brazil. Young girls from poor families originally from rural areas, generally with little education, are employed by families to care for their cleaning, cooking, laundry, and, at times, children. Historically, this work has always been associated with people from the lower classes. In many cases, they work long days, live at their place of employment, have few days off, and are neither formally registered with Social Security nor have other legal worker rights. (According to ILO 2013 there are more than 7 million domestic workers in Brazil.)

On April 2, 2013, the National Congress passed what is called the Domestic Workers Constitutional Amendment, which extended the same rights to domestic workers (not only maids, but gardeners, caretakers, and care providers for the elderly, sick, and many others also) as those of formally contracted employees.

Evaluated from the individual rights point of view, this amendment meets requirements fundamental to democratic societies. However, Brazilian labor legislation produces many economic distortions. For many years, specialists have debated the problems caused by current Brazilian labor legislation, which restricts the creation of jobs and stimulates informality and high labor turnover, as will be considered in Chapter 5, Section 5.7. Instead of seeking to modernize labor rules for all workers (domestic workers included), the political system opted to expand inefficient rules, seeking to benefit a particular segment composed of low-income workers.

Since democratization, the Brazilian Executive and Legislative Branches have not been interested in advancing the reformulation of labor laws, seeking to solve problems in the job market. This reform would seek to balance fundamental rights and contract flexibility so as to benefit formal and informal workers as well as economic productivity.

However, Congress quickly, and almost unanimously, approved a constitutional amendment that presents *visible* benefits (and *hidden* costs to be paid by all of society) to a mass of low-income voters (there were only two votes against and two abstentions in the Chamber of Deputies and unanimity in the Senate).

This episode reflects a reality opposite to that analyzed in Chapter 3, where it was argued that the rich are able to design institutions and policies in their favor. The approval of this amendment, however, shows how, in a democratic system, the poor also benefit from public policies.

This is an example of the type of incentive politicians have to approve legislation to gain popularity among the large contingents of poor voters. In a democracy, politicians are only able to maintain their careers if they have votes. In an unequal society there are typically a large number of poor voters. There is nothing more natural than the political class attending the demands of the poor in exchange for their numerous votes. It was for no other reason that the favorite slogan in the military government (that did not depend on a vote to maintain leadership) "make the product grow before redistributing it," was quickly exchanged for another created by the José Sarney administration (1985-1990), the first President in the current democracy: "everything for social justice."

However, there are negative collateral effects from these redistributive policies on economic growth. As with the ability of the rich to manipulate rules in their favor and consolidate privileges, redistribution in favor of the poor also de-stimulates economic growth, at least in the short and mid terms.

It is possible that redistribution in favor of the poor creates positive growth effects. Such effects, however, tend to manifest themselves in the long term and will be considered in Chapter 6, where it will be shown that under certain conditions such redistribution may, but not necessarily, lead to greater growth potential.

This chapter will consider the redistributive bias in favor of the poor that exists in unequal societies and its adverse impact on short- and mid-term growth.

4.2   WHAT DOES ECONOMIC THEORY HAVE TO SAY?

Ample literature produced in the 1990s[1] proposes models in which redistributionist policies can hinder growth. In an unequal society, there is typically a large quantity of poor and a small nucleus of very rich. This means that a great majority of voters are poor. The politicians, whose careers depend on votes, are induced to seek these votes by offering public policies that propose income

---

1. The main references used in this book are Alesina and Rodrik 1994 and Persson and Tabellini 1994. Bénabou 1996 analyzes 23 studies regarding the relationship between inequality and growth, most of which propose, by means of different theoretical explanations, a causal relationship where inequality reduces growth. Also see Perotti 1992 and Meltzer and Richards 1981.

transfer in favor of the poor. To finance such policies, they tax the rich, which reduces that group's incentive to invest and accumulate capital.

In these theories, simply put, it is assumed that individuals differ in their productive capabilities. In a theoretical model proposed by Alesina and Rodrik, for example, the upper and middle classes possess "accumulated factors," such as capital, qualified labor, and technology (Alesina and Rodrik, 1994). It is said that these factors are "accumulable," which means it is possible to accumulate increasing quantities of capital (machines and equipment), knowledge, ability, and technology, making these instruments available, in increasing quantity, for the production of more and better goods and services.

Meanwhile, the Alesina and Rodrik theoretical model supposes that the poor individual is only gifted with non-qualified labor, which, even though useful in the production process, cannot be accumulated over time. It is not possible to invest in the accumulation of non-qualified labor. Each worker can only offer a limited quantity of non-qualified labor, equivalent to the hours worked.

The rich pay taxes, which are used both to finance transfers to the poor as well as public services, such as infrastructure, provision for the public good and property rights. These services are necessary complements to economic growth.

Growth results from the accumulation of physical capital, human capital, and the increase in productivity, as described in Chapter 1, Section 1.2. Taxation reduces the net returns of accumulative production factors, such as capital and qualified labor. After paying taxes, the rich will have fewer resources to invest in the production of more capital, knowledge, and technology. Moreover, they will have less incentive to invest, because the profit obtained from these activities will be partially taken by the government through taxes. The rate of accumulation for those factors is reduced, therefore affecting growth.

In the models described here, "taxation" is the synthetic manner to refer to cost of government intervention in order to redistribute to the poor. In practice, instead of expanding the tax burden, the government could opt to increase the public deficit. In this case, as seen in Chapter 1, de-stimulus to growth comes from the reduction of aggregate savings in the economy, which reduces the volume of resources available for investments. There will also be an increase in interest rates, which means that the set of investment opportunities with returns above financing costs will be smaller, leading to less investment and less growth.

Another possible way to finance expenditures in favor of the poor is to reduce expenses with other public policies. As discussed in Chapter 1, if cuts in infrastructure investment are made to finance current expenditures in favor of the poor, economic growth will be constrained, since the scarcity of infrastructure will cause an increase in production costs and a reduction in economic productivity.

Theoretical models simplify reality by considering that all redistributive policy is performed by means of monetary transfers to the most poor. Actually, there are other ways, such as raising minimum wage or imposing labor laws. By raising labor costs, these policies reduce the profitability of companies and, as such, reduce the incentive to invest.

Knowing that higher taxes, public deficit, deficient infrastructure, and restrictive regulation reduce economic growth, why does the government opt for these policies? This is due to the fact that budget and regulation decisions are made in the political arena. In a democracy, the government is not an autonomous entity that can make fiscal decisions as it sees fit. The government is run by politicians who seek re-election and political survival. Therefore, they are sensitive to voter preference and tend to follow the choices voiced by the portion of the electorate large enough to guarantee re-election. Fiscal policy and economic regulation are determined by this process.

The poor, who constitute the largest voting bloc in unequal societies, tend to prefer redistribution to growth. Since they receive a small portion of total economic income, growth in production does not benefit them as much as the redistribution of income. If redistribution is intense, income for the poor increases significantly, even if total growth is low. This is exactly what has happened in Brazil in the last years. As seen in Chapter 2, Figure 2.5, in spite of the country having grown little since 2001, income for the poor grew a great deal. This was possible due to redistribution.

Consequently, the political process in an unequal democratic society will tend to choose a greater level of taxation and regulation than what is necessary to finance traditional public goods that would stimulate investment and growth (transportation infrastructure, R&D, protection of property rights, public security, and others). Besides providing such services, it is demanded that the government practice a high level of redistributive policy (cash transfers and free goods and services to the poor), with negative effects on the accumulation of physical capital.

The main conclusion of theoretical work in this area is that more equal societies will prefer less redistributive policies and, consequently, grow more rapidly. Countries where inequality is low count on a large middle class that has assets, such as land and property, and, as such, has little interest in redistributive policies, which would imply taxation of such assets.[2]

As with all theoretical models, the studies cited previously imply simplifications, such as dividing society into rich and poor. Reality is not dual for there are many distinct social groups, each with their own way of being heard by politicians. As will be argued in greater detail in Chapter 5, it is not just the poor, due to being numerous, that benefit from politicians seeking votes. Groups that are able to organize themselves into unions or

---

2. Barro 1999 argues that if the rich were to react to the redistribution demands of the poor, impeding the government to execute such policies, a low-growth scenario would occur just the same. In this case, resources diverted from productive activities and redirected toward lobbying would cause low growth.

associations, as well as those with access to the decision-making process, are also able to obtain public policies in their favor.

This, however, does not void the fact that, due to their great number, the poor are one of politicians' favorite groups. Therefore, redistribution in their favor will occur in a democracy where inequality and poverty are high. The more numerous the poor, the more they attract attention by politicians.

The next section will seek to present evidence that expenditures directed toward the poor have a significant financial impact and are responsible for a relevant part of the increase in public expenditure (shown in Chapter 1, Figures 1.4, 1.5 and 1.6).

4.3   THE FISCAL IMPACT OF INCOME TRANSFER TO THE POOR

According to the literature on Brazilian inequality summarized in Chapter 2, Section 2.2, the main public policy instruments to help in the reduction of poverty were: the *Bolsa Família* program, the BPC program, and increases of Social Security benefits that pay one minimum wage.

Table 4.1 shows the impact of spending increases with these programs on the evolution of primary central government expenditure. (Figure 1.5, in Chapter 1, presents the evolution of primary central government expense between 1997 and 2012.)

What is seen in Table 4.1 is that expenditure with these programs jumped from 2.27% to 3.93% of GDP between 2002 and 2012. In real terms, there was an impressive increase of 179% and, in *per capita* terms, the expense grew 151%. In the same period, the primary Federal Government expenditure "only" doubled (96% growth). In other words, the main monetary transfer programs for the poor, which in 2002 represented 14% of the primary expense, grew to 21% in 2012.

To this nucleus of programs focused on the poor, we can add the expenses of wage bonus (*Abono Salarial*) and unemployment insurance. National Treasury statistics present figures for these two programs together, making it impossible to discriminate the wage bonus (with a higher tie to minimum wage and more focused on the base of the pyramid) from unemployment insurance (which also goes to segments of the middle class). Adding the expense of these two programs to the nucleus of expenses in favor of the poor, one notices that this expanded group of programs grew 183% above inflation, representing 26% of total primary expense in 2012 in contrast to 17.5% in 2002.

One can also see the great importance of adjustments above inflation to the minimum wage as a cause for this tendency of increasing expenditure. Figure 1.16 in Chapter 1 shows that the real growth of the minimum wage was responsible for no less than 51% of the increase in primary central government expense. This impact is included in Table 4.1. With the exception of the *Bolsa Família* program and part of the unemployment insurance, all

TABLE 4.1 Public Expenditure with Monetary Transfer Programs for the Poor: 2002 vs. 2012

	% of GDP		Real Vatiation 2002-2012 (%)	
	2002	*2012*	*Total*	*Per Capita*
Bolsa Família Program (A) [1]	0.11	0.48	606	535
Benefit to low income elderly and physically challenged (LOAS) [2]	0.23	0.66	382	334
Urban social security benefits = 1 SM[3]	0.80	1.26	165	138
Rural social security benefits = 1 SM[3]	1.12	1.53	130	107
Subtotal of expenses with redistributive impact (A)	**2.27**	**3.93**	179	151
Wage bonus and Unemployment Insurance (B)	**0.49**	**0.88**	206	175
Total of expenses with redistributive impact tied to SM (C) = (A) + (B)	**2.75**	**4.81**	183	155
Total primary expense (D)	**15.72**	**18.28**	**96**	**77**
(A) / (D)	14.4%	21.5%		
(C) / (D)	17.5%	26.3%		

Sources: National Treasury Secretariat (Primary result of the Central Government) and the Ministry of Social Development. (1) 2002 values correspond to the sum of assistance programs incorporated into the Bolsa Família Program in 2004. (2) 2002 values provided by the Ministry of Social Development (http://www.mds.gov.br/relcrys/bpc/indice.htm). (3) Calculated by applying the percent participation of urban and rural benefits in total 2011 cost to the total 2012 cost. Deflator: IPCA. Prepared by author.

other programs listed in Table 4.1 have their benefits re-adjusted over time based on the minimum wage.

This high level of expenditures in transfers to the poor caused Lindert and co-authors, from the World Bank, to consider Brazil as one of the "big spenders" in Latin American social policies, in company with Argentina, Chile, and Colombia, and in contrast to other countries in the region (Lindert et al., 2006).

The weight of these policies on the rate of public expense growth is therefore undeniable. According to what is argued in Chapter 1, this expansion in public expense unleashes a movement to increase the tax burden, reduce public savings, and increase interest rates. Furthermore, one cannot forget the adverse effects on expected company profits and the consequent decision to invest (Stylized Fact 6), as well as the decision by companies to remain small and informal, with a negative effect on average economic productivity (Chapter 1, Stylized Fact 9). The result is low growth with dissipative redistribution.

Summarizing, expenditures with transfers to the poor, which help in the reduction of inequality, have a strong collateral effect of fiscal pressure, regulatory distortions, high interest rates and low productivity that hinder economic growth (see estimates of this effect in Chapter 2).

4.4 EXPANSION OF PUBLIC EDUCATION FOR THE POOR AND ITS FISCAL IMPACT

Public policies directed toward the poor are not limited to the income transfer mechanisms already seen. After democratization, the public education system was greatly expanded to include the poor, which in turn had a significant impact on federal, state, and municipal expenses.

The political decision to expand public education was explicitly written into the Constitution, where Article 212 defined minimum percentages of tax revenue to be spent on it.

An important question is to what extent expense on public education was, in fact, directed toward the poor. It is not beyond consideration that the public sector set up an educational system directed toward the elite, and that it excludes the needy. In fact, as will be argued in Chapter 5, Section 5.5, this seems to be the case in Brazilian public universities. What can be said regarding basic education (primary through secondary), however, is that there is sufficient evidence to prove that the poor are, indeed, the main beneficiaries in the expansion of public education after democratization.

Keeping in mind that the primary and secondary education in public schools was, and, on average, continues to be inferior to that of private education, it should be expected that higher-income families prefer private education. In addition to this, not sending children to school is connected with phenomenon such as child labor and the inability to perceive the importance of education in terms of future income (Banerjee and Duflo, 2011). Both characteristics are associated with low-income families. As such, the exclusion of children from the school system, something remarkable throughout Brazil's history before democratization in 1985, was concentrated among the poor.

In 1980, 20% of children between the ages of 7 and 14 were not in school (Oliveira, 2007, based on INEP data). Twenty-nine years later, in 2009, primary education was practically universal, with only 2% of those childhood ages not in school (Veloso, 2011). There was a significant effort in creating approximately 11 million openings in primary education, most of them in public schools (Oliveira, 2007, based on INEP data). Similarly, high school was expanded after the effort to enroll children in elementary school, and increased the enrollment of young people between the ages of 15 and 17 from 64% in 1995 to 85% in

2009 (Veloso, 2011). Between 1995 and 2011, almost 3 million openings were created in public high schools (*Sinopse Estatística da Educação Básica* 1995 and 2011, Statistical Synopsis of Basic Education, 1995 and 2011. Available at http://www.inep.gov.br).

This great effort for educational inclusion was responsible for raising the average education for people over 15 from 2.57 to 7.55 years between 1980 and 2010, as shown in Figure 1.20 in Chapter 1 (Stylized Fact 10). Notwithstanding the low quality of Brazilian public education, this expansion in years of study among the working population is considered by some as a relevant factor in the reduction of wage inequality in the job market, as seen in Chapter 2.

From the point of view of public resource allocation, the expansion of public education represents a substantial increase in expenditures in benefit of the less favored members of society. Table 4.2 shows that public expense with basic education (which includes elementary through secondary education) went from 3.3% to 4.4% of GDP between 2001 and 2011. This represents an expense increase, above inflation, of 125%. In *per capita* terms, the real increase was 102%. This expense represents the sum of federal, state, and municipal expenditures. As thus, it would not be appropriate to compare it with primary federal expense, as done in Table 4.1. Alternately, it is compared with the tax burden imposed by all three levels of government. It can be seen that in 2011, expenditures with basic education consumed no less than 13% of taxes collected in the country, compared with 10% in 2001.

Therefore, expenses with the expansion of basic education, fundamentally offered to the lower income segments of society, represent an important component in the expansion of public expenditure. If on one hand the increase in the supply of education contributes to enhance human capital and reduce poverty and inequality, on the other the increase of expenses feeds the low growth with dissipative redistribution model.

TABLE 4.2 Public Expense for Basic Education: 2001 vs. 2011 (% of GDP)

	% of GDP		Real Variation 2001-2011(%)	
	2001	*2011*	*Total*	*Per Capita*
Basic Education (preschool to high school) (A)	3.30	4.39	125	102
Tax Burden (B)	31.87	33.51	78	60
(A)/(B)	10.4%	13.1%		

Sources: INEP-MEC and Receita Federal do Brasil (Brazil Federal Revenue). Deflator: IPCA. Prepared by author.

4.5 EXPANSION OF PUBLIC HEALTH TO THE POOR AND ITS FISCAL IMPACT

As in the case of education, there was a large expansion in government provided healthcare after democratization. Even though the services offered are far from ideal, one cannot ignore that a relevant part of the increase in expenses benefitted the lower strata of society.

The new Constitution defines health as a right of all citizens and a duty of the state (Federal Constitution, Article 196). The obligation to provide free public health services to the whole population was therefore established. All types of healthcare were to be provided: from preventive to low-, medium-, or high-level complexity procedures. The freedom of the private sector to operate in the healthcare area was also maintained.

The constitutionally defined right of healthcare for all, with the financial responsibility placed on the state, created an obvious fiscal and management problem. From one day to the next, the public sector, which attended only the part of the population that was formally employed, was pressed to attend all. The fiscal and management challenges were quite large, especially in an area such as healthcare, where technological innovation has made medical treatment more sophisticated and expensive.

Since the approval of the 1988 Constitution, pressure for more funding in the area of healthcare has been constant. To solve this problem, Constitutional Amendment 29 was approved in 2000, and obliged the union to annually increase its healthcare expenditure at the rate of GDP growth, while states and municipalities were obliged to apply a minimum of 12% (states) and 15% (municipalities) of their tax revenues to the sector. Such constitutional rule caused an obvious increase in expenses, since GDP and public revenue grow above inflation.

Regardless of the lack of funds during the first years after the approval of the Constitution, there was a significant increase in access by the population to basic health services, which benefitted the poor who were unable to pay for private services or who had insufficient levels of education and information to adopt basic health practices. According to André César Médici, one of the greatest specialists in health economics in Brazil:

> *Between 1994 and 2002, coverage by the Community Agents Health Programs [Programa de Agentes Comunitários de Saúde – PACS] and the Family Health Program [Programa de Saúde da Família – PSF] increased at annual rates of 25% and 73%, respectively. These programs increased their coverage from 10% to 53% and almost nothing for 34% of the population, respectively. During this period, the infant mortality rate fell from 34 to 19 per thousand live births. (…) The positive effect the PSF has had is undeniable among the poor population (…). The PSF has had an impact on the coverage of prenatal care, which increased from 9.8 to 18.2 million between 2003 and 2008; the coverage of family planning care, which increased from 30.2 to 34.5 million during the same period, and the reduction in*

maternal deaths with those covered by the program which, although high, reduced from 52.1 to 50.3 deaths per 100 live births between 2002 and 2007.

(...) voluminous investments were made, especially in basic care, and waiting periods became shorter, at least for basic care. Programs such as PACS and PSF (...) began attending a population that up to that time only had access to hospital beds in desperate cases, and then, many times too late (Médici, 2011, p. 41 e 48).

To measure access by the most poor to healthcare by means of the expansion of basic care is, however, a conservative yardstick. This is due, as this author recognizes, to the fact that the increased life expectancy of the poor has also increased the incidence of chronic diseases in this group and their demand for hospital care and medications (Médici, 2011, p. 65).

Furthermore, as Andrade and Noronha explain, the perception of a low-quality public health service causes a relevant part of the services performed to benefit the most poor simply because those who are able to pay for private service prefer it instead (Andrade and Noronha, 2011). This is the same condition as in the case of basic education. As will be seen in Chapter 5, those who have health insurance only resort to the public health system in cases where treatment reaches such high costs that their private health insurance will not completely cover them.

Table 4.3 shows that the more family income increases, the greater the percentage of people who have private health insurance.

As such, we can assume that a significant share of public health expenditure is directed toward caring for the poor (even though a part of the expense could be lost due to inefficiency and that the service rendered is not the most adequate). Table 4.4 shows that these expenses are not only high, but have grown over the years, with the total expense to all three levels of government going

TABLE 4.3 Percentage of People with Private Health Insurance According to Monthly *per capita* Family Income in Brazil (2008)

Up to 1/4 minimum wage	2.3
Between 1/4 and 1/2 minimum wage	6.4
Between 1/2 and 1 minimum wage	16.1
Between 1 and 2 minimum wages	33.7
Between 2 and 3 minimum wages	54.8
Between 3 and 5 minimum wages	68.8
More than 5 minimum wages	82.5

Source: Menicucci (2013). Primary source: PNAD 2008. Prepared by author.

TABLE 4.4 Expenses with Public Health Services in Brazil: 2002-2012

Year	% of GDP				Real Value (2002 = 100)	
	Federal	State	Municiple	Total	Per Capita	Total
2002	1.7	0.7	0.8	3.2	100	100
2003	1.6	0.8	0.8	3.2	107	109
2004	1.7	0.9	0.8	3.4	128	131
2005	1.7	0.9	0.9	3.6	132	139
2006	1.7	1.0	1.0	3.7	139	149
2007	1.7	1.0	1.0	3.6	145	153
2008	1.6	1.0	1.1	3.7	145	158
2009	1.8	1.0	1.1	3.9	147	161
2010	1.6	1.0	1.0	4.2	151	190
2011	1.7	1.0	1.1	3.8	164	180
2012	1.8	1.0	1.1	4.0	172	192

Source: Vieira (2013). Primary source: SIOPS e IBGE. Note: 2011 and 2012 data are yet incomplete.

from 3.2% to 4% of GDP between 2002 and 2011. In real terms, the total expense almost doubled in 10 years, and in terms of cost per inhabitant, there was a growth of 72%.

Finally, Table 4.5 shows that federal expense for healthcare represents 10% of primary expense. It is a huge amount of money for a single expense category. Health, as in education, has been an important cause of the expansion of public expense (Stylized Fact 1).

Certainly, we cannot attribute all benefits from this level of spending to the most poor. From the available data, it is not possible to ascertain what part of spending with hospital or ambulatory care corresponds to the middle- and high-income population that resorts to the public health system in search of having more expensive procedures performed that are not covered by their health insurance. In fact, it will be shown in Chapter 5 that leeway to increase spending in favor of middle- and high-income individuals is significant.

One cannot deny, however, that part of the expansion in public healthcare was directed toward those most in need. More important yet is the fact that, independently of whether or not healthcare services came to this group, the political demand for more attention to public health has been heard and has given support to those politicians who, in parliament, press for more spending in this area.

TABLE 4.5 Federal Expense with Healthcare: 2002 vs. 2011 (% of GDP)

	2002	2011	% primary expense in 2011
Basic care and prevention[1] (A)	0.35	0.43	2.5
Hospital and ambulatory assistance (B)	0.96	0.88	5.0
Other (C)	0.41	0.43	2.5
Total (D) = (A) + (B) + (C)	1.72	1.74	10.0
Total primary expense (E)	**15.72**	**17.48**	
(D)/(E)	10.9%	10.0%	

Source: SIAFI – Sistema Siga Brasil (Siga Brazil System). (1) Includes: basic health care, basic rural and urban sanitation care, epidemiological surveillance, and sanitary surveillance. Prepared by author.

It is important to note that, even though health care has been greatly expanded, specialists argue that financial resources are small in comparison to the goal of providing universal, complete, and free care (see, for example, Menicucci, 2013). And, the demand by organized groups (hospitals financed by public funds, physician and nurse unions, etc.) for resources for their sector is intense. In 2012 an attempt was made to earmark 10% of gross federal revenue to healthcare. This would have resulted in an expenditure increase of R$46 billion (about US$20 billion) in 1 year alone (a 60% increase in relation to federal expenses in 2012).

Such a proposal was not approved, but the movement in favor of more funds for the healthcare sector gained momentum within the National Congress and several bills came to propose less expensive alternatives, but that would represent expense increases of between R$6 billion and R$19 billion per year (US$2.6 billion to US$8.3 billion). (Piola (2013)) The Executive Branch, at first against any expenditure increase, curved to political pressure and agreed to increase the earmarking of its funds to healthcare, with percentages still being negotiated at the time of writing.

4.6 CONCLUSIONS

Democratization has led to a natural expansion in programs that favor the poor. They stimulate the adoption of legal rules focused on this population. In a political environment where large contingents of poor have the right to vote, politicians have become sensitive to their demands.

There is evidence that income transfer, education, and healthcare policies represent a great increase in public expense. It seems evident, in the face of the statistics shown, that the policies favoring the poor (or that do not target the poor but are used as electoral tools by politicians with pro-poor labels), have had a fundamental role in the expansion of current public expense (Stylized Fact 1). They are, therefore, a central element in the low growth with dissipative redistribution model.

Regulatory policies such as raising the minimum wage above inflation (Stylized Fact 6) and labor market regulation (such as the constitutional amendment for domestic workers presented in the introduction) help feed the cited model as well.

Certainly, improvements in education, healthcare, and the stability and guarantee of a minimum wage for laborers contribute to increase their productivity. This could counterbalance the negative effects on growth. Such effects, however, tend to manifest themselves over the long term, and will be covered in Chapter 6.

REFERENCES

Alesina, A., Rodrik, D., 1994. Distributive politics and economic growth. Q. J. Econ. 109 (2), 465–490.

Andrade, M.V., Noronha, K., 2011. Uma Nota sobre o Princípio da Integralidade do SUS. In: Bacha, E.L., Schwartzman, S. (Eds.), Brasil: A Nova Agenda Social. Gen/LTC.

Banerjee, A., Duflo, E., 2011. Poor Economics. Penguin Books, New York.

Barro, R.J., 1999. Inequality, Growth, and Investment, NBER Working Paper 7038.

Bénabou, R., 1996. Inequality and growth. NBER Macroecon. Annu. 11, 11–74.

Lindert, K., Skoufias, E., Shapiro, J., 2006. Redistributing Income to the Poor and the Rich: Public Transfers in Latin American and the Caribbean. World Bank, Social Protection. SP Discussion Paper No 0605.

Médici, A., 2011. Propostas para Melhorar a Cobertura, a Eficiência e a Qualidade no Setor Saúde. In: Bacha, E.L., Schwartzman, S. (Eds.), Brasil: A Nova Agenda Social. Gen/LTC.

Meltzer, A.H., Richard, S.F., 1981. A rational theory of the size of government. J. Polit. Econ. 89 (5), 914–927.

Menicucci, T.M.G., 2013. A Relação Público-Privado e o Contexto Federativo do SUS: Uma Análise Institucional. ECLAC, Workshop: Aspectos Institucionais do Sistema Único de Saúde Brasileiro. ECLAC, Brasília, 10th October 2013.

Oliveira, R.P., 2007. Da Universalização do Ensino Fundamental ao Desafio da Qualidade: Uma Análise Histórica. Educ. Soc., Campinas 28 (100 - Especia), 661–690.

Perotti, R., 1992. Income distribution, politics, and growth. Am. Econ. Rev. 82 (2), 311–316.

Persson, T., Tabellini, G., 1994. Is inequality harmful for growth? Am. Econ. Rev. 84 (3), 600–621.

Piola, S.F., 2013. Tendências e Perspectivas do Financiamento da Saúde no Brasil. Power Point presentation at the Workshop: Aspectos Institucionais do Sistema Único de Saúde Brasileiro, ECLAC, Brasília, 10th October 2013.

Veloso, F., 2011. A Evolução Recente e Propostas para a Melhoria da Educação. In: Bacha, E.L., Schwartzman, S. (Eds.), Brasil: A Nova Agenda Social. Gen/LTC.

Chapter 5

The Middle Class Joins the Game

Chapter Contents

5.1 INTRODUCTION

In August 2012, a federal law known as the "Youth Statute" (Law 12.852, of 2013) was passed. It provided for a list of rights for young adults between the ages of 18 and 29, among which is the requirement to "provide access for youth to cultural events by means of reduced prices" (Article 22, Clause II, of Law 12.852, of 2013), the so-called "half-fare." This benefit was approved without the issue being discussed of who would pay more so young adults could pay less. What is more, it was not made exactly clear why those between 18 and 29, independent of income level, should be the beneficiaries of such a subsidy.

It is interesting that one of the explicit objectives of the Youth Statute is to promote the liberty and autonomy of young people (Article 2, Clause I, of Law 12.852, of 2013). However, another bill currently in Congress (the very same Congress that approved the statute) proposes increasing dependency of these youth on their parents. This bill (PLS 148, of 2008) already approved in the Senate and being considered by the Chamber of Deputies at the time of writing, proposes that a child continue to be a tax deduction on their parent's income tax until they are 28. If said "youth" is a student, the age limit can be extended to 32. A person who is almost middle age will still be considered a child so their parents can benefit from them as an income-tax deduction! Why? Who's going to pay for this? What are the costs and benefits for this rule? Is it really good to encourage someone to remain a student until they are 32? How can contradictory

167

policies be approved by the same group of lawmakers? Shouldn't those who are in favor of one bill be against the other? Practically nothing has been debated on the issue. Just approve the privilege…and that's that.

How do these facts fit the arguments presented in the previous chapters? After all, what has been said until now is that, in the democratic era beginning in 1985, the poor and rich have had great political ability to extract income from the rest of society by using their political capital in government. Laws such as those described in the two previous paragraphs, however, help neither the rich nor the poor. It makes little difference to the rich if they pay half price for a cultural event or if they have an extra discount on their income tax, or not. Neither does this type of benefit interest the poor who, even with the discount, don't have the money to go to the movies or theater. They probably don't even pay income tax.

How do these laws benefiting middle-income groups find fertile soil to grow?

This chapter shows how intermediate income groups participate in the redistribution game, receiving government advantages and subsidies that are generally funded by taxpayers or the general public. Participation by middle-income groups increases the intensity of the distributive conflict within society and its adverse effects on economic growth.

First, when referring to "intermediate segments of income distribution" it is necessary to understand that it is not as simple as dividing society into clearly defined classes of "poor," "middle" and "rich." As seen in Chapter 2, Section 2.7, the separation of society into income groups can generate quite unequal classifications. In that section, two estimates were cited based on the concept of "poverty and vulnerability" that result in distinct groups of classes. One of them, based on the Commission to Define Middle Class in Brazil (*Comissão para Definição da Classe Média no Brasil*) says that the poor and vulnerable make up 34% of the population, middle class, 48% and upper class, 18% (Brazil Presidency of the Republic, 2012). On the other hand, the estimate presented by Ferreira and co-authors in a study that evaluates the expansion of the middle class in Latin America, believes the poor and vulnerable are responsible for 65% of the population, while the middle class is 30%, and the rich, or upper class, only 5% (Ferreira et al., 2013).

If we use the definition provided by the Commission, the group of "rich" would include a large contingent of independent professionals, those employed in company middle management, mid-level civil servants and others. If we use the definition proposed by Ferreira and co-authors, the "rich" would be a much more select group, containing the richest families in the country, high-level civil servants, well-known independent professionals and those in the upper levels of company hierarchy. Which of the two groups represents the "rich" identified in Chapter 3, able to mold institutions in their favor by political influence and economic power? Similarly, who would be the "poor and vulnerable," whose vote politicians seek by offering redistributive policies: the 34% of the population identified by the Commission, or the 65% shown by Ferreira and co-authors?

In Chapters 3 and 4, a distinction was made between polices directed toward the poor and rich, with the objective of showing, in a didactic way, that there are fundamental differences in the redistribution mechanisms for each group. Intense redistribution to the poor is new in the country's history, only beginning with the re-establishment of democracy in 1985. Redistribution to the rich is not new, going back to the first years of colonization and has occurred independently of the current type of government. Be it monarchical, authoritarian or democratic, strong economic groups and high-income individuals have had privileged access to power and been able to influence institutions in their favor.

These two types of redistribution can co-exist, in fact, have co-existed since 1985. As Lee Alston and co-authors propose, "the new Brazilian constitution has the crucial consequence of directing policies in favor of inclusion, openness and representation. This bias, however, does not hinder the rich from having a disproportional influence over these policies"(Alston et al., 2012, p. 15).

The two types of redistribution (for the rich and for the poor) occur in different political arenas. Redistribution to the poor, in most cases, occurs in a transparent form, by means of public policies that are included in the budget. The public can easily verify, for example, how much is spent on the *Bolsa Família* program or what the impact minimum wage has on Social Security. Programs for the poor are openly debated during electoral campaigns since politicians are interested in promoting what is being done in favor of low-income groups.

Distribution to the rich, however, is done in the shadows, in a disguised way. Decisions are made in closed meetings or in public bank accounting, protected by banking privacy laws. Politicians have no interest in publicizing what is being done in favor of the rich. These policies cover themes that are difficult for the electorate to understand (majority stake in companies, participation in investment consortiums, complex financial instruments, pricing rules for public services operated by private companies). Many times the privileges are justified based on ideology or economic theory (protecting national industry against foreign competition in order to preserve jobs, protecting national assets against foreign exploitation) in which policy in favor of the poor or the whole population is the implicit idea.

This chapter intends to show that there is political room for redistribution in favor of middle-income groups as well. Such redistribution mixes features of the two extremes. It is therefore more difficult to characterize what is middle or upper income. It is not simple to identify a single type of mechanism to implement redistributive policies in favor of heterogeneous middle-income groups.

For example, there are public policies that are clearly visible to the public, shown in the public budget and debated in the Congress, but that have middle-income families as their main beneficiaries. This is the case of retirements and pensions paid by social security, as shown in Chapter 2. On the other side, there are benefits granted to middle-income groups that are not transparent, whose harmful effects on economic growth are not easy to unveil; such are income tax exemptions, complex formulas for civil servant salaries or the implicit subsidy given to high-income families through tuition-free university.

During the military government, many privilege mechanisms for the middle class were developed. They came as result of the low transparency and *accountability* typical of an undemocratic regime. We can take, for example, civil servants in high positions raising their own salaries or those of employees working in their department and ministries. Moreover, the intention of the military regime to placate the resistance and inconformity of urban laborers resulted in policies to please middle-income groups, such as the creation of benefits for the workforce employed in the formal sector: labor legislation, additional payments funded by taxpayers. Sometimes, the middle class profited as an unintended consequence of poor macroeconomic management, as was the case of the depreciation of family real estate debt caused by high inflation, which represented a huge subsidy in the acquisition of housing. Once more the bill was paid by taxpayers and no legislation was approved in order to tax this unexpected gain.

After democratization the middle class expanded its opportunities to obtain privileges. It was not only able to preserve benefits inherited from the previous period, but able to acquire others, by means of political organization. This is what is shown in the next sections.

5.2   WHAT DOES ECONOMIC THEORY HAVE TO SAY?

In Chapter 4, theoretical propositions were presented according to which the co-existence between democracy and a great mass of poor voters led politicians to seek support from this group by means of redistributive policies. This argument, though valid, may be considered simplistic or incomplete. Actually, politicians do not seek votes only from the poor, but any that are easy to get. In a cost-benefit analysis, politicians seek to offer policies that maximize their votes and minimize the cost and effort necessary to obtain them.

As such, some middle-income groups come to be an interesting target because they provide a large number of votes in easy-to-reach niches, which reduces the time and cost necessary to obtain them.

Loukas Karabarbounis, for example, argues that "the political system is more complicated than what the 'one person, one vote' model assumes and various groups of voters may have a 'say' for the equilibrium outcome" (Karabarbounis, 2011, p. 624).

James Robinson, in the article regarding economic redistribution policies that was cited in Chapter 4, shows that politicians respond to the demands of groups that (Robinson, 2008):

- *Are homogenous and numerous*: in an unequal society, the poor are certainly in this category, but they are not necessarily the only ones. Any sufficiently sized group with common interests tends to be privileged by politicians, such as popular religious groups, the elderly, ethnic groups, etc.;

- *Are able to resolve their problem through collective action*: they take advantage of the liberty to organize, as permitted by democracy, to form associations and unions capable of pressuring the government into adopting policies that favor the group. They use their channels of communication to praise politicians that support them and affront the others, as well as guarantee the votes of their members and relatives in favor of allied candidates;
- *Attend the same professional or social locales as politicians* and take advantage of their privileged position to give opinions or influence decisions: civil servants that advise in the design of public policies are an example. This is the case where the means to obtain privileges are closer to those used by the rich (decisions made behind closed doors, with no transparency, based on political connections);
- *Vote in large numbers*: those who vote are more attractive to politicians than those that are not allowed to vote. This would explain, for example, favoring the elderly and youth in detriment to children, given that the latter can't vote.[1]

Intermediate income groups that fit one or more of these categories are more successful when demanding benefits from the government.

Some redistributive government policies can naturally be seen in any country in the world: *lobbying*, redistribution in favor of the poor or by well-connected groups and *rent seeking* are normal characteristics in modern societies and provide a base for the vast amount of literature on the subject.

What makes the Brazilian situation different is that *inequality* generated an elevated level of redistributive pressure. This diffuses throughout society and has become difficult to dismantle. The more a society is divided (levels of schooling, purchasing power, etc.) the more difficult it is to form majorities to revoke privileges accrued by each of these groups.

An ex-Chief Economist for the International Monetary Fund and current president of the Reserve Bank of India, Rajan shows how inequality is a crucial factor in blocking reforms, which if taken forward, could place most of society in a better position (Rajan, 2006). Even in a democratic society, where all groups have the right to vote and express their preferences, attempts by each group to preserve rent extracted from other groups paralyzes reforms that could favor the majority.

Suppose, as the author argues, that there are three types of individuals in a given society: a capitalist who earns extra profit due to his monopolistic production of goods, a group of highly educated laborers and a group of workers with little or no education. The two working groups are employed by the capitalist, but those with a better education have access to jobs with greater technological content and better pay. They may be able to open their own businesses, but cannot because the monopolist is the only one with legal right to own a business.

---

1. In Brazil, everyone between the ages of 18 and 70 is obligated by law to vote. For those between 16 and 18 or over 70, voting is optional.

The poorly educated workers only have access to lower-paying jobs that require less qualification.

If confronted with the option of a complete reform composed by two partial reforms (one, the extension of education to all workers and the other, opening the market to new firms by ending monopolistic control), there is a good chance of a collective choice for no reform.

The basic argument is that at least one of the groups is damaged by at least one of the two partial reforms. As such it is not easy to form a majority in favor of the complete reform (i.e., in favor of the two partial reforms).

The workers with a higher level of education would like to end the monopoly. With this reform, they could set up their own companies and the expansion of the economy would open new high-technology jobs, which would be favorable to them. However, they are not interested in expanding education in general. This would reduce their competitive advantage in relation to those with little or no education, since if low-skilled workers had a better education, they could also set up companies or have access to good jobs, thereby intensifying the competition for positions that originally were available only to the group of high-skilled workers.

The capitalist is not interested in freeing the market for fear of losing their monopolistic position. He may even support an increase in the level of education, because this would increase worker productivity, which would make his company more profitable. However, he fears that with the increase in the level of education, both groups of workers (both able to open their own businesses after the educational reform) would unite in favor of ending the monopoly. As such, the capitalist tends to position himself against reform.

The low education workers tend to be favorable to the expansion of education, but if not approved, they have no interest in ending the monopoly. First, because without a high level of education they won't be able to take advantage of the end of the monopoly by opening their own companies. Second, because the end of the monopoly could prompt a technological improvement in the economy that would substitute unskilled labor by machines, worsening the position of those with a low education.

Therefore, Rajan shows that there is a low probability for a consensus to be formed to approve a complete reform, since each of the groups disapproves of at least one of the two partial reforms.

What is happening in this case is the fact that, due to *inequality* among the groups, each has different endowments (education and market power) and the dismantling of a restriction imposed on one group means the end of a rent enjoyed by another. In other words, inequality is a central factor to blocking reform and preserving a sub-optimum equilibrium where each group has incentives to extract rents from the others.

Notice that this model abstracts a series of complications in real life. In it, each individual or group knows exactly if they will win or lose with the reform. There is no transition period until gains begin to appear. The individuals are not risk averse and all act in a rational way, with complete access to information. Even then, there is bias in favor of the *status quo*, and entrenched privileges tend to have a long life.

Fernandez and Rodrik show how uncertainty plays an additional role in maintaining the *status quo* (Fernandez and Rodrik, 1991). They present a model in which a reform that would revoke privileges and openly benefit the greater part of society (it is supposed that all know this *ex ante*) cannot be approved because the individuals do not know exactly *who* the winners or losers will be.

For example, when a country opens its market to international trade, companies do not know if they will be able to adapt to the new market conditions or if they will succumb to competition. They know that most will prosper, while others will fail, but they are unable to distinguish *who* will be part of which group. Fernandez and Rodrik show that uncertainty is enough to form a majority in favor of maintaining the *status quo*.

This model also supposes that individuals are rational and there is no risk aversion or uncertainty as to the *aggregate* result of the reform.

Add to the basic scenario all the additional real-life features, along with the costs of collective action for those who want to end privileges, and you have a scenario even more favorable to the preservation of the *status quo*. Mechanisms to create and preserve rents, once established, are able to perpetuate themselves.

Since there are no means to credibly coordinate collective action to end rent seeking by each individual group, the best strategy is to try to increase the rent it extracts for itself, which results in an ever-increasing demand for rents and privileges made to the government.

In this dispute, the groups with the advantage are those with the above mentioned attributes: they are numerous and homogeneous; have privileged access to political institutions where decisions are taken; are able to solve collective action problems; and that vote more frequently, or who simply have the right to vote.

A refining of the argument presented in Chapter 4 regarding the redistribution models for the poor should be noted here. In it, a relevant cause for low growth came from the fact that the assets and income of the very rich were taxed to finance redistribution, discouraging investment. In the present context, where there are redistributive policies demanded by groups situated in all the social pyramid, public expenditure grows rapidly (Chapter 1, Stylized Fact 1) and forces the government to seek all possible forms to obtain revenue (Stylized Fact 2). It is no longer the specific taxing of the rich that binds the propensity to invest. It is the excess taxation of all social groups and its distortionary effects (cumulative taxation, administrative costs to pay taxes, competitive differences due to tax evasion) that discourage investment and corrode productivity.

Rent seeking ceases to be an exclusive behavior for high-income groups, being present in middle-income groups as well, or even in low-income groups. In general, it is assumed that the poor are unable to solve their collective-action problems, and are therefore unable to promote rent-seeking activities. However, in Brazil there are many organized interest groups that incorporate segments of the poor, such as women farmers, landless rural workers or the urban homeless.

Lisboa and Latif upon analyzing the high degree of rent seeking in Brazil, synthesize the theoretical literature on the theme (Lisboa and Latif, 2013). (Classic texts on the theme are Krueger, 1974; Olson, 1965.) The authors describe such phenomenon as that which presents the following characteristics.

- Privileges (subsidies, income transfers, market access restrictions) are focussed on specific groups in contrast to disseminated benefits that traditional public services (policing, urbanization, public sanitation, property rights) provide to the whole population.
- Costs are disseminated and, therefore, difficult to be identified. There is not a specific tax to pay for each type of government-provided benefit that allows society to identify how much each program costs. For each new privilege or subsidy conceded, financing comes from a pool of resources collected via taxation. Likewise, the negative impacts on productivity, interest rates or budget deficit, are not easily perceived.
- The benefited groups have strong incentives to lobby to maintain those privileges and invest in obtaining governmental protection, while the rest of society does not know the costs or does not consider them sufficiently significant to justify the effort to mobilize.
- The concession of privileges is not preceded by a unbiased study to calculate the general impact on society (costs, benefits and collateral effects), which allows the potential beneficiaries to exaggerate in propagating the social benefits and hiding the costs to be paid by society.
- Rules and procedures are tailor made to specifically attend the beneficiaries to which they are directed.
- Lack of transparency: many operations are performed outside the public budget (credit conceded by public banks, operations performed by autonomous state companies) or are based on diverse tax exemptions or special tax regimes within a complex system.
- Once a policy is adopted, no posterior study is performed to evaluate its effects in order to decide if it should be continued or terminated; the tendency is that, due to lobbying, inertia or the difficulty in changing laws, the privileges survive the test of time.
- Incentive policies that are justifiable due to their cost-benefit to society, but that should be temporary (some types of commercial protection for a strategically important sector or region, for example) are perennial since interest groups fight for their continuance. Paradoxically, the less successful a policy (and therefore, incapable of inducing sectors to firmly establish and compete in the market without the incentive), the greater the pressure to maintain the policy. If repealed, it will lead to the death of the protected companies and the elimination of jobs. This causes the beneficiaries to fight to maintain the subsidy.

		BENEFITS	
		Scattered	Focussed
COSTS	Scattered	**A** - General interest policies (weak lobby for and against)	**B** - Preferential policies (strong lobby for and weak lobby against)
	Focussed	**C** - Threatened minorities (weak lobby for and strong lobby against)	**D** - Minority conflicts (strong lobby for and against)

FIGURE 5.1   Standards for Public Policy Choices. *(Source: Monteiro 2013, p. 217)*

Jorge Viana Monteiro, specialist in institutional economics, presents a very didactic figure (reproduced here as Figure 5.1) that summarizes the essence of the previously cited characteristics.

Cells A and D present policies that *do not* induce rent-seeking behavior. Cell A contains general-interest policies, such as pollution control or disease prevention. They are typical public service actions that attend the whole population. As they are of general interest, there is no one who acts out of personal interest either to defend or to criticize such policies.

Cell D contains those policies that attend a particular interest group, but face direct opposition by another. In 2013, for example, legislation was passed regarding the practice of medicine (Law 12.842, of 2013) in which different procedures performed by other professionals (physical therapists, psychologists, nurses) were exclusively destined to physicians. A conflict arose between the interests of the physicians on one side and those of the other professionals on the other. In this case, there was incentive on the part of both sides to explicitly show the benefits (doctors) and costs (other professions) of the bill approval. The argument came up for public debate and politicians were squeezed between the interests of both parts. There is no way to hide or disperse costs. The conflict between interest groups restricts the concession of privileges to one of them.

Rent seeking will more easily flourish in Cell B cases, while Cell C explains why privileges, once gained, perpetuate over time.

All policies that result in benefits to a specific group and where the cost is paid by society in a diffused manner, fit into Cell B: financial aid to bankrupt businesses, loans from public banks given at subsidized interest rates, job positions in government with above average salaries, labor law that protects certain labor positions, etc. The incentive to mobilize the beneficiaries (in terms of mobilization costs *vis-a-vis* the expected benefit) is much greater than the incentive to mobilize those who will pay the bill. It is not easy to clearly identify the losers in order to assemble them to lobby against the benefit. Furthermore, the individual cost paid by each citizen is small when compared to the loss of time and effort to organize the collective action against the privilege.

Cell C contains the cases of groups that organize to resist reforms that could result in the repeal of existing privileges. For example, social security reforms to control real increases in retirement and pension income would save public funds that could be applied, say, to public sanitation, benefitting all of society. Retirees and pensioners have great incentive to resist such measures because they represent a loss of income for that group. However, the potential beneficiaries (people that do not get sick thanks to an expansion in sanitation, workers and businesses that do not lose days of work due to sickness) are dispersed and how much each would effectively gain cannot clearly be quantified.

The next sections represent some concrete examples of how intermediate segments of income distribution have increased their benefits in the new democratic era by means of rent-seeking behavior and how they have resisted institutional reforms.

It will initially be described how the new constitutional order opened breaches to legally demand "rights" that, actually, generate individual privileges and collective costs.

5.3   RENT SEEKING IN LEGAL DISPUTES

Chapter 3, Section 3.4.1 showed how the 1988 Constitution not only increased access to the courts, but also the body of subjects about which they could rule, increasing the number of cases filed. It was presented that this greater access did not benefit the whole population, but rather some specific groups. This section will show how organized groups are able to become the beneficiaries of the legal system implanted by the new Constitution.

The 1988 Constitution was written under the presupposition that social inequality is an evil that must be eradicated by government action. The reduction of inequality is a point central to the constitution of the new Brazilian democracy, which considers direct access to public services and the court, and even that to private goods and services, such as employment and housing, a "right of every citizen." As Maria Teresa Sadek, a sociologist dedicated to studying the Brazilian legal system, writes:

> (...) social inequality – and this is the central point – ceased to be seen as natural. (...) any and all inequality came to be understood as an inequality caused by social order (...) the more unequal a society, the greater the effects of the universal rights agenda. (...) As such, the preparation and adoption of policies that have the end of inequality as their goal, were defended. (...) Civil and political rights have the individual as their base, demanding the limitation of government power for its execution, a minimalist state. Social rights, however, (...) require public policies that, when recognizing exclusion, have redistribution as their objective. In other terms, it needs a state that is active in the sense of providing the rights of health, work, education, housing, retirement and etc. (...) In the last decades, so called third generation rights have been added to these, no longer applicable to individuals, but to groups. These are rights of consumers, children, elderly, minority, etc. (Sadek, 2013, pp. 7-9).

Add another important characteristic of the 1988 Constitution to this universal concept of rights: an increase in the power of the court to interfere in public policies, associated with the increased access to the court. Once more quoting Maria Teresa Sadek:

> From the point of view of rights, the 1988 Constitution promoted many funda-mental changes: on one side, besides recognizing individual rights, it recog-nizes the so-called social rights, such as employment, housing, education and health. On the other side, it strengthens mechanisms for protecting rights. (...) To protect collective rights, an innovative legal instrument was devised: pub-lic civil suits (ação civil pública). (...) the objective of protecting public civil rights covers any diffused societal interest, covering: rights pertaining to health, social security, social aid, education, healthy environment, maternity, infancy, adolescence, physically challenged individuals, and the social use of property. The greatest gain resulting from the protection of diffused and collective rights is equal access to the court; since it covers groups and community (...) it is a legal instrument to correct inequalities, an instrument for redistributive justice. (...) The citizen came to have access to the institution to solve disputes and to guarantee the most varied rights (...) the consecration of an ample set of rights (...) and, equal access to the court stimulated an extraordinary pursuit of judi-cial solutions (Sadek, 2013, pp. 15-18).

The redistributive impetus and promotion of social justice included in the text of the new Constitution, added to the increase in means to access the court, resulted, actually, in giving opportunity to organized segments, many of them from the middle and upper classes, to appeal for individual or restricted group rights. Paradoxically, the prevalence of these specific interests reduced the qual-ity of public policies. With it, the effective ability to promote global benefits and reach the highly desired reduction of inequality is compromised.

The constitutional intent to guarantee ample benefits and aid to the popula-tion was not tempered by a definition of how to finance said benefits. Given the inability of the state to finance everything the constitution promises, a fa-vorable scene is created for people to go to court in order to fight to gain what is promised to everybody. Given that the right is "ensured" by constitution, a well-informed citizen, union or class entity able to retain a good lawyer, will go to court whenever possible to "make their rights count." The judges consider the rights of the petitioner without considering those of the part of society not participating in that legal case, which ends up being negatively affected by the concession of the benefit.

A classic case with strong financial and public administration repercussions is the dispute for access to public healthcare. As cited in Chapter 1, Section 1.3, after approval of the 1988 Constitution, public healthcare was considered a "right of all and duty of the state."

With the intent of fulfilling the constitutional mandate, the government pro-vided public access to health services by means of the Unified Health System

(*Sistema Único de Saúde* – SUS), where the different types of treatment and medications were defined that would be provided to the population free of charge. Many individuals, however, go to court demanding that the government pay for treatments and medications not included in the SUS service protocol, arguing that the Constitution establishes the universal right to health, without limits to such rights.

The treatments and medications demanded are generally expensive and the service required by one individual consumes public resources that could be applied to regular treatments offered to a greater number of patients. Given the cost of high-technology treatments or latest-generation medications, it is impossible to provide this level of treatment to the whole population. However, some use the courts to force the public sector to pay for such therapies. The amount of legal cases and the costs involved disrupt health planning at the state government level, which many times must suspend other activities or services in order to finance the special treatments mandated by court.

The suspension of treatments provided for by the SUS protocol, partly due to the financial chaos caused by court decisions, generates more court cases, this time by those denied the promised basic treatment, such as a bed in the ICU, medications designated as free or a medical appointment in a reasonable amount of time.

The perverse magic has been performed: the instrument that was intended to reduce inequalities and provide universal access has been changed into a privilege mechanism. In other words, whoever gets to court first, takes the prize! The one who doesn't have access to information or the means to demand their "rights" through legal procedures must conform themselves to the lack of service and the negative effects of court action on the quality of regularly provided services. (For more information regarding this kind of litigation, see Sabino, 2013; Machado, 2010; Romero, 2008.)

André César Medici states, for example, that:

> In 2004, the total expenditure for basic and strategic medications (excluding medications for SDT-AIDS) was practically the same as that spent on special medications (about R$830 million). In 2009, expenditures on special medications [which most of the time were required by court mandate] were 2.5 times higher than the total expense for basic and strategic medications (R$.1 billion), in a context where the low-income population is far from having complete access to this set of basic and strategic medications (Medici, 2011, p. 64).

People tend to resort to legal action if, after calculating the costs and benefits, they believe they can profit. This is the case in the situation above, where the expected high-cost treatment or medication is worth paying the legal fees involved. But the expected result is not always positive and some social groups may avoid seeking a court decision due to the implicitly high costs. According to Armando Castelar Pinheiro:

The Brazilian courts are seen as being very slow and a significant number of businesses also complain of the high costs. Small businesses, in particular, see the cost of going to court as prohibitive and only resort to this when pressured to do so. Large companies also assume a similar behavior and structure their operations in such a way as to avoid contact with the courts, except in the area of taxes, where the sluggishness of the courts is seen by a minor portion of companies as being eventually beneficial (Pinheiro, 2005, p. 246).

In other words, in cases where resorting to court is expensive (due to legal fees, or the time spent on the case), people and companies prefer avoiding it. When the sluggishness is beneficial, as in the possibility of taking advantage of the slowness to delay paying duties, using the courts becomes an interesting option, which, frequently happens in cases related to loans, rent payments and commercial and labor disputes. (Pinheiro (2005))

On the other hand, as identified in a report produced by the Catholic University of Rio Grande do Sul (*Universidade Católica do Rio Grande do Sul*), by request of the National Justice Council (*Conselho Nacional de Justiça*), there are cases where legal fees are practically zero (Santos Filho and Timm, 2010). In these cases, lawyers are paid by means of a percentage of the damages awarded in the case with no cost to the person who joins the suit. This encourages some people to participate in a lawsuit simply because it costs them nothing and there is the possibility of receiving damages (typical of "free-rider" behavior).

There are, in this case, incentives to create a market where lawyers set up class action suits for the remediation of damages or payment of labor rights and try to enlist the greatest number of clients possible to join. They offer the attractive features of no retainer fees, no court costs (the law office develops the case) and not paying damages if the case is not won.

This results in repetitive cases, with a large number of plaintiffs, where lawyers receive a percentage of the damages and the clients have little to lose. Typical examples are: suing for wage adjustments due to inflation not considered in the past; labor cases against former employers; and suits that demand the recalculation of taxes paid on financial investments made many years before.

The usual defendants in these cases (governments, public service providers and banks) also exploit the ample number of appeals to delay payment of damages. Court congestion increases due to the opportunistic behavior of both parts, reducing access by people that need the courts for cases of a different nature.

Summarizing, the combination of the intent to increase access to the courts and expand the "rights" that can be vindicated in them, along with the congestion and sluggishness of the court, provides openings for all types of strategic behavior. Some individuals do not pay their bills and take advantage of the financial gain they will receive due to the slowness of the collection process. Others count on the low cost of joining a class action suit that, many times, is no more than an exploitation of legal loopholes to generate unfounded economic gains. There are also those who count on the courts in order to gain access to special and expensive services in detriment to society. As has been argued, the results, in terms of inequality, can be opposite of those expected.

Once more, inequality is a relevant variable, a fundamental motive for the inscription of ample "social and collective rights" contained in the Constitution. Such rights come to give organized groups advantages in the distributive conflict and feed the logic of seeking private benefits, with their costs being charged to others.

5.4   THE ELDERLY AS A POLITICALLY PREFERRED PUBLIC

The political preference to concede benefits to the elderly is a typical case of a policy that fits Cell B in Figure 5.1: benefits concentrated on a group with costs paid by all of society. In the classification proposed by James Robinson, in his work on redistributive policies, the elderly are a group of voters that bring together several features that are interesting to those in search of votes (Robinson, 2008). They have similar needs related to retirement and health. A good part of them are able to organize due to having lived in an urban environment, and being retired from formal positions, are accustomed to union organization. Another part is poor and a traditional client of social-assistance policies (rural retirees, for example).

It is no coincidence that they have been the object of preferential policies since democratization. During the military government, the idea was formed that the elderly composed an underprivileged group. The military contributed to this with low retirement pensions (that were corroded by inflation), restricted access to health services and the abandonment of rural retirees. If social assistance was bad for all, it was even worse for the poor elderly who could not compensate for their lack of income and basic services in the private work market.

With the advent of democracy, the situation of the elderly changed radically. There was intense policymaking to concede retirement to rural workers, with weak restrictions on concessions and loose verification of time of service. Such retirements, equivalent to one minimum wage, had a considerable increase in their unitary value, as shown in Figure 1.14 in Chapter 1. At the same time, the so-called BPC program was established, which, as seen in Chapter 2, pays one minimum wage to the elderly and physically challenged people who are members of families with a *per capita* income inferior to one-quarter of one minimum salary.

In the urban environment, the increase in life expectancy was not followed, in the same intensity, by a reformulation of the parameters that defined the retirement age or eligibility for pensions due to death. Social security reforms, even though performed, were insufficient to avoid early retirement and long-term high-value pensions. Retirement for civil servants is especially notable since it is conceded under better conditions than for those workers in the private sector.

Table 5.1 shows how the elderly are more privileged in the allocation of federal resources. No less than 50% of total primary federal expense refers to budget lines that directly favor the elderly: retirement and pensions (public and private) and the BPC program. Expense in favor of the elderly grew 92% above inflation between 2002 and 2012. In *per capita* terms, growth was 72%.

Notice especially the intense growth of the three first items on Table 5.1, all with adjustments tied to variations in the minimum wage, which grew considerable above inflation (Chapter 1, Stylized Fact 6).

The only item on Table 5.1 that does not represent a retirement benefit expense is the BPC program, paid with regular National Treasury resources. The remaining retirement, pension and other benefit payments are the responsibility of social security, whose revenue comes from employer and employee contributions.

TABLE 5.1 Primary Federal Government Expense in Favor of the Elderly: 2002 vs. 2012 (% of GDP)

	% of GDP		Real Variation 2002-2012(%)	
	2002	*2012*	*Total*	*Per Capita*
BPC Benefits to the elderly [1][2]	0.08	0.29	479	421
Urban social security benefits = 1 minimum-wage[3]	0.80	1.26	165	138
Rural social security benefits = 1 minimum-wage[3]	1.12	1.53	130	107
Other social security benefits (private sector employees)	4.04	4.41	84	66
Federal civil servant retirements and pensions[4]	2.03	1.68	40	26
Total expense in favor of elderly (A)	**8.07**	**9.16**	92	72
Total primary expense (B)	**15.72**	**18.28**	96	77
(A)/(B)	51.3%	50.1%		

Sources: National Treasury Secretariat (primary result from the central government), Statistical Personnel Bulletin, Ministry of Social Development and Hunger Alleviation (MDS) and Social Security Annual Statistic. (1) Excludes benefits paid do physically challenged in the LOAS ambit. (2) MDS (http://www.mds.gov.br/relcrys/bpc/indice.htm). (3) Calculated by applying the percent participation of urban and rural benefits in the total 2011 expense to the total 2012 expense. (4) Ministry of Planning, Budget and Management. Statistical Personnel Bulletin. Note: calculations for the opening of benefits up to one minimum salary and other benefits were authored by Marcelo Abi-Rama Caetano and graciously conceded to the author. Deflator: IPCA. Prepared by the author.

Is this social security expense excessive? In an international comparison, one of the main Brazilian specialists on the issue, Marcelo Abi-Rama Caetano, shows that "Brazil spends a proportion of its GDP on social security equivalent to countries such as Belgium, France, Germany, Finland and Sweden, which present dependent demographic ratios [relation between number of beneficiaries and number of active contributors to social security] of near 27%, about triple that of Brazil. Analogously, (...) countries with demographics more similar to Brazil have social security spending in the neighborhood of 4% of GDP, practically one-third that spent in Brazil" (Caetano, 2006, p. 9).

Even though it is not within the scope of this book to provide a detailed discussion on the problems of Brazilian Social Security, the comparison given above makes the great weight of social security on total expenses evident. (Regarding problems and Social Security reform proposals, see: Afonso, 2005; Pinheiro and Giambiagi, 2006; Caetano, 2006; Amaro, 2011; Caetano, 2008, 2011a, 2011b; Tafner and Giambiagi, 2011.) The expansion of this type of expense has a fundamental role in the low growth with dissipative redistribution model presented in Chapter 1. It was this economic weight that stimulated three governments, led by two distinct parties, to propose reforms in social security to Congress. Reforms were approved in 1998, 2003 and 2012, which imposed control mechanisms on social security expense and the reduction of benefits, increased the retirement age and promoted a reduction in the amounts received for those opting for early retirement. The last reform, in 2012, established a pension fund for civil servants in order to avoid the federal government covering retirement costs above the maximum amount paid to workers in the private sector. (Regarding the introduction of the Civil Servant Retirement Fund (*Fundo de Previdência dos Servidores Públicos*), see Guerzoni Filho, 2011; Rangel and Sabóia, 2013.)

The approval of such reforms, however, went against the existing political incentives, which led politicians to try to please and not antagonize well-organized social groups. As such, those reforms met with great resistance in Congress: the final approved texts were much different (and made fewer changes) than what had been originally proposed.

Furthermore, several projects presented to the National Congress constitute counter reforms. In 2013, a special retirement for the physically challenged was passed (regulated by Complementary Law 142, of 2013) There are a series of bills being supported by unions and retirement associations that propose, for example: the removal of a device called the "retirement factor" (which, if approved, would allow early retirement and higher pensions); special retirement (less time of contribution) for specific professional categories; the end of retirement contributions by retirees who return to active work (there are bills in Congress and cases in court); higher re-adjustment index for benefits; and the calculation of benefits based on the highest salaries received during the work life (Velloso et al., 2010).

The pro-elderly policies are not restricted, however, to retirement benefits. Table 5.1 shows that expenses for the BPC program more than doubled in proportion to GDP between 2002 and 2010. This happened not only due to real adjustments to the minimum wage, but also due to reducing the minimum age for an elderly person to be eligible for the program. When the Social Assistance Organic Law was approved (*Lei Orgânica de Assistência Social*) (Law 8.742, of 1993) the minimum age to receive the benefit was 70. The age was reduced to 67 (Law 9.720, of 1998) and later to 65 due to the "Elderly Statute"(Law 10.741, of 2003).

The Elderly Statute is a symbol of the political preference for this group. Besides reducing the minimum age to receive the BPC allowance, the statute created several other benefits for its target public. Some of them are: the right to pay half-fare for cultural presentations, free urban and semi-urban public transportation, two reserved seats on interstate transportation and a 50% discount on all others (in this case for the low-income elderly), priority in receiving income tax refunds, free medications and prostheses, no health insurance premium increases for clients 60 or over and the prohibition to charge legal fees in cases involving rights established in the statute.

All of these benefits generate costs to be paid by someone. Take, for example, the prohibition to readjust health-insurance premiums for those over 60. There are several consequences: (a) younger clients pay more than they should in order to compensate for less expensive health insurance for the elderly; (b) monthly premiums are significantly raised when the client turns 59; (c) health insurance companies create bureaucratic and operational barriers to accept elderly clients or do not offer them individual coverage. In other words, both the younger and elderly clients must pay the costs of regulatory restrictions and society as a whole loses due to the price distortions and bureaucracy resulting from the rule. Some elderly are able to get less expensive coverage, but this is far from being a cost-free regulation for society.

Besides those benefits explicit in the Elderly Statute, there are a series of generic declarations in the statute that serve as a legal basis for eventual court cases against the public sector. In the spirit described in the previous section (rent seeking in legal cases), take, for example:

Article 9 – It is the obligation of the state to guarantee protection of life and health to the elderly by means of approving public social policies that allow aging with health and dignity.

This type of generic guarantee, associated with the gratuitous use of the courts to defend the rights included in the statute, can stimulate the filing of collective-interest law suits.

What is the problem with giving so much emphasis to the elderly? Should they not be, as a matter of fact, a group under the special watch care of the government due to the vulnerabilities brought on by age?

The problem is that public resources are scarce and, to obtain the best possible results, should be allocated in an efficient manner. If the government objective is to direct expenditure and regulation in favor of the elderly *in order to reduce inequality and poverty*, they are aiming at the wrong target. The already mentioned study by Barros and co-authors states:

> *(...) poverty is still 10 times greater among children than among the elderly, but the average noncontributory public transfer for an elderly person is at least 20 times greater than the average non-contributory public transfer for a child. (...) optimizing social policy design gives Brazilian policymakers plenty of room to further reduce inequality, without the need of additional resources (Barros et al., 2009, pp. 71-72).*

Armando Castelar Pinheiro and Fábio Giambiagi state that in 2000 44.8% of the indigents in Brazil were under the age of 15 in contrast to 1.9% who were 65 or older (Giambiagi and Pinheiro, 2012). In the same vein, Ferreira and co-authors argue that:

> *(...) in Brazil, for instance, half of all children live in households below the US$4-per-day poverty line, and another 30 percent live in vulnerable households; therefore, 80 percent of Brazilian children are growing up in households that are not middle or upper class (Ferreira et al., 2013, p. 148).*

In other words, focussing social spending on the elderly is grossly missing the target of poverty in Brazil. In fact, as seen in Chapter 2, social security expenses, both public and private, concentrate income, exactly because the elderly population concentrates in the middle- and high-income ranges. On the other hand, the *Bolsa Família* program, which is partially tied to children in the home, has, as seen in Chapter 2, the power to reduce poverty and inequality.

Spending a large part of available resources on the elderly and leaving children to a second level is not only an error in terms of policies to reduce poverty. It is also undermining future economic growth since it forms a future generation of adults and workers with all sorts of cognitive and educational deficiencies, making them less capable and productive. There are also opportunity costs in preferring to spend on retirement and aid to the elderly in preference to investments in infrastructure, education and health, which, in turn, have obvious positive impacts on productivity and economic growth.

Furthermore, it would be possible to attend the poor elderly along with the rest of the family at a lower cost to the government. There are policies that favor the elderly who are not poor (retirement and pensions from the public sector and those for the private sector retirees that are above one minimum wage). On the other hand, there are programs that are relatively focussed on the poor elderly (BPC and minimum wage retirement and pensions), but that are high cost. Finally, there are policies in favor of the elderly that may be enjoyed by high-income elderly (privileges guaranteed by the Elderly Statute). The ideal would be to focus policies in favor of the poor elderly at the least possible cost.

However, what can be seen, firstly, is that a substantial portion of expense in favor of the elderly does not go to the poor. The total expenditure for benefits of social security above one minimum wage and for retirement and pensions for civil servants reached no less than 6.1% of GDP in 2012, or 66% of the total expenditure in favor of the elderly. This portion should not be treated as a poverty-reduction policy simply because it is not directed toward the poor. As such, parameters of financial sustainability adapted to life expectancy, restrictions to special retirement and other privileged treatment should be part of a social security reform, in order to reduce its regressive effect on income distribution.

Secondly, it is necessary to question the logic that supports the privileges contained in the Elderly Statute that affect both the elderly that are poor, or those that are not. The 70-year-old from the middle class has as much right to ride the bus for free as the poor. There is no moral or ethical justification to provide this benefit to a person who can afford the service and pass the cost on to others. Therefore, it is necessary to adjust the privileges and concessions to help those clients who are poor.

Thirdly, one notices the possibility of a superimposition of policies in favor of the poor. While the *Bolsa Família* program cares for low-income families, the BPC and one-salary retirements care for low-income families with elderly. Certainly, there is room to rationalize this superimposition by means of, for example, substituting the BPC and retirements obtained without due contribution for a policy of complete family aid, a type of extended *Bolsa Família* program, which would take into account the presence of needy elderly in the poor family being cared for.

Above all, this should be done because benefits for the poor elderly indexed to the minimum wage are expensive. As Table 5.1 shows, the BPC benefit paid to the elderly costs 0.29% of GDP per year, which is more than half of the total cost for the *Bolsa Família* program, which was 0.48% of GDP in 2012 (see Table 4.1 in Chapter 4). When we consider the number of beneficiaries considered, however, the *Bolsa Família* program covers 13.4 million families (Brazil Ministry of Social Development and Hunger Alleviation, 2012), while the BPC supports only 1.75 million elderly (http://www.mds.gov.br/relcrys/bpc/docs/downloads/2013/AgoTodos.pdf). It is inevitable to conclude that, even though BPC is a program that reduces poverty and redistributes income (Chapter 2), it is not cost-effective. It is therefore necessary to try to reach the poor elderly in a way with greater scope at less cost.

It is, nevertheless, not easy to implant this type of fine-tuning of social programs. It does not interest the groups of elderly or future retirees that are not poor, but that use poverty as an argument for their political pleas. To those who wish to maintain their privileges, the ideal is to mix themselves with rural and poor urban retirees, using the poor as a symbol of the "injustice" committed by those who want to reform social security. It is necessary to maintain, for bargaining purposes, the incorrect image that all elderly are poor and need preferential public policies.

Certainly, the bias in favor of the elderly is not a case of political shortsightedness. As has been stated, it is a calculated political move to receive votes. Children, who do not vote, will probably be the ones at risk, unless they have a retired parent or grandparent in their home.

An extreme example of the political class-pleasing elderly voters is the program "Travel for the Elderly" (*Viaja Mais Terceira Idade*). Through this program, the Ministry of Tourism signed agreements with tour agencies to offer travel packages to the elderly, with discounts, under the pretext of "social inclusion." It is known that travel packages are something availed by the middle and upper classes and are far from being necessary. Therefore, one must ask, "What type of social inclusion is this?" In defense of the program, it may be argued that there is no public subsidy involved (which is not clear since public banks finance the packages and subsidies may be hidden in low-interest rates). The simple fact is, however, that a public-service structure that consumes work hours, materials and physical space in the Ministry for this type of program is questionable. If there is a market niche to expand tourism among the elderly, the private market can take care of it, with no necessary involvement of public resources. There is no "market failure" that justifies governmental intervention in this case.

Summarizing, the elderly seem to attract political attention by being a large group with collective demands (especially retirement and health care) that counts on well-structured organizations and unions, and has a public image of being vulnerable. It is not easy to remodel these policies in order to reduce adverse impacts on inequality, poverty and growth. Behind them there is a political *motive* and rent-seeking dispute, as described in Section 5.2.

5.5 PUBLIC EDUCATION THAT DOES NOT SERVE THE POOR

In Chapter 4, Section 4.4, it was argued that the expansion of public education, from primary to secondary, was an expression of redistribution to the poor. Not all public education, however, preferentially aids the poor. Brazilian public universities are traditionally elitist, being attended in large part by the middle and upper classes.

This is a historic characteristic of the country, which stood out during the military government. With the onset of democracy, the privilege was maintained by the middle-and upper-income classes and has been very resistant to higher-education reforms. It has especially resisted the implantation of paid public universities, remaining free to all, and independent of income level or ability to pay tuition.

This is a situation that, in Figure 5.1, could be classified in Cell C: a privileged minority with a strong incentive to fight to maintain a privilege. On the other hand, the potential beneficiaries (public-school students who would have more resources for their schools if part of the money spent on universities were directed to other levels of education) are not mobilized and do not perceive the potential benefit a reform would provide.

The fact that the middle- and upper-income classes have captured a substantial part of public funds for university education is not exclusively Brazilian. Nancy Birdsall and Estelle James from the World Bank describe this as being true in many developing countries:

> *Many countries spend a disproportionate share of their total educational budgets at the tertiary level. This is also the level which heavily benefits upper income groups; a large expenditure is concentrated on a small number of advantaged students in contrast to primary education which disproportionately benefits the poor (...). Public universities typically do not have price barriers to entry. However, they have academic barriers which are more likely to be surmounted by high income families, whose children complete primary school, attend a high quality secondary school, pay for after-school tutoring, and pass the entrance exam to the prestigious public institution (Birdsall and James, 1990, p. 10).*

Addison and Rahman, in a study commissioned by the United Nation, present statistical evidence of the correlation between economic inequality and the relation of disbursements for higher education in relation to basic education for a set of developing countries: the greater the inequality, the greater the financial advantage of the college education (Addison and Rahman, 2001).

Table 5.2 presents statistics, compiled by Veloso (2011) that show the prevalence of spending in favor of higher education in detriment to others. It can be seen that, in Brazil, 93% of the country *per capita* GDP is spent on each student in public universities. But, in primary education, only 18% of *per capita* GDP is spent. This means that 5.2 times as much is spent on a university student as what is spent on a student in their first years of education. Of the countries presented, only India has a greater proportion than Brazil. The neighboring countries of Chile and Argentina, for example, spend about the same amount on public elementary education as on public universities. South Korea, an international reference in educational excellence, spends more on elementary education than on universities. In the relation between secondary education and higher education, Brazil is by far the country with the greatest bias in favor of the university student.

In dollar values, Brazil spent 2,800 dollars *per capita* on elementary public-education students in 2010 compared with the 8,000-dollar-average *per capita* spending in OECD countries, a difference of 186% in favor of the latter. Whereas Brazil spent 13,100 dollars per student in higher education, the OECD spent an average of 13,500. In this case, there is a difference in favor of the OECD of only 3% (OECD – Education at a Glance. In dollars, adjusted by purchasing-power parity).

This pro-university bias has a significant impact on total spending. Table 5.3 shows that, even though there was a great increase in spending on elementary public education between 2001 and 2011 (considered in Section 4.4), higher education was able to maintain its participation in total spending, with a small reduction from 18 to 17%.

TABLE 5.2 Public Spending on Education per Student in Relation to *per capita* GDP, per Level of Instruction – Selected Countries (2008)

	Elementary	High School	College	College/Elementary	College/High School
	(A)	(B)	(C)	(D)=(C)/(A)	(E)=(C)/(B)
India	8.9	16.2	55.0	6.2	3.4
Brazil	**18.0**	**13.4**	**93.2**	**5.2**	**7.0**
Mexico	13.4	13.8	35.4	2.6	2.6
Uruguay	8.5	10.4	18.1	2.1	1.7
France	17.1	26.6	33.5	2.0	1.3
Ireland	15.0	22.8	26.4	1.8	1.2
United Kingdom	22.1	27.3	29.2	1.3	1.1
Portugal	22.4	34.0	28.8	1.3	0.8
Spain	19.4	24.0	23.5	1.2	1.0
United States	22.2	24.6	25.4	1.1	1.0
Argentina	13.2	20.3	14.2	1.1	0.7
Chile	11.1	12.4	11.5	1.0	0.9
Japan	21.9	22.4	19.1	0.9	0.9
South Korea	17.2	22.2	9.5	0.6	0.4

Source: Veloso, 2011.

TABLE 5.3 Public Spending in Education in Brazil per Level of Instruction: 2001 vs. 2011

	% of GDP		Real Variation 2001-2011(%)
	2001	*2011*	*Total*
Basic Education (primary through high school) (A)	3.30	4.39	125
College (B)	0.74	0.88	99
Total (C)	4.05	5.26	120
(B)/(C)	18%	17%	

Sources: INEP-MEC and Brazil Federal Revenue. Deflator: IPCA. Prepared by the author.

This prevalence in higher education can be considered a victory by those privileged by it: the middle- and upper-income students who have a greater ability to pass the competitive entrance exams. The political means to maintain this privilege is similar to that used to bar social security reforms (Section 5.4).

In that case, middle- and upper-income workers and retirees mix with the poor retirees and present political propaganda against social security reform by calling it an assault on the "poor elderly." In the public university case, it is very common to hear discourses on "free, quality, public, universities for everyone." Such universalist discourse uses the fallacious argument that paying for university education would bar access by the poor. Actually, access by the poor is already barred due to the difficulty of the entrance exams and the fragility of elementary and secondary public education.

Furthermore, the argument makes little of budget restrictions to the public sector and the need to make choices. It simply claims the best for all. It does not consider that charging university tuition would cover part of the cost of education, freeing resources to be applied to elementary education, improving its quality and raising the general level of education. Neither does it consider that scholarships for poorer students would solve the problem of social inclusion.

Notwithstanding the frailty of this point of view, the universalist argument for higher education for all has a strong political appeal. It reproduces the central phenomenon pictured in this book: the quest for inclusion of the poor with voting power without eliminating the privileges enjoyed by middle-income and rich groups. As in the case of using the legal system to obtain privileges in health treatment, free tertiary education is another example of the contradictory idea of "privileges for everybody."

In fact, the federal government higher-education policy has followed a universalist approach. There has been a large increase of openings in the public universities, which has allowed the entrance of students who have achieved low scores on the admission exams. Besides this, quotas have been created, both to include the poor, coming from public schools and ethnic groups (a typical category of group that gained a voice after democratization). The racial quotas tend to disproportionately benefit black and mulatto individuals from middle-income families who are able afford good primary and secondary education and to prepare for university entrance exams.

The federal government has also bought, by means of tax exemptions, openings in private universities, offering them to public school students by means of the University for All Program (ProUni). Little demand is made on the quality of the subsidized courses. Such increase in openings has lowered the average quality of university education. This type of policy increases the weight of university education costs on total educational expense and has had dubious results from the educational point of view.

The high weight of public universities on the cost of education does not only reflect the maintenance of historical privileges for the middle- and upper-income layers. Superimposed on this phenomenon is another layer of privileges: those of the university professors and administrative staff. As they are civil servants, they enjoy job security and many other privileges (which will be considered in the next section) that stimulate lower productivity and quality of education.

Summarizing, the high financial cost and low quality of Brazilian university education seem to flow from the combination of different privileges, both from those that demand the services (students) and from the service providers (professors and staff). Government policy tries to maintain the old privileges (no tuition for students, job security, preferential remuneration and retirement for professors and staff), while at the same time attempts to provide increased access to poor voters or those with the ability to demand (organized ethnic groups).

Quality falls while costs rise. Once more the cycle of financial pressure and low productivity, that characterize low growth with dissipative redistribution, begins.

5.6   THE POLITICAL POWER OF CIVIL SERVANTS

Brazilian civil servants earn more than their counterparts in the private sector. Many studies (see Barbosa and Barbosa Filho, 2012; Belluzo et al., 2005; Bender and Fernandes, 2006) show that, when comparing Brazilians with the same socioeconomic characteristics (level of education, place of residence, gender, race, work experience, etc.), those employed in the public sector earn more. In the most recent estimate it was estimated that male civil servants earn, on average, 12.8% more than their counterparts in the private sector. The differential between women was even higher, 18%. In addition to this, civil servants enjoy other substantial advantages, such as higher-paying retirements (despite the recent reforms in Social Security) and job tenure. (For Social Security reforms approved between 1998 and 2012 see Afonso, 2005; Pinheiro and Giambiagi, 2006; Caetano, 2006; Amaro, 2011; Caetano, 2008, 2011a, 2011b; Tafner and Giambiagi, 2011.)

TABLE 5.4 Public and Private Employment by Class: Workers between 25 and 65 – 2009 (%)

	Private	Public
Poor	94.6	5.4
Vulnerable	90.1	9.9
Middle Class	81.4	18.6
Upper Class	70.2	29.8

Source: Ferreira et al., 2013, p. 153. Note: Poor = daily *per capita* income less than US$4; Vulnerable = daily *per capita* income between US$4 and US$10; Middle Class = daily *per capita* income between US$10 and US$50; Upper Class = daily *per capita* income greater than US$50. Values expressed in US$ in 2005 by purchasing power parity.

In terms of income level, civil servants, for the most part, are considered members of the middle and upper classes. Table 5.4 shows that public-sector employees represent about 30% of upper-class workers (daily *per capita* income above US$50 per day) and only 5.5% of the poor (less than US$4 per day). The profile is inverted in the private sector, where participation decreases as income increases.

Notice that the income stratification presented in Chapter 2, proposed by Ferreira and co-authors, and used in Table 5.4, is the one that establishes higher limits to define the middle and upper classes. Even using this classification, which raises the minimum remuneration necessary to classify a person as middle or upper income, civil servants still maintain a significant presence at the top.

Here is another example, using a different measure of income stratification. Remember that in Chapter 2, Section 2.7, it was seen that, using Family Budget Research based on 2002 values, the upper class begins with a monthly per capita household income of R$1661.00 (about US$722). A three-member family with a single source of income would move from being middle class to upper class with an income of about R$5000 (about US$2200). Consulting the wage structure of federal civil servants, rarely does one find a middle- or upper-level career position with remuneration inferior to this amount (Statistical Personnel Bulletin, http://www.servidor.gov.br/index.asp?index=65&ler=s712). An upper-level professional in the Central Bank, for example, receives a lower salary when compared to other similar careers. Their beginning wage is R$5100 and goes to R$8900. There are, however, many gratifications that accumulate over the course of their career that can double their basic income. It is easy to find careers on the pay charts with gross salaries, before gratifications, of over R$12,000 thousand (about US$5200) a month.

This result is consistent with findings by Pedro de Souza and Marcelo Medeiros, reported in Chapter 2, Section 2.2, according to which the remuneration of civil servants has an intense regressive effect on income distribution. This means it is received in large part by people at the upper levels of income distribution.

A full-time university professor in the United States earns, on average, US$135,000 per year (*The Economist* 2013). Frequently, they do not possess tenure and work in a highly competitive market where thousands of earned doctorates are added yearly. They must regularly publish papers in high-reputation periodicals and are under constant evaluation by their students and peers. In a Brazilian public university, the professors are civil servants with tenure and very little pressure to produce. Their salaries can reach US$85,000 per year, not counting the innumerable gratifications added to their base salary (Ministry of Planning. Statistical Personnel Bulletin, 2013).

The difference in remuneration between a North American professor and a Brazilian, according to the numbers above, is only 60%, while the difference in *per capita* GDP between the two countries is 377% (Penn World Table versão 7.1.).

Another category of civil servants, Brazilian judges, are among the best paid in the world. A report published by the Secretary of Judicial Reform (*Secretaria de Reforma do Judiciário*), a department in the Ministry of Justice, states that:

> Brazilian federal judges of the first level have salaries superior to all countries, with exception of Canada. Magistrates of the second level have salaries higher than all other countries, with the exception of Colombia and Canada (Brazil Ministry of Justice, 2004).

Obviously there are poorly paid categories in public service and much inequality between professions. For example, Moriconi (2008) states that elementary teachers, who are college graduates, can find better paying employment in the private sector. Even in these cases, however, remuneration in the private sector may not be better. Teachers who are beginning their careers, who are not graduates or are female, earn more in the public sector than in the private sector. One must also consider the additional advantages of higher retirement salaries and job tenure.

In Brazil, one must pass exams to be hired as a civil servant. The high salary and advantages offered by public employment have made those exams a national fever. The civil servant exam for the Public Attorney's Office in 2013, for example, had over 800,000 applicants for only 147 openings. That is almost 5500 candidates per opening (http://congressoemfoco.uol.com.br/noticias/maior-concurso-do-pais-mpu-registra-800-mil-inscritos/). There is an ample market of tutoring classes for these exams as well as the sale of preparatory study materials. Radio broadcasters present special programs with tips for these competitions. The electronic versions of the main newspapers in the country have popular *blogs* regarding the theme. The National Congress was forced to pass a general law to establish rules that guarantee fairness in exams for civil servant hiring due to the great amount of social interest in the subject. The search for public employment has taken on such a social dimension that it came to inspire a very successful theater comedy: In "How to Pass a Directed

Civil Servant Exam" (*Como passar em concurso público*), the actors parody the routine common among young people of studying for years to obtain the dream job. A topic to be researched is the economic impact of the time dedicated to preparatory studies (and not other more productive activities) by millions of youth at the peak of their productive age, including those very talented people who have just graduated from university.

Civil servants are able to reach this privileged position due to a combination of factors that allow them a politically strong position to voice their demands. In the terms proposed by Robinson in his oft-cited work on redistributive policy (Robinson, 2008) some groups of civil servants are near the decision-making center and are in the same professional and social environment as politicians. Other groups have the great ability to use collective action by means of unions and associations. Together, they are able to pressure politicians for Cell B type policies, shown in Figure 5.1: concentrated benefits in their favor and costs diffused to all society by means of taxation.

As with any place in the world, there are groups of civil servants who take advantage of their great proximity to political decision making. They advise politicians on salary increases, opening new job positions, etc. They are therefore able to exercise their influence in topics of interest to them. Others detain power due to their professional activities. For example, if those responsible for collecting taxes decide to strike, the flow of revenue is placed in check and the state may find it difficult to honor its commitments.

This typical type of privilege was reinforced by devices in the 1988 Constitution, which increased civil servant ability to use collective action. The constitution gave government employees the right to strike (Federal Constitution, Article 37, Clause VII), which prior to this was not only prohibited but was considered a crime. At the same time, civil servant job security was preserved (Federal Constitution, Article 41). Limits on the right to strike must be regimented by a specific law, which yet awaits approval.

The combination of these factors made striking profitable for civil servants. They can strike with no fear of being fired. The inexistence of a law defining limits and conditions for strikes leaves room for long strikes with no significant restrictions or punishment. It also allows for strikes in services considered essential, such as health services and police. Neither are there limiting rules for strikes, such as a minimum number of servants to provide services, advanced notice of an impending strike, discounting pay for days on strike, etc.

In September 2007, the Supreme Court, faced with the inexistence of regulations for civil servant strikes, determined that the law in force governing the private sector be followed (Court Injunction 670) in "what applied." Based on the legislation, it would be possible to deduct pay or restrict the length of strikes. In practice, however, the political pressure of the civil servants and the fact that the lawyers who were supposed to act in favor of the government in this case, are themselves civil servants (and therefore not interested in enforcing the rule), has resulted in the non-application of the judicial determination.

TABLE 5.5 Total Strikes and Hours of Work Stoppage in the Public and Private Sectors (2012)

	Strikes		Hours Off		Average
	Number (A)	% of Total	Number (B)	% of Total	Hours Off (C) = (B)/(A)
Public Service	380	43.7	65,393	74	172
State Companies	28	3.2	1,434	2	51
Private Sector	461	53.0	21,223	24	46
TOTAL	869	100.0	88,050	100	101

Source: DIEESE (2013). Prepared by the author.

The consequence is that civil servants proportionally strike more than the private sector and their strikes last much longer. Table 5.5 reflects this reality. Even though public servants represent 25% of the formal workforce, they are responsible for 44% of the strikes held in 2012 (Brazil Ministry of Work and Employment, 2013). What is surprising is the difference in respect to hours on strike: 74% of time away is attributed to civil servants. On average, a public servant strike lasts 172 hours, compared to only 46 in the private sector.

As an example, in 2012, there was a strike of federal university professors that lasted 120 days. At the time of writing, there was a public school teacher strike in Rio de Janeiro that had lasted for over 60 days. These are not isolated cases, but a simple fact of daily life in the many areas of public service.

Consequently, the state weakens and is incapable of imposing sanctions on striking civil servants, leaving little to do but attend the demands presented or see the popularity of government leaders fall during the time the servants are on strike and public services are discontinued. Even ex-President Luiz Inácio Lula da Silva, a former union leader, was exasperated at the excessive liberty of strikes in the public sector. He stated in an interview:

What is not possible, what no Brazilian can accept, is that someone spends 90 days on strike and gets paid for the days off. It then ceases to be a strike and becomes a vacation (Guerreiro and Zimmermann, 2007).

Parallel to this phenomenon is another characteristic of the new constitutional order. It granted political power to civil servants in the form of financial autonomy for the Judicial and Legislative Branches and the Public Attorney's Office. To ensure that the autonomy of these institutions would not be threatened by the Executive Branch by means of funding rationing, the constitution gave them administrative and financial autonomy. Article 168 of the Constitution prohibits the curtailment of those institutions' expenses, while other devices give them the liberty to determine the total amount of their own budgets.

This autonomy was used, in the best rent-seeking style, to raise salaries in those public institutions. Political and administrative leaders in the Legislative and Judiciary branch, as well as in the Public Attorney's Office, are able to increase their institutional budget (and their own salaries) year after year. As consequence, some careers in the Executive Branch, which are well organized and work in strategic services (such as the revenue service or public security officials), take advantage of their strength and demand salary parity with the financially autonomous Branches. (Regarding this point, see Mendes, 2006.)

In Figure 5.2, one can see that in the initial years of the series, the Legislative, the Judiciary and Public Attorney's Office had a more intense payroll increase than the Executive Branch. Up to 2003, the Executive Branch payroll remained nearly constant in real terms, while the other branches had substantial increases. After 2003, two facts occurred. First, the Worker's Party (PT) gained control of the federal government, with the election of the President Lula da Silva. Since the PT has strong ties to the unions, Executive Branch employee unions took advantage of this situation to obtain pay raises (see Guerzoni Filho, 2006). Second, the country left a turbulent period of international financial crises (1997-2002) and entered the commodities boom, which increased the fiscal space of the public sector to pay higher salaries. With this, the demands for pay equality by the Executive Branch in relation to the other branches were met and expenses for the Executive began to rise more intensely.

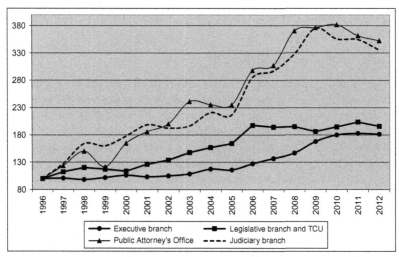

FIGURE 5.2   Index of Personnel Expense per Federal Public Service Branch (1996 = 100). *(Source: Ministry of Planning, Budget and Administration. Statistical Personnel Bulletin. Several numbers. Prepared by the author.)*

TABLE 5.6 Expenses with Personnel in the Federal Government, States and Municipalities 2001 vs. 2011

	% of GDP		
	2001	*2011*	**Real Variation 2001-2011 (%)**
Federal	5.55	5.24	61
States	4.37	6.00	134
Municipalities	2.49	3.99	173
Total (A)	12.40	15.37	109
Tax Burden (B)	31.87	33.51	
(A)/(B)	39%	46%	

Sources: Ministry of Planning. Statistical Personnel Bulletin (several issues) and Brazil Federal Revenue. Deflator: IPCA. Prepared by the author.

Table 5.6 shows the great importance of personnel expense in aggregated public finances. Between 2001 and 2011, spending with federal employees grew 61% in real terms, almost the same as GDP growth. Expenses in states and municipalities grew at a much greater rate. (In Section 5.10, considerations will be made regarding the motives for rapid expansion in personnel expenses in the states and municipalities.) Considering the expense of the three levels of government, we see that expenses for personnel more than doubled in real terms, representing the equivalent of 46% of total tax revenues in 2011.[2] This is, therefore, a high-cost expense that over time has been a determinant for the trajectory of high public expenditure.

Seeking rent in the legal details

Some episodes in recent years show the ability of civil servants to exploit legal rules in their favor, resorting to their intimacy with power and the strength of their unions. The first of these episodes regards the transformation of employees hired under the Consolidation of Labor Laws (*Consolidação das Leis do Trabalho* – CLT) – a typical private sector contract – into government civil servants covered by the so-called "Unified Judicial Regime" (*Regime Jurídico Único* – RJU) – the law that governs civil servant work contracts and guarantees them many benefits not provided to workers in the private sector. Changing from a CLT contract to a RJU contract brings a lot of gains, such as job tenure, high salaries and better retirement pensions.

---

2. Attention is called to the fact that one cannot add the values of Tables 4.2, 4.5 and 5.3 with those shown in Table 5.6, since the expenses with health and education include expenses with personnel in their respective areas.

This transformation allowed approximately 550,000 employees, hired without taking a directed civil service exam and, therefore, had no job security, to receive all the advantages inherent to their new situation. (The description to follow is based on Guerzoni Filho, 2000.)

The new Constitution imposed conditions for the transfer of CLT employees to the RJU regime. Those who had not entered public service by means of a directed civil servant exam could only be transferred if they had been actively employed for at least 5 continuous years before the approval of the new Constitution (Article 37, Clause II, of the Constitution and Article 19 of the Transitory Constitutional Dispositions Act (*Ato das Disposições Constitucionais Transitórias*).

Law 8.112, of 1990, which created the RJU, however, simply ignored the requirements set forth in the Constitution and determined the immediate transfer of all CLT employees to the RJU regime, even those who had been hired on the eve the law was passed. From one day to the next, 550,000 federal employees came to enjoy the benefits of job tenure and, especially, public retirement benefits, expanding the actuarial imbalance of civil servant retirement system. There was a boom in retirements soon after the approval of the new law. In 1991 there were 542,000 retired federal civil servants. This number went up to 793,000 in 1994, an increase of 46% in only 3 years, thanks to the inclusion of ex-CLT employees in the RJU system (Brazil Ministry of Social Security and Social Assistance, 2002). People who had not contributed to civil servant retirement (they only paid into private sector retirement at a rate well below that paid by civil servants) were now eligible to receive a pension equivalent to 100% of their last salary.

Discussion of Law 8.112 of 1990 in Congress was obviously of great interest to CLT civil servants. The Collor government (1989-1992) tried to block the passage of the bill, which had been sent to the Chamber of Deputies by the previous president (José Sarney), but without success. Even presidential vetoes to some parts of the law were overturned by Congress.

A similar story later occurred with the employees of the Central Bank. In 1996, they were transferred from CLT job contracts to RJU contracts. Migrating to the new system, where they would begin to receive full retirement and pensions paid by the Treasury, Central Bank employees were refunded all they had paid into their private retirement fund. A prudent financial decision would be for the Central Bank private retirement fund to pay the Treasury the amount accumulated in each employee account in order to fund future pension payments. However, there was no reckoning between the pension fund and the Treasury. All the money was refunded to Central Bank employees. They simply gained a "free" retirement pension, paying contributions to the Treasury only when they started their new job contract under RJU law. Those who were close to their retirement date paid almost nothing.

The decision was made by the pension fund (CENTRUS) leadership, which was composed almost entirely of Central Bank employees, direct beneficiaries of the awkward decision. The amount of money received by each employee was so large that a car dealer opened a showroom in front of the Central Bank building offering luxury models to the lucky civil servants.

It is also worth mentioning the episode in the 1990s when, in order to reduce the size of government, the Collor administration (1990-1992) decided to sell about 20,760 properties, most of them apartments leased to civil servants. (Number of properties placed for sale obtained from the *Correio Braziliense* 1990.)

There is nothing abnormal about the government selling assets it deems unnecessary for its use. To do this, a bidding process should be opened and the property sold in auction to the highest bidder. The legislation (Law 8.025, of 1990, Article 6), however, included one small detail: the property had to be sold to its current resident. Whoever, by a stroke of luck, was living in one of these apartments in 1990 was privileged to buy it.

Even though the law determined that they should be sold at current market prices, in practice the prices, defined by an evaluation done by the *Caixa Econômica Federal* (a bank controlled by the Federal Government), and payment conditions were quite favorable to the civil servants.

Payment was financed in a 25-year mortgage. It is known that inflationary spikes promote increases in the real values of real-estate assets because they represent a safe harbor for the owner's personal worth. In the long term, civil servants that had bought apartments from the government obtained large capital gains.

Despite of the fact that the sale was a real bargain for civil servants, organized groups were formed to lobby for additional subsidies. As usual, they argued that it was a question of "social justice." Those groups, (the "Movement for the Sale of Government Employee Housing" and its dissident, the "Movement to Mobilize the Purchase of Government Employee Housing"), gained ample support among congressmen.

One dissident voice in Congress stated the obvious, but was ignored:

> *The jurist and Senator José Paulo Bisol stated yesterday that he intended to file a case in the Federal Supreme Court requesting the annulment of the sale of government apartments on the basis of unconstitutionality.*
>
> *Bisol said, however, that he did not believe in the "impartiality" of the Supreme Court, being that its ministers, as reported in the Folha [a newspaper], had signed intent to purchase documents for the apartments where they reside. "The Court runs the risk of corruption," the Senator stated.*
>
> *According to Bisol, it is unconstitutional to give sale preference to those who reside in the property, which would be a violation of the principle of equality before the law. The sale should be public and available to all interested. The illegality, according to the Senator, is the "privilege" conceded to civil servants residing in the property. (Dimenstein, 1990)*

Another interesting episode occurred in 2003, when an employee in the Federal Court of Audits requested acknowledgement of the time they had worked for the postal service (a public company that contracts its employees under the CLT job contract), as time of service in the Court of Audits, with all legal effects (including retirement). The Court of Audits granted his request (Acórdão (Agreement) 1.871 of 2003). As a postal service employee, the employee had contributed to a private sector retirement program and to the postal-service pension fund, and not the civil servant retirement, which is a much higher contribution. Having his time of service recognized, the Court of Audits employee could consider the years worked before entering the civil service in the calculation of his full retirement, being able to retire early and to receive a higher pension, to which he had not fully contributed.

This decision was immediately extended to all Court of Audits employees that were in the same position and unleashed a wave of similar requests in the entire federal administration. Once more, costs were paid by society.

It is also worth mentioning a tangled story in which a bonus expressly revoked by law was resurrected thanks to the ability of high bureaucracy to produce creative interpretations of legal texts.

Until 1997, civil servants that held positions of leadership had the right to receive a yearly bonus of one-fifth of the amount received as gratification in addition to salary. This pay bonus was expressly revoked by Law 9.257 of 1997, which prohibited payment of fifths to newly occupied leadership positions, while maintaining those already being received.

Later, the legal devices that had been revoked were mistakenly cited in other legislation that sought to regulate pending situations relative to the already extinct fifths. The simple fact of the revoked devices being mentioned in laws opened loopholes for the creative interpretation that they were again considered legal: a resurrection of a revoked privilege! (These laws were Law 9.624, of 1998, Article 3, and Provisional Measure 2.225-45, of 2001, Article 3.)

According to this interpretation, the bonus that had been extinct since December 1997 had been resurrected during the period between April 1998 and September 2001, ending from that time forward. This not only allowed servants the right to increase their pay for leadership functions exercised during such period, but to receive back pay in reference to this gratification.

The procedure began in the courts, more specifically the Superior Labor Court (TST) and was, according to Hugo Cavalcanti, President of the National Association of Labor Court Magistrates at that time, "a judicial invention constructed by the high bureaucracy of the TST [Supreme Labor Court] to benefit a privileged group" (Folha de São Paulo, 2002). The interpretation quickly spread to other branches of the courts.

Due to articles published in the press, the Public Prosecutor's Office filed a suit with the Federal Court of Audits requesting the termination of payments and to prohibit this type of creative interpretation. After being considered for 2 years by the Court of Audits, during which time several unions came on as interested parties requesting approval of the interpretation, the

Court of Audits decided in favor of the legality of the payments (Acórdão (Agreement) 2.248, of 2005 – TCU/Plenário).[3]

These stories have many interesting elements: the ability of public bureaucracy to seek rents and exploit the labyrinths of the law in search of interpretations that allow pay raises; the active role of the unions, which use both traditional union tactics (strikes) and the contacts and influence of its members with decision makers; the conflict of interests by high bureaucrats who make decisions that affect their own salaries and assets; a greater predisposition by those areas of public administration that have autonomous administration and budgets protected against cuts (Legislative, Judiciary, Court of Audits and Public Attorney's Office) to embark on procedures to increase their salaries; and the support of the Court of Audits (TCU), which should defend public interests, to such procedures and to polemic questions that are in the private interests of its own employees.

5.7 LABOR UNIONS AND RESISTANCE TO LABOR LEGISLATION REFORM

A classic dilemma that exists in any capitalist economy deals with the degree of regulation in the labor market. Labor laws have as their objective the immediate improvement of the worker's quality of life, defining minimum pay, regulating the work day or week, establishing the right to vacation and restricting dismissals, etc. As nothing is free, the benefits given to employees can represent a loss to the unemployed or to those who, even though employed, are not protected by legislation (informal sector). Labor laws represent costs to companies, which in turn react to the laws by reducing the amount of labor hired, substituting manual labor with automation, contracting illegally, etc.

Balance is therefore necessary: labor legislation that is not so liberal as to demean worker dignity, but not so strict as to negatively affect employment or stimulate informal work contracts. Protectionist labor legislation privileges unionized workers and those in better companies (able to abide by the legislation) in detriment to all others.

As stated by Heckman and Pagés in an article on Latin American labor legislation:

> (...) as is often true in economics, benefits usually come at a cost: mandated benefits may reduce employment; job security provisions may protect some workers at the expense of others.(...) job security policies have a substantial impact on the

---

3. The branches and departments with budgetary autonomy (Legislative, Judiciary, Public Prosecutor's Office and the Court of Audits) decided to pay the back wages and raised civil servant salaries in accordance with the new benefit. A judicial dispute blocked some of these payments. The Executive Branch refused to concede. It is possible that, in the future, outstanding payments will be made following a judicial final decision.

level and the distribution of employment in Latin America. (...) While the benefits to recipients are well-documented, the costs are often unintended and less well understood (...) Thus, while the evidence suggests that regulations promoting job security reduce covered workers exit rates out of employment, it also indicates that demand curves are downward sloping, that regulation reduces aggregate employment and that the greatest adverse impact of regulation is on youth and groups marginal to the workforce. Insiders and entrenched workers gain from regulation but outsiders suffer. As a consequence, job security regulations reduce employment and promote inequality across workers (Heckman and Pagés, 2000, pp. 1-2).

Similarly, Di Tella and MacCulloch, considering the case of OECD countries, conclude that "increasing the flexibility of the labor market increases both the employment rate and the rate of participation in the labor force (...) There is also some evidence that more flexibility leads to lower unemployment rates and to lower rates of long-term unemployment" (Di Tella and MacCulloch, 2005, p. 1225).

It deals with, therefore, privileging middle-income workers in detriment to those with less income, those less organized or those less qualified. Resistance to labor reform (which occurs anywhere in the world) can be seen as a type of Cell C case, as seen in Figure 5.1: unionized labor (potential loser in a reform) resists legal changes while potential winners are demobilized and do not know the benefits they would enjoy.

In Brazil, the 1988 Constitution was extremely benevolent with laborers included in the protective system, broadening such protection as illustrated in Figure 5.3.

Thus, in 1988 on the eve of the fall of the Berlin Wall and worldwide economic globalization and liberalization, Brazil established high-cost, anticompetitive labor legislation. According to what was shown in Chapter 1 (Stylized Fact 9), Brazilian labor law causes a company that hires an employee, and that obeys all the legal rules, to pay almost double the amount of salary, which is proportionately one of the highest in the world.

Benefit	Before Constitution	After Constitution
Maximum weekly work hours	48 hours	44 hours
Maximum continuous daily work hours	8 hours	6 hours
Minimum overtime pay	1.2 times normal hourly wage	1.5 times normal hourly wage
Additional pay for vacation period	1 monthly wage	4/3 monthly wage
Maternity leave	3 months	4 months
Fine for unjustified dismissal	10% of FGTS	40% of FGTS
Paternity leave	none	5 days

FIGURE 5.3 Changes in Labor Benefits Introduced by the 1988 Constitution. *(Source: Barros and Corseuil 2001. Note: see Federal Constitution, Article 7. Prepared by the author.)*

Before Constitution	After Constitution
Ministry of Labor can intervene in unions and remove leadership.	Ministry of Labor intervention in unions not permitted.
Every union must be registered and approved by the Ministry of Labor.	Union registration and approval by the Ministry of Labor not required
Nationalized union representation only permitted in special cases.	Nationalized unions permitted
Union administration elected by a 2/3 minimum quorum of members in first vote, 1/3 votes in second vote and 2/5 in third. If a minimum quorum not achieved, the Ministry of Labor could choose the administration and call for new elections.	Unions establish own election rules
Unions represent only one professional category	Unions can represent many categories
The decision to strike required a 2/3 quorum of votes in first round and 1/3 quorum in second round for approval.	Unions free to define criteria to decide and to strike
In case a strike was called, the employer was to receive a 5-day advance notice.	In case of strike, 48-hour advance notice is required
Strikes prohibited in essential areas (power, gas, hospital and funeral services, for example) as well as the public sector.	All sectors may strike. Only minimum provision of services is required in essential sectors.

FIGURE 5.4   Changes in Unions Rights and Restrictions Introduced by 1988 Constitution. *(Source: Barros and Corseuil 2001. Note: see Federal Constitution, Articles 8 and 9. Prepared by author.)*

It happens that, parallel to the increase in labor rights, the new Constitution also increased the power of unions to resist future legislative reforms. Figure 5.4 describes this increase in power:

It is not about advocating in favor of the restrictive rules imposed during the dictatorship. It is necessary, however, to recognize that the increase of union power, including that of the incorporation of civil servants (See Section 5.6), raised the ability of "insider" workers to bar policies that go against their interests, but that would be favorable to the "outsiders" and to economic growth.

It is interesting to note that, even though the unions have become independent of the state in terms of regulation, their financial dependence on the Treasury has been maintained. The so-called "union tax," instituted by law in the 1940s, survived the new Constitution. Payment of this contribution (supported by Article 8, Clause IV, of the Constitution) is compulsory for employees and employers, independently, whether they are unionized or not. The collection goes to the Ministry of Labor and is distributed to unions, their federations and confederations.

This tax, on one side, strengthens the political power of the unions since they have a guaranteed source of income. They do not need to provide services or be efficient to attract members. All workers (and companies) are required to contribute to finance the unions. On the other side, it generates typical rent-seeking incentives because it is a good business opportunity to create a union in order to receive public funds, independently of the ability to provide services or representation.

Instead of being reformed, this system has become more entrenched. In 2008, for example, a law was approved to formally recognize the national union federations as part of the union system, giving them the right to receive 10% of the total union tax (Law 11.648, of 2008).

The unions also have financial ties to the state by means of worker training programs, funded by the Worker Support Fund (*Fundo de Amparo ao Trabalhador* – FAT). Such training programs have been a source of successive embezzlement scandals involving inexistent training programs.

The social costs of an excessively controlled labor market include a large and expensive labor court charged with mediating the labor relations written in the Constitution. With such explicit labor rights in the Constitution, there is little margin to negotiate between employers and employees and even small conflicts end up in court. (Regarding labor court institutional expansion and costs, see Mendes, 2006.) The high number of restrictions and details contained in labor law stimulates litigation, with thousands of labor suits filed every year. According to federal budget data, in 2012, the Labor Court consumed R$13.6 billion (about US$6.5 billion) (Brazil Federal Senate, 2013).

If the labor market was less regulated, one would certainly not see the impressive number of 3.9 million new lawsuits annually. However, this would deprive 44,000.5 civil servants of their employment in the Regional Labor Tribunals scattered around the country, not counting the lawyers that work in the area and those that work in the labor unions and confederations (court numbers (*Justiça em Números*) (http://www.cnj.jus.br).

It's no wonder that liberalizing reforms in labor relations hardly ever make it onto the political agenda, for there are many interests that are threatened in an environment characterized by endless rent-seeking opportunities. Changes in labor legislation have been made with the intention of reinforcing regulation (such as in the Domestic Workers Constitutional Amendment mentioned in the introduction to Chapter 4), and not aiming to reduce regulation.

5.8 INCOME-TAX EXEMPTIONS

An analysis of bills before Congress that propose exemptions or reductions in personal income tax (*Imposto de Renda da Pessoa Física* – IRPF) is an interesting way to see how the demand of the middle- and upper-income groups are attended by the Brazilian political system. This is because the IRPF almost exclusively falls on the more rich. Figure 5.5, based on estimates provided by

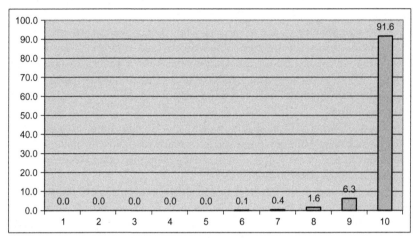

FIGURE 5.5 Incidence of Personal Income Tax by Income Decile (2009). *(Source: Siqueira et al., 2012.)*

Siqueira and co-authors show that no less than 91.6% of all personal income-tax revenue is paid by the wealthiest 10% of the population (Siqueira et al., 2012). The poorer 60% do not pay this tax, be it because the minimum taxable income is high or due to simple tax evasion by those who work in the informal market.

Therefore, the IRPF is a highly progressive tax. This means that any exemption or reduction proposal will especially benefit the wealthiest 10% of the population.

Regardless of this, the National Congress is swamped with bills that propose the reduction of personal income tax, be it in a generalized way for all taxpayers, or for specific groups. Table 5.7 shows that in a period of less than 13 years (January 2001 to September 2013), 215 bills were put before Congress with this objective, most of them dealing with demands by specific groups.

Almost a quarter of the proposals had the goal of giving some benefit to people with chronic diseases or physical disabilities. Such is the case with a bill that intends to "exempt those with albinism from paying income tax on retirement income received" (PLS 245/2012). This bill does nothing more than add this disability to a long list of others that already guarantee partially or total exemption from paying income tax (Parkinson's, multiple sclerosis, neoplasty, leprosy and others). The argument, as in other cases, is that treatment is costly.

Notice, however, that this law does not help *all* those with the disease, but only those with high income (those who pay income tax). Those who are poor are not benefitted and continue to wait for aid from the public health system.

Another type of project that is quite common (10% of the total included in Table 5.7) is that which either increases values or extends the term of a legislation that allows those who employ domestic workers to reduce the amount of income tax they pay, in order to compensate them for employer contributions to the social security of their domestic workers. This type of project provides

TABLE 5.7 Bills Put Before Congress between January 2011 and November 2013 to Concede Personal Income Tax (IRPF) Benefits

	Amount	% of Total
TOTAL	215	100
Originate in the Executive branch	4	2
Originate in the Legislative branch	211	98
Benefitted Groups		
Pacients	51	24
Household Employers/Employees	22	10
Elderly	19	9

Source: Senate and Chamber of Deputies. Prepared by the author.

a high political return. On one side it pleases the middle- and upper-income classes that employ domestic workers. On the other, it stimulates the formal employment of a mass of domestic employees estimated at 7.2 million, a considerable number of votes (estimate given by the International Labour Organization).

Many times there are bills that also benefit the elderly. Consistent with what was presented in Section 5.4, which showed how politicians were attracted to this group, one notices a considerable number of bills similar to PLS 76/2011, which exempts taxpayers over 60 from paying income tax. There does not seem to be any logical justification to exempt an upper-income person from paying income tax when reaching a certain age. The tax is on income, not age! As a matter of fact, as seen in Figure 5.5, the poor of all ages are exempt from paying personal income tax in Brazil.

There are other interesting cases that allow discounts on personal income tax for items common to those in the upper-income bracket, such as payments for nutritionists, gym memberships and auto insurance (e.g., PL 935/2011; PL 1.717/2011; PL 5.087/2013; PL 5.195/2013). Also common are those projects that seek to benefit workers, conceding income-tax exemptions for some instances of extra payments, such as shared profits or additional payment for vacation periods (e.g., PL 1.186/2011; PL 2.581/2011; PLS 266/2012). Some specific professions are courted with tax-benefit proposals, such as the case of the bill that proposes that teachers not pay income tax (e.g., PLS 445/2012 and PL 6.167/2013) or another that reduces the base to calculate taxes paid by taxi drivers (e.g., PL 4.842/2012).

It is true that a great part of these bills will never become law, either being rejected by Congress or vetoed by the President. But, year after year, some of them are approved. Since the exemptions and benefits are conceded, for the most part, without expiration, the accumulation of tax exemptions has a significant impact on Treasury finances. (According to the Federal Revenue Service, exemptions from income tax in 2013 due to concessions made to attend public policy objectives, the so-called "tax expenditures," come to no less than R$218.2 billion (about US$95 billion), the equivalent of 4.5% of GDP.)

5.9   18 GREAT FARM DEBT RENEGOTIATIONS IN 19 YEARS

An interesting coalition case (occasional, non-intentional and unplanned) between the rich, poor and middle classes, with the goal of extracting rent from the National Treasury, is in the form of farm debt renegotiation. Small, medium and large farms are constantly benefited by the renegotiation of loans taken from banks (especially state banks) backed by public resources. These renegotiations are made under favorable conditions, are heavily subsidized and forgive a significant portion of the debt. The cost is absorbed by the National Treasury or by public funds that, sooner or later, are refunded by the Treasury. Between 1995 and 2013, there were no less than 16 laws and 2 resolutions by the National Monetary Council (a department that provides monetary policy directives and defines the rules for Central Bank operation), for a total of 18 rounds of socializing private costs in 19 years. That is almost one per year!

Fernando Lagares Távora presents a detailed description of each of these renegotiations (Távora, 2014). From reading his study, one notices that there is an oft-repeated script. The first step is the concession of credit to agricultural businesses of all sizes, from the small family farm to large-scale projects, with funding backed by the Treasury. This credit is distributed by the public and private banking network, mostly through the Bank of Brazil, whose controlling share belongs to the federal government.

Viability studies, even though done, seem to be insufficient to avoid financing unprofitable or high-risk crops. The lender does not adequately evaluate if the agricultural enterprise requesting financing would employ the funds in an economically viable activity, planting the correct crop, on an adequate scale, or using efficient production methods, much less evaluate the climactic risks where the rural property is located. Bad weather conditions during one growing season (for example, a drought) are all that are needed for certain loss, especially for small farmers who have fewer modern instruments (such as irrigation) to deal with such adverse scenarios.

When a majority of low-income farmers who depend on their crops to sustain themselves enter in default, a social problem is created. The federal government, the final "guarantor," is called upon to renegotiate the debt to prevent this poor population from starving.

To make the debt forgiveness possible, a bill by the Executive Branch must be approved by Congress to permit renegotiation. Since the legislature has a strong group of representatives that defend the interests of large producers, Congress amends the bill submitted in favor of low-income farmers to include large producers as well. The formula for state loss is relatively simple: when all goes well in planting and harvesting, the farmers pocket the profit; when there is bad weather or other negative effects, the losses are paid by the Treasury and, therefore, passed on to the taxpayer.

The study by Távora presents clear and repeated examples of this logic. Take the case of the 2013 debt renegotiation. The original bill submitted to Congress covered debts of up to R$35,000 (about US$15,000), restricted to financing given to small family farms located in areas of extreme poverty where a state of emergency or public calamity had been declared due to drought. Debate in Congress, however, increased the group of beneficiaries on two levels. First, it removed a restriction that the bailout only be applied to poor drought areas. Second, it expanded the debt ceiling to R$100,000 (about US$43,000).

With these changes, the cost of financial aid multiplied four times over, going from R$870 million (about US$380 million) to R$3.5 billion (about US$1.5 billion). Even though the debt included in the bailout by Congress (those between R$35,000 and R$100,000) represented only 2% of the contracts, it was equal to 25% of the outstanding debt. Therefore, a significant part of the renegotiated benefits were taken by a small group of big debtors (Távora, 2014, pp. 94-95).

Some of the renegotiations are quite complex and non-transparent, many times reflecting parameters from previous negotiations, making it impossible to obtain an approximate evaluation of the amounts involved. The author compiled estimated costs from eight operations where such calculation was possible. Figure 5.6 shows the relative values compared to GDP for their respective years.

The values presented in Figure 5.6 are far from being the total cost, since there are 10 other renegotiations whose costs could not be estimated. These values are sufficiently large to have had a fiscal impact and affect macroeconomic management.

The discounts in the debt balance made in renegotiations are not merely exemptions from late fees or other penalties resultant from non-payment. They

Renegotiation Bill	% of GDP
Law 9138/1995	1.64
Resolution CMN 2.471/1998	0.29
Resolution CMN 2.666/1999	0.14
Law 10177/2001	0.88
Law 11322/2006	0.12
Law 11755/2008	2.47
Law 12249/2010	0.07
Law 12844/2013	0.06

FIGURE 5.6 Some Agriculture Renegotiation Bills and their Estimated Cost to the Federal Treasury. *(Source: Távora, 2014.)*

are real debt forgiveness, many times with the debt being reduced to less than half the original amount. For example, in the 2013 renegotiation presented above, the debt forgiven, in some cases, was no less than 85% of the outstanding amount.

It would be expected that this high frequency of renegotiations would cause the agents involved to include future renegotiations in their estimates, causing them to adopt strategic behavior that has negative collective results.

First, the poor, small farmer, given his very low capital, is extremely dependent on credit. The most adequate would be to offer them direct public subsidies and removing them from the credit market. Once in the credit market, they become a "trigger" for renegotiations. When there are a large number of small farmers in trouble, new pressure for renegotiation is always applied.

The financial agent that distributes subsidized credit has no incentive to carefully evaluate those who will receive credit, much less demand quality guarantees. First, because the lender, in most cases, is a mere distributor of public resources: if there is default, the loss will be to the government. Second, because they are paid based on a percentage of the total lent, they are prompted to lend as much as possible.

The large farmer sees the failure of the small farmer as an opportunity to catch a ride and, with the support of his representatives in Congress, transfer a part of his costs to the Treasury.

Even though the creation of a rural insurance market has been exhaustively debated in Congress, the many beneficiaries of public bailouts have not shown much interest in creating it or in developing policies governing agro-climactic zoning and the regulation of rural credit to reduce the need for government bailouts. After all, if credit insurance were created, with premiums paid by the insured, the large farmers with the financial ability to be covered by the scheme would not be eligible to receive debt forgiveness and be required to assume at least part of the risk of their operations.

From the public policy point of view, it is not easy to structure legislation on which to base a rural insurance system. A central problem is the difficulty in diversifying risk (a large drought, for example, would affect a large portion of the insured). Furthermore, there is the need to think of a specific insurance model for small farmers and a way to relieve the effects of high administrative costs. Therefore, it is not easy to create insurance with economically viable premiums that producers will voluntarily participate in.

Furthermore, maintaining the status quo is not all bad for the political class. After all, when they pressure for new renegotiations and debt forgiveness, the parliamentarians who support the big and medium-sized famers make their campaign financing and re-election easier.

Besides this, given that new renegotiations are always possible and that new payment conditions are always more favorable than the previous ones, the farmers no sooner renegotiate their debt than they again enter into default and force a second round of renegotiations.

The loss of resources to the economy is not only in the way of costs assumed by the Treasury. There is also the loss of efficiency by not restricting the planting of crops in inappropriate locales. Furthermore, what is spent on these repeated financial bailouts could be alternatively invested in storage and transportation infrastructure, increasing rural productivity.

There is, therefore, a confluence of interest between the small, medium and large farmers, financial agents and political groups in Congress that results in a transfer of costs to the Treasury and, consequently, to all of society.

5.10 THE WIDESPREAD DISTRIBUTIVE CONFLICT

Sections 5.3 to 5.9 illustrate how groups seek privileges and resist reforms, forcing society as a whole to pay the fiscal costs and suffer negative consequences such as economic inefficiency and low growth. Such examples are only a small fraction of a much greater set of redistribution and rent-seeking behavior that has spread like a plague throughout Brazilian society. Many other cases could be presented, such as the following.

A famous case is that of the increase in number of municipalities. In 1980, Brazil had 3991 municipal governments, while 20 years later, in 2000, there were 5507, a growth of 38% (IBGE, 2011). This would not have been a problem if the creation of new administrative units had occurred due to the economic and population expansion of certain areas, which demanded the creation of new government bodies. With intense economic activity and a growing population, these new towns would have sufficient financial revenue to pay their administrative costs as well as have a sufficiently large population to justify building hospitals, schools and other local public services.

Actually, this was not the case. Most new municipalities had less than 10,000 inhabitants. This was due to a simple reason: to be eligible to receive federal funds, by means of transfers through the Municipalities Participation Fund (*Fundo de Participação dos Municípios* – FPM). This Fund, established by the Constitution, transfers part of some federal taxes to municipalities. The sharing criteria, however, is biased in favor of small municipalities. As such, if a town of 15,000 divides into 3 of 5000, these three new cities, together, would come to receive 50% more than originally. Therefore, it is profitable to fraction a large municipality into many small ones in order to obtain more transfers from the federal government.

This *rentist* motivation, to receive more federal funds, subverts the logic of creating new towns. Instead of creating cities because the local private economy is prospering and attracting more people, economically stagnant towns are founded as a form to receive more federal resources. This money, instead of supporting the expansion of public infrastructure in areas of population growth, is used to pay the salaries of mayors, aldermen and employees, leaving very little to provide services. (Regarding this theme, see Mendes et al., 2008; Gasparini and Cossio, 2006.)

Also very interesting is the fact that the voluminous income some municipal governments receive from royalties paid for oil extraction on the continental platform contiguous to their territories is not used to pay for public services to their constituents. Caselli and Michaels show that the amount of expenses registered in the books of towns that receive oil royalties is disproportionately large in relation to the expansion of public services offered to the population, while at the same time there is abundant evidence of government and civil servant corruption (Caselli and Michaels, 2009). In the same vein, another study shows that municipalities that receive oil royalties, on average, spend 50% more than other municipalities on their city council (mostly on salaries to councilmen and civil servants; Mendes, 2002).

In the National Congress, the rent-seeking behavior is also very strong. One of the main priorities of parliamentarians is to obtain federal funds for their home cities and states. This is done through the so-called "parliamentary amendments" to the budget. David Samuels, who has performed many studies on the Brazilian political system, shows how these amendments work (Samuels, 2001a and 2001b). On one side, the politician tells his constituents that he is bringing a federal project to his electoral district. On the other, such a project, in general an investment in public works such as urbanization, school building, etc., is executed by a company that promises to contribute to the politician's next campaign fund. With a certain frequency, these amendments lead to corruption, with the embezzlement of public money.

Another interesting case is the Manaus Free Zone (*Zona Franca de Manaus* – ZFM). It was established in 1967 by means of tax incentives and property sales to industries at low prices. The plan was for the tax incentives to last until 1997. The idea of the ZFM was to integrate the distant Amazon region into the national economy, creating a technological center capable of generating high-qualification employment and giving fiscal and economic autonomy to the region. Almost 40 years after its creation, and several extensions of its financial benefits,[4] the ZFM still cannot stand alone without the incentives. The cost of such incentives is high (about R$18 billion in 2011 or about US$11 billion), the quality of the jobs created is low and the industries are basically assembly plants, with no real contribution to innovation (Miranda, 2013).

Summarizing, the rest of the country subsidizes the ZFM. It is a curious case in which a policy failure determines it survival. If the incentives were taken away, the ZFM would quickly become an economic void. Obviously, the local residents have good reasons to fight for the incentives, while the rest of the population is not sufficiently informed or organized against the cost imposed on it: a typical case of a threatened minority (Figure 5.1, Cell C). At the time of writing, Congress was about to approve a constitutional amendment that would extend tax incentives for the ZFM up to 2073.

---

4. The last promoted by Constitutional Amendment 42, of 2003, extended benefits until 2023.

Another type of common rent-seeking behavior is the appropriation of funds administered by public agency employees. For example, it is the responsibility of the *Banco da Amazônia* (Bank of Amazon, a federal state-owned bank) to manage federal funds allocated to the Amazon Development Fund (*Fundo de Desenvolvimento da Amazônia*) that offers subsidized credit for infrastructure investment and private business in the Amazon region. The Amazon Development Fund is 100% funded by the Federal Treasury.

According to data compiled in a study by Ricardo Miranda in 2009, the Bank of Amazon lent R$1.84 billion from the Amazon Development Fund, and appropriated, as service fees, R$572 million. In other words, the Bank of Amazon charged the Amazon Development Fund fees that represented no less than 31% of the total Fund disbursement. According to 2009 Bank of Amazon records, its payroll cost R$271 million. This means that administrative fees charged to the Fund were sufficient for 2 years' of bank payroll. Instead of being used to finance investments, a huge part of the Amazon Development Fund is being used to pay for Bank of Amazon administrative costs.

This high payment would be justifiable if the Bank of Amazon assumed operational risks, but, as stated on their website, the Amazon Development Fund is responsible for 97.5% and the Bank for only 2.5%! Similar mechanisms benefit the Bank of the Northeast (which is the financial agent for the Northeast Development Fund and the Northeast Constitutional Fund) and the Bank of Brazil (which manages the Mid-West Constitutional Fund) (Miranda, 2012).

In the same way, the *Caixa Econômica Federal* earns a high, risk-free income by administering the resources of the Time of Service Guarantee Fund (*Fundo de Garantia do Tempo de Serviço* – FGTS). The gains *Caixa* makes administering the FGTS are more than sufficient to cover its large payroll. Or rather, the institution does not need to be efficient and compete in the market with other banks since it has the privilege of a "captive market," which provides cheap funds and easy profits.[5]

Another interesting case is the federal government concession of roads to private companies beginning in 2007. The main electoral risk for this type of contract is the high toll charged. After all, this is a highly visible cost. Every time a driver goes through the toll booth, they must take money from their wallet and feel the agony of paying. To minimize the loss of popularity, the federal government decided to base bidding for road concessions on who would charge the cheapest toll.

The results couldn't have been better from the political point of view. In 2007, contracts were signed based on a toll of R$1.00 (about US$52 cents at 2007 average exchange rates). It so happens that this fee was not enough to cover road management costs. To solve this problem, in a way little noticed by the electorate, the government conceded subsidized financing to the companies responsible for road management. That is, a visible benefit was provided to

---

5. The author is grateful to Marcos Kohler for calling attention to this point.

voters – cheap tolls – and the cost – subsidized credit – was passed on (in a hidden way) to all taxpayers (including those who would never use the subsidized roads). (Regarding road concession in Brazil, see Velloso et al., 2012.)

In an attempt to create electoral impact, in 2013 the federal government announced a reduction of about 20% in the price of electrical power to consumers. This was widely publicized, and even supported with an official speech by the President of the Republic on radio and TV. The cost of this measure, duly omitted in all the publicity, was divided between: (a) taxpayers in general (by means of the National Treasury to cover the contractual imbalance for companies in the electric sector), (b) the power-generating companies, which, under threat of not renewing their contracts, were required to reduce rates charged for their power, a typical case of judicial uncertainty (Chapter 1, Stylized Fact 8). Once more, politicians pleased voters with explicit benefits, while hiding the costs.

5.11   CONCLUSIONS

Behind the many examples provided in this chapter there is one common feature: they result in private benefits for specific groups and hidden costs dispersed among society. When benefits bring votes to the politicians that support them, they are explicitly shown off to society (job creation, "pork barrel" projects, cheap road toll, benefits to the elderly, etc.). While benefits that do not have social approval (subsidies to big companies, legal maneuvers to increase civil servant wages, etc.) they are hidden in off-the-budget operations.

Politicians, the bureaucracy and interest groups have learned this game well and play it masterfully. Be it the distribution by means of the "half fare," in the approval of the elderly or youth statues, or the concession of subsidized financing, the rule is to do it at "another's expense" or to "feather one's own nest."

Middle- and upper-income groups are the main beneficiaries of these mechanisms. The rich have always had access to financial benefits and the legal rules biased in their favor. They continued to have this privileged access after democratization (Chapter 3). The poor began receiving social aid, healthcare and education with democratization (Chapter 4). The middle-income groups, which had some privileges before democratization, did not only maintain such privileges, but benefitted from the new political scene to increase them.

These three redistributive movements taken together (the rich, the poor and some middle-income groups) generate innumerable public policies directed toward creating privileges and market protection mechanisms that are mutually contradictory, high-cost and that significantly hinder the incentive to invest, economic productivity and, therefore, long-term growth. The result is the low growth with dissipative redistribution model.

The Brazilian state has not developed its ability to be a traditional public services provider (public security; protection of liberty and of contracts; provide public services such as transportation, sanitation or urbanization), and has become, primarily, a mediator for income transfer: taxing some to give to others.

Sometimes in a Robin Hood style: taking from the rich to give to the poor, but sometimes in reverse, and most of the time taking from everybody to give to specific (poor, rich or middle-income) groups.

According to statistics presented by economists Raul Velloso and Cláudio Hamilton to the Senate Economic Committee (*Comissão de Assuntos Econômicos do Senado*), no less than 49.2 million people receive income financed by public resources. This figure is equal to 26% of the Brazilian population. More than a quarter of the population has the government as a source of income in the form of civil servant salaries, payments to retirees, pensioners and social assistance program beneficiaries (Velloso and Hamilton, 2013).

As someone must finance this, the tax burden rises and society must pay the cost. Everyone struggles to earn more and pay less. The situation is so confusing that it is difficult to clearly identify who the winners and losers are. Take, for example, a low-skill worker employed in the informal sector. At first glance, this person could be considered a loser. After all, they are not covered by labor legislation, receive a low wage and have little perspective of moving up socially. Furthermore, they pay high indirect taxes built-into the prices of every good they consume. But, if they receive a cash transfer from the *Bolsa Família* program or have a relative who is beneficiary of rural retirement pension (without having contributed) or of BPC program, their situation improves. What more, they do not pay income tax or make contributions to social security.

At the other extreme, we have a business owner who earns rents from subsidized credit offered by public banks and protection against the competition of imported goods. But, at the same time, they pay a lot of tax, use a low-quality and high-cost public infrastructure and see the market for their products narrowed by bleak economic growth perspectives.

After all the income transfers promoted by the government and their negative effects on the economy it is hard to know who are the winners and losers.

Analyzing the mass demonstrations that arose in June 2013, Samuel Pessôa vividly describes this redistributive confusion:

> (...) *probably, many of those who took to the streets were the children or grandchildren of people who receive benevolent lifetime pensions paid by the government, for example, and others who receive and accumulate more than one social security benefit. Many were civil servants from the health sector whose request was to make their health career into a special career, such as in the judiciary (you can imagine the consequence of this measure to the public coffers). Others are probably the children of individuals who retired due to disability [and got a job in other company] or are receiving medical aid or unemployment benefits (several defrauded the program, that is, forced their dismissal in order to work informally and to receive a salary in addition to the benefits). Others, a few, probably have parents or grandparents who benefit from the program to repair damages by the Brazilian dictatorship (we know that the Brazilian dictatorship killed or tortured*

only a fraction of what Argentina or Chile did, but we spend many times over what they do, only as another example of how we prodigiously distribute individual lifelong benefits). (…) individuals who benefit from subsidized loans with lower rates that are paid for by other loans at higher rates (…) people who had a good tuition free education financed by taxes (…). In other words, we created an infinite amount of "half fares." (…) The problem is that, those many "half fares" introduce inefficiency into the system and reduce growth. (…) Each one sees the benefit they receive as of first importance. (…) Everyone wants to keep their half fare and eliminate all others (Pessôa, 2013).

In spite of the great dissipation of resources, the most poor still receive something. After all, as was shown in Chapter 2, poverty and inequality are going down, in part due to public programs. However, the fall in inequality and poverty could be much greater if there weren't so many privileges distributed among the rich and middle-income groups. (Siqueira and Nogueira, 2013 shows how government intervention reduces the Gini Index in a more intense way in OECD countries than in Brazil. In other words, the public policies in those countries are much more redistributive to the poor than the Brazilian.) As such, the price paid by the country (fiscal cost plus economic inefficiency) for a given distribution of income and a given reduction in poverty is much greater than it should be. The poor miss opportunities not only due to these "leaks" in distributive policy, but also because the lack of potential growth hinders new employment opportunities.

If the problem sharpens to the point that all feel they are losing due to low growth, the incentive for a new social contract should naturally arise where all benefits and privileges are eliminated. In this case, institutional reform would gain political support. Unfortunately, as shown in Section 5.2, this is a collective-action problem where, in a highly unequal society, uncertainty and risk aversion could lead to blocking reforms, even in situations where society as a whole is losing.

Another factor that makes dismantling the innumerous and conflicting redistributive policies difficult is the occasional coincidence of interests between the rich and poor. For example, the rural pensioner (poor) is afraid that a social security reform directed toward reducing benefits to the rich may splash over onto them. As a precaution, they oppose such reform. The same thing is true for free university education, which could be interpreted by poor families as a threat to free elementary education.

Associations and unions that represent middle- and upper-income groups use this confusion to package their interests. They use generic labels such as "free public education for all" or "protection for the retired elderly" to hide their intent to preserve privileges. The ideological demonization of the privatization of state companies speaks of "national interests and the defense of national capital," but actually seeks to preserve state-company-employee rents, who receive above average salaries and have little risk of dismissal.

The next chapter will analyze the possible long-term consequences of the low growth with dissipative distribution model.

REFERENCES

Addison, T., Rahman, A., 2001. Why is so Little Spent in Educating the Poor? United Nations University, WIDER. Discussion Paper 2001/29.

Afonso, L.E., 2005. Seguridade Social. In: Biderman, C., Arvate, P.R. (Eds.), Economia do Setor Público no Brasil. Elsevier-Campus.

Alston, L.J., et al., 2012. Changing Social Contracts: Beliefs and Dissipative Inclusion in Brazil. NBER Working Paper 18588.

Amaro, M.N., 2011. Terceira Reforma da Previdência: Até Quando Esperar? Núcleo de Estudos e Pesquisas do Senado Federal. Texto para Discussão n. 84, February. Available from, http://www12.senado.gov.br/publicacoes/estudos-legislativos/tipos-de-estudos/textos-para-discussao/td-84-terceira-reforma-da-previdencia-ate-quando-esperar.

Barbosa, A.L.H., Barbosa Filho, F.H., 2012. Diferencial de Salários entre os Setores Público e Privado no Brasil: um Modelo de Escolha Endógena. IPEA. Texto para Discussão 1713. Available from, http://www.ipea.gov.br/agencia/images/stories/PDFs/TDs/td_1713.pdf.

Barros, R.P., et al., 2009. Markets, the State and the Dynamics of Inequality: Brazil's Case Study. UNDP, Research for Public Policy Inclusive Development, ID-14-2009.

Belluzo, W., Neto, F.A., Pazello, E.T., 2005. Distribuição de Salários e o Diferencial Público-Privado no Brasil. *Revista Brasileira de Economia* 59 (4), 511–533.

Bender, S., Fernandes, R., 2006. Gastos Públicos com Pessoal: uma Análise de Emprego e Salário no Setor Público Brasileiro no Período 1992–2004. ANPEC. Available from, http://www.anpec.org.br/encontro_2006.htm#trabalhos.

Birdsall, N., James, E., 1990. Efficiency and Equity in Social Spending: How and Why Governments Misbehave. The World Bank. Country Department I, Latin America, WP 0274.

Brazil Federal Senate, 2013. Sistema Siga Brasil - Budget databank. [On Line]. Available from http://www12.senado.gov.br/orcamento/sigabrasil (accessed 21.03.14).

Brazil Ministry of Justice, 2004. Diagnóstico do Poder Judiciário. [On Line] . Available from http://portal.mj.gov.br/reforma/main.asp?View={597BC4FE-7844-402D-BC4B-06C93AF009F0} (accessed 14.02.2014).

Brazil Ministry of Planning, Budget and Management, 2013. Boletim Estatístico de Pessoal. [On Line] February 2014. Available from http://www.servidor.gov.br/index.asp?.index=82&ler=s1025 (accessed 23.04.14).

Brazil Ministry of Social Development and Hunger Alleviation, 2012. Relatório de Gestão 2011 - Secretaria Nacional de Renda de Cidadania.

Brazil Ministry of Social Security and Social Assistance, 2002. Livro Branco da Previdência Social.

Brazil Ministry of Work and Employment, 2013. Relação Anual de Informações Sociais 2012. [On Line]. Available from http://www.rais.gov.br/download.asp (accessed 15.03.13).

Brazil Presidency of the Republic, 2012. Relatório da Comissão para Definição da Classe Média no Brasil. Secretaria de Assuntos Estratégicos. Available from, http://www.sae.gov.br/vozesdaclassemedia/wp-content/uploads/Relat%C3%B3rio-Defini%C3%A7%C3%A3o-da-Classe-M%C3%A9dia-no-Brasil.pdf.

Caetano, M.A.R., 2006. Determinantes da Sustentabilidade e do Custo Previdenciário: Aspectos Conceituais e Comparações Internacionais. IPEA, Texto para Discussão n. 1226.

Caetano, M.A.R. (Ed.), 2008. Previdência Social no Brasil: Debates e Desafios. IPEA.

Caetano, M.A.R., 2011a. Por Que a Previdência Social Brasileira Gasta Tanto com o Pagamento de Pensões por Morte? *Brasil, Economia e Governo*. [Online] 1st August. Available from, http://www.brasil-economia-governo.org.br/2011/08/01/por-que-a-previdencia-social-brasileira-gasta-tanto-com-o-pagamento-de-pensoes-por-morte/.

Caetano, M.A.R., 2011b. Reformas Infraconstitucionais nas Previdências Privada e Pública: Possibilidades e Limites. In: Bacha, E.L., Schwartzman, S. (Eds.), Brasil: A Nova Agenda Social. Gen/LTC.

Caselli, F., Michaels, G., 2009. Do Oil Windfalls Improve Living Standards? Evidence from Brazil, NBER Working Paper Series w15550.

DIEESE, 2013. Balanço das Greves em 2012. DIEESE - *Estudos e Pesquisas*, n. 66, maio.

Dimenstein, G., 1990. Bisol diz que vai ao Supremo para Anular Venda de Imóveis Funcionais. *Folha de S. Paulo* 23 November 1990. Available from: Brazilian Federal Senate Library archive.

Di Tella, R., MacCulloch, R., 2005. The consequences of market flexibility: panel evidence based on survey data. *Eur. Econ. Rev.* 49, 1225–1259.

Fernandez, R., Rodrik, D., 1991. Resistance to Reform: Status Quo Bias in the Presence of Individual-Specific Uncertainty. *Am. Econ. Rev.* 81 (5), 1146–1155.

Ferreira, F.H.G., et al., 2013. Economic mobility and the rise of Latin American middle class. World Bank Latin American and Caribbean Studies, The World Bank.

Folha de São Paulo, 2002. Reajuste Disfarçado Chega a R$ 500 mi. [On Line]. Available from http://www1.folha.uol.com.br/fsp/brasil/fc1308200235.htm (accessed 22.05.13).

Gasparini, C.E., Cossio, F.A.B., 2006. Transferências Intergovernamentais. In: Mendes, M.J. (Ed.), Gasto público eficiente: 91 propostas para o desenvolvimento do Brasil. Topbooks/Instituto Fernand Braudel.

Giambiagi, F., Pinheiro, A.C., 2012. Além da Euforia: Riscos e Lacunas do Modelo Brasileiro de Desenvolvimento. Elsevier-Campus.

Guerreiro, G., Zimmermann, P., 2007. Lula Rejeita Terceiro Mandato, Chama Greve de 90 dias de Férias e Indica Queda de Juros. *Folha de São Paulo*. [On Line] 16 March 2007. Available from http://www1.folha.uol.com.br/folha/brasil/ult96u92417.shtml (accessed 15.03.14).

Guerzoni Filho, G., 2000. Análise da Lei n. 9.962, de 22 de fevereiro de 2000: a contratação de servidores públicos pela CLT. *Revista de Informação Legislativa* 37 (146), 25–53, Brasília.

Guerzoni Filho, G., 2006. Política de pessoal em um ambiente de economia estável. In: Mendes, M.J. (Ed.), Gasto público eficiente: 91 propostas para o desenvolvimento do Brasil. Topbooks/Instituto Fernand Braudel.

Guerzoni Filho, G., 2011. Observações sobre o Projeto de Lei n. 1.992, de 2007: o Regime de Previdência Complementar dos Servidores da União. Núcleo de Estudos e Pesquisas da Consultoria Legislativa. Texto para Discussão n. 106. Available from, http://www12.senado.gov.br/publicacoes/estudos-legislativos/tipos-de-estudos/textos-para-discussao/td-106-observacoes-sobre-o-projeto-de-lei-no-1.992-de-2007-o-regime-de-previdencia-complementar-dos-servidores-publicos-da-uniao.

Heckman, J.J., Pagés, C., 2000. The Cost of Job Security Regulation: Evidence from Latin American Labor Market, NBER Working Papers n. 7773.

IBGE, 2011. Evolução da Divisão Territorial do Brasil 1872-2010. [On Line]. Available from http://www.ibge.gov.br/home/presidencia/noticias/imprensa/ppts/00000006841812102011183809 11960.pdf (accessed 22.03.13).

Karabarbounis, L., 2011. One dollar, one vote. *Econ. J.* 121, 621–651, June.

Krueger, A., 1974. The Political Economy of the Rent-Seeking Society. *Am. Econ. Rev.* 64 (3), 291–303.

Lisboa, M.B., Latif, Z.A., 2013. Democracy and Growth in Brazil. INSPER Working Papers. Available from: http://www.insper.edu.br/working-papers/working-papers-2013/democracy-and-growth-in-brazil/.

Machado, M.A.A., 2010. Acesso a Medicamentos via Poder Judiciário no Estado de Minas Gerais. Universidade Federal de Minas Gerais. Faculdade de Farmácia. Available from, http://www.bibliotecadigital.ufmg.br/dspace/bitstream/handle/1843/LFSA-87UMKE/disserta__o_marina_machado_fev_2010.pdf?sequence=1.

Médici, A., 2011. Propostas para Melhorar a Cobertura, a Eficiência e a Qualidade no Setor Saúde. In: Bacha, E.L., Schwartzman, S. (Eds.), Brasil: A Nova Agenda Social. Gen/LTC.

Mendes, M.J., 2002. Descentralização Fiscal Baseada em Transferências e Captura de Recursos Públicos nos Municípios Brasileiros. Universidade de São Paulo. Departamento de Economia. Doctoral thesis.

Mendes, M.J., 2006. Despesa dos Poderes Autônomos: Legislativo, Judiciário e Ministério Público. In: Mendes, M.J. (Ed.), Gasto público eficiente: 91 propostas para o desenvolvimento do Brasil. Topbooks/Instituto Fernand Braudel.

Mendes, M.J., Miranda, R.B., Cosio, F.A.B., 2008. Transferências Intergovernamentais no Brasil: Diagnóstico e Proposta de Reforma. Núcleo de Estudos e Pesquisas da Consultoria Legislativa. Texto para Discussão n. 40. Available from, http://www12.senado.gov.br/publicacoes/estudos-legislativos/tipos-de-estudos/textos-para-discussao/td-40-transferencias-intergovernamentais-no-brasil-diagnostico-e-proposta-de-reforma.

Miranda, R.N., 2012. Nota Informativa sobre o Fundo Constitucional do Norte (FNO) e a Perspectiva de Desenvolvimento da Amazônia. Consultoria Legislativa do Senado Federal, Nota Informativa n. 1.764/2012.

Miranda, R.N., 2013. Zona Franca de Manaus: Desafios e Vulnerabilidades. Núcleo de Estudos e Pesquisas do Senado Federal – Texto para Discussão n. 126, Available from, http://www12.senado.gov.br/publicacoes/estudos-legislativos/tipos-de-estudos/textos-para-discussao/td-126-zona-franca-de-manaus-desafios-e-vulnerabilidades.

Monteiro, J.V., 2013. O ambiente institucional-constitucional da política de gasto público e das escolhas orçamentárias em geral. In: Rezende, F., Cunha, A. (Eds.), A Reforma Esquecida: Orçamento, Gestão Pública e Desenvolvimento. Fundação Getúlio Vargas.

Moriconi, G., 2008. Os Professores Públicos são Mal Remunerados nas Escolas Brasileiras? Uma Análise da Atratividade da Carreira do Magistério sob o Aspecto da Remuneração. Fundação Getúlio Vargas, São Paulo. Mestrado em Administração Pública e Governo.

Olson, M., 1965. The Logic of Collective Action: Public Goods and the Theory of Groups. Harvard University Press.

Pessôa, S.A., 2013. As manifestações de rua e o direito à meia-entrada. Simon Schwartzman's Blog. [Online] 7th July. Available from, http://www.schwartzman.org.br/sitesimon/?p=4545&lang=pt-br (accessed 01.07.14.).

Pinheiro, A.C., 2005. Magistrados, Judiciário e Economia no Brasil. In: Zylbersztajn, D., Sztajn, R. (Eds.), Direito e Economia: Análise Econômica do Direito e das Organizações. Elsevier-Campus.

Pinheiro, A.C., Giambiagi, F., 2006. Rompendo o marasmo: a retomada do desenvolvimento no Brasil. Elsevier-Campus.

Rajan, R., 2006. Competitive Rent Preservation, Reform Paralysis, and the Persistence of Underdevelopment. NBER Working Paper 12093.

Rangel, L.A., Sabóia, J.L., 2013. Criação da Previdência Complementar dos Servidores Federais: Motivações e Implicações na Taxa de Reposição das Futuras Aposentadorias. IPEA. Texto para Discussão n. 1.847. Available from, http://www.ipea.gov.br/portal/index.php?option=com_content&view=article&id=18997.

Robinson, J.A., 2008. The Political Economy of Redistributive Policies. UNDP – Research for Public Policy Inclusive Development, ID-09-2009. Available from, http://www.rrojasdatabank. info/09_RPPLAC_ID.pdf.

Romero, L.C.P., 2008. Judicialização das Políticas de Assistência Farmaceutica: O Caso do Distrito Federal. Núcleo de Estudos e Pesquisas do Senado Federal. Texto para Discussão n. 41. Available from, http://www12.senado.gov.br/publicacoes/estudos-legislativos/tipos-de-estudos/ textos-para-discussao/td-41-judicializacao-das-politicas-de-assistencia-farmaceutica-o-caso-do-distrito-federal.

Sabino, M.A.C., 2013. Quando o Judiciário Ultrapassa os seus Limites Constitucionais e Institucionais: o Caso da Saúde. In: Grinover, A.P., Watanabe, K. (Eds.), O Controle Jurisdicional de Políticas Públicas. second ed. GEN/Forense.

Sadek, M.T., 2013. Judiciário e Arena Pública: Um Olhar a Partir da Ciência Política. In: Grinover, A.P., Watanabe, K. (Eds.), O Controle Jurisdicional de Políticas Públicas. second ed. GEN/ Forense.

Samuels, D., 2001a. Money, elections and democracy in Brazil. Lat. Am. Polit. Soc. 43 (2), 27–48.

Samuels, D., 2001b. Does money matter? Campaign finance in newly democratic countries: theory and evidence from Brazil. Comp. Polit. 34, 23–42.

Santos Filho, H., Timm, L. (Eds.), 2010. Diagnóstico Sobre as Causas do Progressivo Aumento das Demandas Judiciais Cíveis no Brasil, em Especial Demandas Repetitivas, bem como da Morosidade da Justiça Civil. Pontifícia Universidade Católica do Rio Grande do Sul/Conselho Nacional de Justiça.

Siqueira, R.B., Nogueira, J.R.B., 2013. Taxation, inequality and the illusion of the social contract in Brazil. In: IARIW-IBGE Conference on Income, Wealth and Well-Being in Latin America. Rio de Janeiro, Brazil, September 2013.

Siqueira, R.B., Nogueira, J.R.B., Souza, E.S., 2012. O Sistema Tributário Brasileiro é Regressivo? Universidade Federal de Pernambuco. Departamento de Economia.

Tafner, P., Giambiagi, F., 2011. Previdência Social: Uma Agenda de Reformas. In: Bacha, E.L., Schwartzman, S. (Eds.), Brasil: A Nova Agenda Social. Gen/LTC.

Távora, F.L., 2014. A Renegociação da Dívida Rural: Reflexões sobre o Financiamento da Agricultura Brasileira. Núcleo de Estudos e Pesquisas da Consultoria Legislativa. Senado Federal. Texto para Discussão n. 146. Available from, http://www12.senado.gov.br/ publicacoes/estudos-legislativos/tipos-de-estudos/textos-para-discussao/td-146-renegociacao-de-divida-rural-reflexoes-sobre-o-financiamento-da-agricultura-brasileira.

Velloso, R., Hamilton, C., 2013. Pagamentos a Pessoas no Orçamento da União. Power Point presentation, Comissão de Assuntos Econômicos do Senado Federal. Public Meeting in 26th August 2013.

Velloso, R., Mendes, M., Caetano, M.A.R., 2010. Redirecionar os Gastos para Investir e Crescer Mais. In: Velloso, J.P.R. (Ed.), Construindo Sociedade Ativa e Moderna: Consolidando o Crescimento com Inclusão Social. XXII Fórum Nacional. José Olympio.

Velloso, R., et al., 2012. Infraestrutura: os Caminhos para Sair do Buraco. Fórum Nacional. Available from, http://www.raulvelloso.com.br/infraestrutura-os-caminhos-para-sair-do-buraco/.

Veloso, F., 2011. A Evolução Recente e Propostas para a Melhoria da Educação. In: Bacha, E.L., Schwartzman, S. (Eds.), Brasil: A Nova Agenda Social. Gen/LTC.

Chapter 6

Redistribution and Long-Term Growth

Chapter Outline

6.1 INTRODUCTION

The main argument developed in the previous chapters is that high inequality in a democratic environment has created incentives for a rent-seeking dispute that has blocked economic growth. What remains to be asked is: Since inequality is at the root of the problem, what would happen if it continues to fall as fast as in the recent past? Would there be a decrease in the distributive conflict and the disincentives to growth? Would the country be able to grow at higher rates?

If the answer to these questions is "yes," then redistribution to the poor is "a good deal." The weak short- and mid-range economic performance, due to these policies, could be considered a cost to be paid so that, in the long term, society was less unequal and able to grow at greater rates.

In spite of the ability of the middle and upper classes to create and preserve privileges (Chapters 3 and 4), inequality in Brazil has systematically fallen during the first years of the 21st century (Chapter 2).

Could Brazil finally be in a long-term, virtuous cycle? Have the first three decades of democracy been the negative trajectory that now is turning upward, leading to a more equal and dynamic society?

This is a possible economic trajectory for Brazil, but not the only one. It is not written in the stars that the country will be a success. There is also the possibility that the fall in inequality slows or stops (as considered in Chapter 2, Section 2.4) and that for many years to come Brazil continues to be an unequal society, involved in rent-seeking disputes among the different social groups, stuck in a model of low growth with dissipative redistribution.

The recent fall in inequality and the increase in the middle class have shown that the virtuous path is possible. A *possibility*, not a fact! The future of the country is at a crossroads. Just like a car that comes to a fork in the road, Brazil must choose: either the road to persistent and sustainable reduction in inequality and to growth, or the road to rent seeking and the unsustainable reduction of inequality and chronic low growth. These two perspectives are available, each reasonably possible and dependent on the choices to be made by those who run government in the next years.

6.2   WHAT DOES ECONOMIC THEORY HAVE TO SAY?

Many authors have called attention to the effects of redistribution on long-term growth. At the same time that redistributive policies can harm short- and mid-term growth, they may create the necessary conditions for long-term growth if they promote a significant and permanent reduction in inequality.

Abhijit Banerjee and Esther Duflo, authors of the outstanding book "Poor Economics," argue in one of their academic papers that:

> (...) in our model high inequality is bad for growth because it create incentives for hold ups, intended to reduce inequality. But the resulting reduction in inequality makes it less likely that in the subsequent period there will be a hold up and therefore the expected growth rate in that period will be higher than what it would have been, absent the costly change in inequality in the previous period. (...) we can clearly have shocks to inequality that are costly in the short run but beneficial over a longer horizon (Banerjee and Duflo, 2003, p. 276).

The economy would begin in a "bad equilibrium" with high inequality and low growth, but, with time and thanks to redistributive government policies (and eventually a favorable market dynamic), it would migrate toward a "good equilibrium," which would reduce inequality. A time of greater equality would arrive, where redistributive policies lose support and growth is stimulated. The less people depend on social aid and the greater the amount of those able to venture and earn income by means of productive labor in the private market, the less interest society will have in the redistributive rules and programs that impose costs and restrictions on companies.

The previously poor will demand better schools, less time wasted in slow and inefficient public transportation, conditions favorable to opening small businesses, less income tax, etc. They will pressure politicians to dismantle part of the income-transfer mechanisms (for the rich and poor) and find themselves in a state that is more focused on providing public services and promoting productivity gains.

This is the idea behind the notion of a "middle-class consensus," proposed by William Easterly. To the point that society becomes more equal, the degree of conflict for income distribution reduces and it becomes easier to arrive at a consensus regarding which policies should be adopted in favor of prosperity for the majority of the population:

(...) societies that are not polarized are able to reach a consensus on public goods and overall economic development. (...) Countries with a middle class consensus have a higher level of income and growth, they have more human capital and infrastructure accumulation, they have better national economic policies, more democracy, less political instability, more 'modern' sectorial structure, and more urbanization (Easterly, 2001, p. 318, 332).

Saint-Paul and Verdier draw attention to a special redistributive policy: public education (Saint-Paul and Verdier, 1993). The increase in human capital among the poor reduces inequality and increase worker productivity, which induces the virtuous cycle described above: redistribution stimulates growth. Increasing education among the poor represents a redistribution of opportunities, allowing them to increase their income, which is more efficient than taking income from others to give to the poor (World Bank, 2006). Bringing the educational level of the poor up to that of the rich reduces the persistence of inequality over time: with each generation, the level of education of the parents is a less important predictor of the educational level attained by the children, which accelerates social mobility and the fall of inequality from one generation to the next (Ferreira et al., 2013).

Economic literature has also advanced an analysis of *behavioral* arguments to explain the persistence of poverty and justify the use of redistributive policies to help the poor adopt behaviors favorable to social mobility and economic growth. (A synthesis of this literature can be found in Banerjee and Duflo, 2011. Ray, 2006 proposed the "aspiration gap" idea.) It is derived from the idea that poverty imprisons a person to the short-term. The extremely poor individual is a person who cannot plan for their future and make decisions that would provide an improvement in their life over the next years because they are focused on daily survival and, therefore, do not have the "mental space" to deal with mid- and long-term planning. Government help, by means of a conditional transfer such as the *Bolsa Família* program, or by providing basic healthcare service, for example, would be the "nudge" needed to set the poor in the right direction. By not needing to seek daily survival at any cost and being free of the uncertainties of income (including eliminating child labor) and healthcare, poor families would have stability necessary to plan for the education of their children and begin the process of social mobility.

A similar line of reasoning based on the concept of "aspirations," points toward the inability of the very poor to save and invest in the future. The poor who feel they have the opportunity to make their aspirations come true (improve future income, educate their children, and buy a better house) will be motivated to work arduously, increase their level of savings, carefully evaluate daily expenses and avoid waste. Looking toward a promising future, for themselves and their children, these people will be able to resist adversity and the temptation to spend now and change their attitude in respect to increasing the family's physical and human capital. By doing this, they contribute to the economic growth of society.

On the other hand, there are those very poor individuals who, even after making a great effort to save and invest well, are not able to advance because their total savings are very little. The effort to work hard, save and make daily sacrifices, things necessary to attain a better life, will be enormous in comparison to the results obtained. Those who do not feel they have any hope of having a better life, have nothing to lose. As such, they tend to make decisions that reflect such despair and are concerned only with the present. Only with an initial incentive by the government, by means of a minimum income, can the very poor have their "aspiration gap" reduced, being stimulated to dream of a better life in the long-term.

Public policies designed to reduce extreme poverty and inequality and guarantee access to fundamental services, such as healthcare and education, would fulfill an important role in reducing the contingent of discouraged poor (with a wide aspiration gap) and increase the amount of those with a dream of a better future (with a narrow aspiration gap). With this, redistributive policies would positively affect economic growth since they would be another channel by which a virtuous cycle of social inclusion and long-term expansion could be created.

Another path by which redistribution could generate this effect would be the reduction of *credit restrictions* faced by the poor (Mendes, 2013, Section 6 synthesizes the literature regarding the relationship between poverty, inequality, and access to credit). A fundamental issue in the credit market is that debtors can decide to not pay their bills. With the objective of reducing the probability of this event, banks, and lenders in general, demand that borrowers offer some type of collateral. This way, in the case of nonpayment, the bank sells the asset to recover part of the loss and at the same time punish the one in default. In general, the poor do not have sufficient assets to give as collateral and are excluded from the credit market.

A redistributive policy that allows the poor to accumulate assets that can be used as loan collateral (property, financial assets) would be to "remove" credit restrictions. Credit opens doors to invest in one's own business, finance private education for children and overcome critical periods when there is a substantial decrease in income. This would allow the poor to program their lives for a horizon that goes beyond the quest for immediate survival and permit them a vision of social mobility (Banerjee and Newman, 1993; Galor and Zeira, 1993; Ray, 1998, p. 227; Ghatak and Jiang, 2002).

For the economy as a whole, this means a greater number of entrepreneurs, increased education (greater human capital) and a greater propensity to invest. All this, added to the reduction in redistributive pressure, due to the reduction of inequality, would help raise the rate of economic growth.

There would also be a greater incentive, on the part of those entrepreneurs financed by credit, to work hard to prosper and avoid default, given that a greater level of individual wealth used as collateral would mean the borrower would have more to lose (the collateral) in the case they were unsuccessful (Aghion et al., 1999).

As such, the increase of credit would stimulate a greater productive effort with benefits to economic growth.

This virtuous cycle of redistribution generating growth after the reduction of inequality is not necessarily the only possible evolution of a redistributive policy. If a country is at the point of extreme inequality and the growth rate resulting from redistribution is low or negative (due to the negative effects of the redistributive policies on the economy), this society could be in a growth trap: the product the government redistributes reduces every year. In this case, "income inequality is or becomes so pronounced that it discourages further accumulation and growth" (Persson and Tabellini, 1994, p. 605).

There could also be an intermediate situation, where redistributive policies are not efficient enough to result in a substantial fall in inequality, but produce negative effects that are strong enough to hinder growth, which would block a virtuous cycle of redistribution and growth. In this case, redistribution in favor of the poor can generate instability and inconsistency in macroeconomic policy (high inflation, chronic unbalance in public accounts, and balance of payments). Therefore, the policy of redistribution to the poor would be a waste of resources for it would only temporarily improve the quality of life for the poor, or not improve it sufficiently to unleash the effects favorable to long-term growth.

Therefore, the *quality* of the redistributive policy can be decisive in this process. The more effective the redistribution policies to the poor are, the less their cost, and the lower the pressure for income redistribution to the upper (Chapter 3) and middle (Chapter 5) classes, the greater the chances that society will embark on a virtuous cycle.

6.3 WHICH PATH WILL BRAZIL TAKE?

The previously cited study by Lee Alston and co-authors (Alston et al., 2012) presents an optimistic view of the redistribution process in Brazil. They believe that Brazilian society has already attained a consensus regarding two fundamental points: (a) the need to reduce inequality, and (b) the importance of fiscal balance and price stability. As such, even if slowly, the country would be moving in the direction of a virtuous cycle, but yet needs to go through the dissipative redistribution stage (which they call "dissipative inclusion") to a state of "efficient inclusion": the reduction of inequality together with accelerated growth.

Thanks to the supposed consensus regarding the need for fiscal stability, the authors believe that macroeconomic policy would maintain its consistency, with no risk of redistributive pressures taking the public deficit to an excess, a return of high inflation, a crisis in balance payments or uncontrolled public debt.

A negative outlook, where redistribution (to the poor, rich, and intermediate classes) would occur in such an intense way so as to stunt growth, would therefore be avoided. This undesirable scenario, considered unlikely by the authors, is referred to by them as "populist inclusion." In such a scenario, income redistribution would only be temporary and later be corroded by inflation and low growth.

The arguments and examples presented in the previous chapters do not allow us to be as optimistic as the cited authors. Brazilian society does not seem to be reaching a consensus regarding the need to reduce inequality. What does exist, as shown in the previous chapters, is an intense distributive conflict, with the low ability of the different groups to coordinate their actions and, consequently, reduce pressure on the state.

Furthermore, it is not clear that the greater part of Brazilian society, or the political class that decides in its name, is convinced that a sound fiscal stance is a necessary condition for macroeconomic stability and growth, and that, as such, should be pursued by whatever political party is in power.

There is a great amount of resistance (and apprehension by politicians to touch on the subject) to reforms in social security and to alter the policy to adjust the minimum wage above work productivity, even though they are the main sources of fiscal instability for the present and future. One does not see, besides critiques by specialists, a reaction by voters against the fiscal deterioration that occurred between 2010 and 2013, and that has shown a tendency to worsen in the next years.

The less the financial discipline, the greater the ability of pressure groups to obtain more public spending in their favor. This feeds the low growth with dissipative redistribution model.

Furthermore, as seen in Chapter 2, nothing guarantees that inequality will continue to fall, because many components of this redistribution have lost strength. There is a tendency for inequality to stabilize at a still high level, distant from what is necessary for society to progress in the direction of a middle-class consensus.

A large part of the "ex-poor" could be considered a population that is still vulnerable to return to poverty, not having attained the economic security typical of the middle class. Many years of frustrating GDP performance added to a stagnation in the fall of inequality can lead this population back to poverty, or keep them in a vulnerable situation and, therefore, dependent on governmental aid policies.

In this context, redistributive pressures and the motivation for rent seeking remain strong and tend to intensify if the country remains in a low-growth situation.

A fall in demands for manufactured products leads to pressure for more commercial protection; high inflation unleashes demands for salary raises by pressure groups; a lower perspective of poverty reduction by means of the labor market resounds in a greater demand for social aid policies. A scenario of low growth, low productivity, expansion in public debt and increase in political pressure for income and preservation of privileges cannot be disregarded. "Populist inclusion," to use the term suggested by Lee Alston and co-authors, is not an unlikely scenario for Brazil.

To aggravate this scenario, there is the fact that the Brazilian population is aging quickly. This means that, in the next decades, the pressure on social security and the public healthcare system will increase. In 2012, social security and healthcare were responsible for no less than 45% of primary government expense (Siafi—Sistema Siga Brasil). It will be even more difficult to financially sustain the model of dissipative redistribution or "populist inclusion," especially if the economy continues to grow slowly.

There are those who have an optimist point of view and believe the demonstrations held in June 2013 are a sign that a significant portion of the population is migrating away from the demand for income and toward that of quality public services. The inclusion of millions of people in the middle class would be changing the perception of this group regarding the role of government in the economy. According to this interpretation, in demanding better public services, the new middle class, who now pays taxes and can plan their life beyond that of daily survival, would have acquired higher expectations regarding the transportation, healthcare, and education services offered by the government. This is, for instance, the opinion of Ricardo Paes e Barros, a specialist in poverty and inequality (World Bank, 2013b). The persistence of this movement would help the country move into a virtuous cycle of growth and less inequality.

However, as argued by the IMF economist, Carlo Cottarelli, the experience of developed countries that experienced social protests in the 1960s and 1970s similar to what Brazil has today, shows that the result was an expansion of public expenditure to finance more public services (Cottarelli, 2013). A large part of such expenditures were financed by increases in inflation, higher taxes, and a growing public debt. Brazil simply cannot afford this kind of solution. As shown in Chapter 1, the tax burden is at its limit, the public deficit already compromises a significant part of domestic savings and expenses are high and growing. Inflation is also quite high.

Furthermore, it is not clear if the protests were only a demand for better public services. There were a myriad of typical rent-seeking demands by organized groups, with no concern for fiscal consistency in what was demanded, as illustrated by the quote from Samuel Pessôa in Chapter 5. The main theme of the demonstrations, for example, was the demand for free public transportation for students. The cost of this subsidy to a specific group, if conceded, could reach something in the neighborhood of R$16 billion (about US$7 billion) per year (Balbim et al., 2013; 0.35% of estimated 2013 GDP). Not only would the expense be high, but adopting the measure would not result in a better public service, but an increased demand on an already congested and inefficient system, reducing speed and transportation capacity, with a negative effect on productivity and economic growth.

In other words, the protests could be seen by future historians as a symptom of the lack of resources to maintain the current system of "privileges for all." Everyone began to complain because the cover was getting too small and it is no longer possible to maintain the system of generalized distribution of benefits. Furthermore, diffused and hidden costs began to be noticed in the form of inflation, low growth, and high taxes. The sum of the innumerable expenditures generated by policies to create privileges grew too much. If this conflict intensifies, a political crisis could arise and even democracy would be at risk.

One cannot forget that the country also has important institutions able to trim expenses and contain the greed of some organized groups, thereby reinforcing democracy. The free press regularly investigates and exposes cases of corruption and inefficiency and pressures the three levels of government (federal, state, and municipal) to increase their efficiency and transparency. The autonomous Public Attorney's Office is another institution that acts in the same sphere. Control administrations, such as the Federal Court of Audits (TCU), have improved their organization and performance and evolved from being passive, bureaucratic organizations to being active and managerial in their evaluation of public programs.

This, however, does not seem to be enough. Brazilian society is far from demanding a change in the way government works, especially in respect to providing privileges and subsidies to specific groups. As seen in Chapter 5, even some institutions charged with refraining privileges and inefficiency, such as the TCU, did not miss the opportunity to guarantee privileges for their own members.

6.4 CONCLUSIONS

The central argument of this book is that the combination of high inequality with democracy has generated a model of low growth with dissipative redistribution. In the long term, this can lead to either a virtuous cycle of growth or a vicious cycle of low growth, inequality, and an eventual political crisis that may even threaten democracy.

If this is correct, and the combination of inequality and democracy is, in fact, a *deep cause* of Brazilian low growth, then it does not make much sense to form policy proposals that only address the *immediate causes* of low economic performance. There is no point in recommending that government control its expenses if there is strong motivation to continue expansion of these expenses in the form of benefits to the poor, the rich, or the middle class. It would also be unproductive to recommend a reduction in taxes since the high and growing expense would create an unsustainable fiscal deficit. Greater efficiency in the courts, greater independence of the regulatory agencies, greater economic openness and many other reforms that could stimulate growth, have little chances of occurring due to the political opposition of the beneficiaries of the status quo in a context of fragmented interests due to high inequality.

So, now what? What reforms would be feasible? How do we untie the knot of high inequality and low growth?

The main insight that occurs from the analyses made in this book is that the starting point may be in the reforms and policies that, *at the same time*, stimulate growth and reduce inequality.

Given that high inequality intensifies resistance to any type of reform that affects privileges, it is necessary to carefully choose a small set of reforms and put all of the government's political weight into it. The greater the number of reforms proposed, the greater the possibility of coalitions to form among the different affected groups to oppose them.

It is therefore fundamental to select a small set of reforms and public policy goals, giving priority to those that, at the same time, reduce inequality and stimulate growth. As the first reforms increase growth and reduce inequality, the other reforms will be easier to pass.

Within this perspective, the number one priority should be a revamp of social security. As shown in Chapter 2, the Brazilian retirement system is expensive, unsustainable in the long term and concentrates income. As it consumes 11% of GDP, the dimension of the retirement problem is great and only tends to worsen with the aging of the Brazilian population.

A social security reform that reduces privileges to middle- and upper-income groups and, at the same time, gives financial support to the poorer and assures the long-term actuarial balance, certainly would be an important push for the country to move in the direction of the virtuous cycle. It certainly will not be done without any resistance, just as those done in the past were not. A gradual transition policy and the concern to keep the poor from suffering loss would certainly make the change viable.

Second, obviously, is education. This would increase worker productivity and create the perspective of reducing inequality. Facing the problem of low-quality education in Brazil does not seem to be an easy task. Even though everyone declares themselves in favor of better public education, it is necessary to keep in mind that it is not at all interesting to the middle- and high-income groups that the poor have access to quality education. Even though this might seem inhumane, what really matters, after all, is that keeping the poor at a lower educational level reduces competition for openings in public universities and for good jobs in the labor market (Rajan, 2006). As a counter example, one only needs to notice the youth in the Asian societies that have created an efficient and inclusive educational system. They go through a lot of stress and long hours of study to enter and graduate from university in order to land a job in a top-shelf company. In comparison, Brazilian middle- and high-income students simply do not fear the competition of a mass of poor students who go to low-quality public schools for their primary and secondary education.

The urgent expansion of infrastructure (Chapter 1, Stylized Fact 5) must be done with the intent of reducing inequality. It would be interesting to give priority to infrastructure investments that have a positive impact on the lives of the poor. These are not hard to find: basic sanitation, collective transportation systems in the large cities, investments in drainage and housing policy to prevent homes from being built in high-risk areas. It would be interesting to change the profile of social inclusion policy: less real adjustments to the minimum wage, less expansion of social aid and more investments that have an immediate impact on the quality of life of the poor.

Politicians interested in placing the country in a virtuous cycle of inequality reduction and increased growth need to choose the primary reforms and throw all their political weight into them. They must also play defense, defending fiscal control rules that impede the populist expansion of policies in favor of specific groups. The more rigid the fiscal restriction imposed by the country, the more difficult it will be for interest groups to approve benefits in their favor. Regarding the Fiscal Responsibility Law, obeying the debt limits, respecting accounting rules and the transparency of public accounts are necessary. Playing "defense" also means working to block "counter reforms" that have recovering previously abolished privileges or expanding those existent as their objective.

In a society as unequal as the Brazilian, only in times of severe political and economic crises are there opportunities to implement deep reforms. In the recent history of the country, there have been only two periods of intense reform, both resulting from acute economic crises. The first was between 1964 and 1967 when there were modernizing reforms that reestablished fiscal balance, controlled inflation, and deregulated the credit market. Significant reforms, like the creation of the Central Bank and taxes, modernized the economy and allowed for a period of growth (see Veloso et al., 2013; Cardoso, 2013). The second period, with similar characteristics, occurred at the end of the 1990s, when it was possible to privatize public companies, adjust public accounts, reform financial relations among federal, states, and municipal governments and open the economy.

In both cases, after the worst part of each crisis, interest-group pressure on government led to the slow dismantling of institutional advances. In the case of the 1964–1967 reforms, for example, the Central Bank, at first created to be independent, was placed under the authority of the Executive Branch; the ICMS (tax on goods and services), conceived as a modern VAT (value-added tax), received exemptions and exceptions, which accumulated distortions and generated loss of efficiency; the model of import substitution and heavy state intervention was reestablished. In the more recent period, history seems to have repeated itself: fiscal control institutions were gradually taken apart, rules in the Fiscal Responsibility Law were bypassed, commercial barriers rebuilt and state control of the economy was increased by means of the expansion of public financial institutions, credit subsidies, and casuistic tax exemptions. (Regarding temporal inconsistency and changes in macroeconomic policies in Latin America, see Dornbusch and Edwards, 1991.)

What differentiates the two instances of reform was that the first happened under a dictatorship and the second under democracy. In the first case, dismantling of the reforms came due to the pleas of the upper- and middle-income classes with access to power. In the second, the poor and ample segments of intermediate classes also had a voice to demand privileges.

If the crises open opportunity for reform, they also bring the risk of damaging democracy (as what happened in the 1964 crisis). Democracy has been maintained thanks to the ability of the state to please ample social groups by means of privileges. As dysfunctional and prejudicial to growth the current model of "privileges for all" adopted by Brazilian democracy is, it has the merit of having been able to guarantee political stability for almost 30 years, a significant period by Brazilian standards. Nothing guarantees that this model will survive in the future, seeing that it is threatened by financial depletion. However, fiscal reforms must maintain political balance and avoid excessive damage to some social groups, which would otherwise generate political instability.

This is the challenge that is posed for those who next rule the country: proceed in the direction of the virtuous cycle without breaking with democracy. It is necessary to make concessions in the name of maintaining democracy, reducing the rhythm of desired reforms to maintain political harmony always when necessary. As Acemoglu and Robinson, teach in *Why Nations Fail*, experience from history shows that democracy is a necessary condition (though not sufficient) for inclusive institutions to be built (Acemoglu and Robinson, 2011), which are fundamental to sustainable economic development. It is therefore necessary to choose the most important reforms and throw a lot of political weight into their execution, for Brazil to walk in the direction of the virtuous cycle and be able to slowly advance other reforms in order to increase the rhythm of economic growth and lower the inequality and distributive conflict it creates.

REFERENCES

Acemoglu, D., Robinson, J.A., 2011. Why Nations Fail: The Origins of Power, Prosperity and Poverty. Profile Books Ltd. London, UK.

Aghion, P., García-Peñaloza, C., Caroli, E., 1999. Inequality and economic growth. In: Aghion, P., Williamson, J. (Eds.), Growth, Inequality and Globalization. Cambridge University Press, Cambridge, UK.

Alston, L.J., et al., 2012. Changing Social Contracts: Beliefs and Dissipative Inclusion in Brazil, NBER Working Paper 18588.

Balbim, R., et al., 2013. Ampliação ao Acesso ao Transporte Público Urbano—Propostas em Tramitação no Congresso Nacional. IPEA, Nota Técnica n. 3.

Banerjee, A., Duflo, E., 2003. Inequality and growth: what can the data say? J. Econ. Growth 8, 267–299.

Banerjee, A., Duflo, E., 2011. Poor Economics. Penguin Books, London, UK.

Banerjee, A., Newman, A., 1993. Occupational choice and the process of development. J. Polit. Econ. 101 (2), 274–298.

Cardoso, R.F., 2013. Política Econômica, Reformas Institucionais e Crescimento: a Experiência Brasileira (1945–2010). In: Veloso, F., et al. (Eds.), Desenvolvimento Econômico: Uma Perspectiva Brasileira. Elsevier-Campus.

Cottarelli, C., 2013. The times they are A-Changin': will (Fiscal) history repeat itself? The Huffington Post. [Online] 25th July. Available from: http://www.huffingtonpost.com/carlo-cottarelli/the-times-they-are-a-changin_b_3653163.html

Dornbusch, R., Edwards, S., 1991. The macroeconomics of populism. In: Dornbusch, R., Edwards, S. (Eds.), The Macroeconomics of Populism in Latin America. University of Chicago Press, Chicago, IL, USA.

Easterly, W., 2001. The middle class consensus and economic development. J. Econ. Growth 6 (4), 317–335.

Ferreira, F.H.G., et al., 2013. Economic mobility and the rise of Latin American middle class. World Bank Latin American and Caribbean Studies, The World Bank, Washington D.C.

Galor, O., Zeira, J., 1993. Income distribution and macroeconomics. Rev. Econ. Stud. 60, 35–52.

Ghatak, M., Jiang, N., 2002. A simple model of inequality, occupational choice, and development. J. Dev. Econ. 69, 205–226.

Mendes, M.J., 2013. Inequality and Growth: An Overview of the Theory. Núcleo de Estudos e Pesquisas do Senado Federal. Texto para Discussão n. 131. Available from: http://www12. senado.gov.br/publicacoes/estudos-legislativos/tipos-de-estudos/textos-para-discussao/td-131-inequality-and-growth-an-overview-of-the-theory

Persson, T., Tabellini, G., 1994. Is inequality harmful for growth? Am. Econ. Rev. 84 (3), 600–621.

Rajan, R., 2006. Competitive Rent Preservation, Reform Paralysis, and the Persistence of Underdevelopment, NBER Working Paper 12093.

Ray, D., 1998. Development Economics. Princeton University Press, Princeton, New Jersey, USA.

Ray, D., 2006. Aspirations, poverty and economic change. In: Banerjee, A., Benábou, R., Mookherjee, D. (Eds.), Understanding Poverty. Oxford University Press, New York.

Saint-Paul, G., Verdier, T., 1993. Education, democracy and growth. J. Dev. Econ. 42, 399–407.

The World Bank, 2013. Inequality in Focus. The World Bank, Poverty Reduction and Equity Department, vol. 2, no. 2.

Veloso, F., Ferreira, P.C., Pessôa, S.A., 2013. Experiências Comparadas de Crescimento Econômico no Pós-Guerra. In: Veloso, F., et al. (Eds.), Desenvolvimento Econômico: Uma Perspectiva Brasileira. Elsevier-Campus.

World Bank, 2006. Equity and Development. World Development Report 2006, The World Bank, Washington, D.C., USA.

Glossary

1) Most used acronyms

Acronym	Original name	Name in free translation	Description
ANA	Agência Nacional de Águas	National Water Agency	Federal water use and preservation agency
ANAC	Agência Nacional de Aviação Civil	National Civil Aviation Agency	Federal civil aviation regulatory agency
ANATEL	Agência Nacional de Telecomunicações	National Telecommunications Agency	Federal telecommunication regulatory agency
ANEEL	Agência Nacional de Energia Elétrica	Brazilian Electricity Regulatory Agency	Federal electrical energy regulatory agency
ANP	Agência Nacional do Petróleo, Gás Natural e Biocombustíveis	National Agency of Petroleum, Natural Gas and Biofuels	Federal oil, natural gas and biofuel regulatory agency
ANTAQ	Agência Nacional de Transportes Aquaviários	National Waterway Transportation Agency	Federal waterway transportation regulatory agency
ANTT	Agência Nacional de Transportes Terrestres	National Land Transportation Agency	Federal land transportation regulatory agency
BASA	Banco da Amazônia	Bank of Amazon	Bank (100% owned by the federal government)
BB	Banco do Brasil	Bank of Brazil	Bank (majority shares belongs to the federal government)
BCB	Banco Central do Brasil	Brazil Central Bank	Equivalent to Federal Reserve Board
BNB	Banco do Nordeste do Brasil	Bank of the Northeast of Brazil	Bank (majority shares belongs to the federal government)

Continued

Acronym	Original name	Name in free translation	Description
BNDES	Banco Nacional de Desenvolvimento Econômico e Social	National Bank for Economic and Social Development	Development Bank (100% owned by the federal government)
BOVESPA	Bolsa de Valores de São Paulo	São Paulo Stock Exchange	
BPC	Benefício de Prestação Continuada	Continued Benefit	Cash transfer to low-income elderly and low-income physically challenged citizens
CEF	Caixa Econômica Federal	Federal Savings Bank	Bank (100% owned by the federal government)
CENTRUS	Fundação Banco Central de Previdência Privada	Central Bank Pension Foundation	Central Bank employee pension fund
CLT	Consolidação das Leis do Trabalho	Consolidated Labor Laws	Federal Law that regulates the job market (not applied to civil servants)
CNJ	Conselho Nacional de Justiça	National Justice Council	Agency for overseeing, planning and monitoring judicial institutions
CVM	Comissão de Valores Mobiliários	Securities Commission	Securities market regulatory agency
FAT	Fundo de Amparo ao Trabalhador	Workers Support Fund	Federal government budgetary fund used to finance unemployment insurance and other worker benefits
FCO	Fundo Constitucional do Centro-Oeste	Mid-West Constitutional Fund	Budgetary fund created by the 1988 Constitution to subsidize private investments in the Mid-West region of Brazil
FDA	Fundo de Desenvolvimento da Amazônia	Amazon Development Fund	Budgetary fund to subsidize private investments in the Brazilian Amazon
FDNE	Fundo de Desenvolvimento do Nordeste	Northeast Development Fund	Budgetary fund to subsidize private investments in the Brazilian Amazon

Continued

Acronym	Original name	Name in free translation	Description
FGTS	Fundo de Garantia do Tempo de Serviço	Time of Service Guarantee Fund	Forced saving device to which employers and employees make mandatory deposits in the name of the employee; the balance may be withdrawn when the employee is dismissed or in other special circumstances
FNE	Fundo Constitucional de Financiamento do Nordeste	Northeast Constitutional Fund	Budgetary fund created by the 1988 Constitution to subsidize private investments in the Northeast region of Brazil
FNO	Fundo Constitucional do Norte	North Constitutional Fund	Budgetary fund created by the 1988 Constitution to subsidize private investments in the North region of Brazil
IBGE	Instituto Brasileiro de Geografia e Estatística	Brazilian Institute of Geography and Statistics	Main research agency for economic and social inquires in Brazil
IPEA	Instituto de Pesquisa Econômica Aplicada	Applied Economic Research Institute	Public think tank
IRPF	Imposto de Renda Pessoa Física	Personal Income Tax	Charged by the federal government
PETROBRAS	Petróleo Brasileiro	Brazilian Oil Company	Oil company (federal government has majority share)
PETROS	Fundação Petrobras de Seguridade Social	Petrobras Pension Foundation	Petrobras employee pension fund
PL	Projeto de Lei	Legislative Bill in the Chamber of Deputies	
PLS	Projeto de Lei do Senado	Legislative Bill in the Senate	
PME	Pesquisa Mensal de Emprego	Monthly Employment Inquiry	Research performed by the IBGE

Continued

Acronym	Original name	Name in free translation	Description
PNAD	Pesquisa Nacional por Amostra de Domicílios	National Research by Sample Households	Inquiry made by IBGE
POF	Pesquisa de Orçamento Familiar	Family Budget Research	IBGE research on family income and budget
PREVI	Caixa de Previdência dos Funcionários do Banco do Brasil	Bank of Brazil Pension Foundation	Bank of Brazil employee pension fund
PREVIC	Superintendência Nacional de Previdência Complementar	National Pension Fund Superintendence	Federal Pension Fund Regulatory Agency
PSF	Programa Saúde da Família	Family Health Program	Federal government health program
RJU	Regime Jurídico Único	Unified Judicial Regime	Law that regulates civil servant work contracts
STF	Supremo Tribunal Federal	Federal Supreme Court	Highest level of the Brazilian judicial system
SUDAM	Superintendência de Desenvolvimento da Amazônia	Amazon Development Superintendence	Public agency in charge of supplying subsidized credit for private investment in the Amazon region
SUDENE	Superintendência de Desenvolvimento do Nordeste	Northeast Development Superintendence	Public agency in charge of supplying subsidized credit for private investment in the Northeast region
SUS	Sistema Único de Saúde	Unified Health System	Public health system managed by the Ministry of Health
TCU	Tribunal de Contas da União	Federal Court of Audits	Agency for auditing federal government expenses
TST	Tribunal Superior do Trabalho	Supreme Labor Court	Higher level of the branch of the judicial system that is specialized in labor issues
ZFM	Zona Franca de Manaus	Manaus Free Zone	Tax-free industrial district in Manaus (capital city of the state of Amazon)

2) Other acronyms

Acronym	Original name	Name in free translation	Description
AMBEV	Companhia de Bebidas das Américas	Americas' Beverage Company	Private beverage and beer producer
ANFAVEA	Associação Nacional dos Fabricantes de Veículos Automotores	National Association of Motor Vehicles Producers	Private association of automobile producers operating in Brazil
CCX	Carvão da Colômbia	Colombia Coal	Private coal explorer—belonged to the bankrupt EBX Group
CHESF	Companhia Hidro Elétrica do São Francisco	São Francisco Hydroelectric Company	State-owned power-generating company
COFINS	Contribuição para o Financiamento da Seguridade Social	Contribution to Social Security Fund	Tax to finance social security
CPI	Comissão Parlamentar de Inquérito	Parliamentary Inquiry Commission	Temporary committees created by Federal Congress to investigate crimes or relevant problems
DIEESE	Departamento Intersindical de Estatísticas e Estudos Sócio-Econômicos	Inter-union Department for Statistics and Socioeconomic Studies	Institute for statistics and socioeconomic research funded by worker unions
EBX	EBX Holding		Bankrupt EBX Group holding company
ECLAC	Economic Commission for Latin America		Branch of the United Nations
FACHESF	Fundação CHESF de Seguridade e Assistência Social	CHESF Pension Foundation	State-owned power supply company employee pension fund
FAPES	Fundação de Previdência e Assistência Social do BNDES	BNDES Pension Foundation	BNDES employee pension fund
FEBRABAN	Federação Brasileira de Bancos	Brazilian Banking Federation	National Federation of Banks (includes private and state-owned banks)

Continued

Acronym	Original name	Name in free translation	Description
FGV	Fundação Getúlio Vargas	Getúlio Vargas Foundation	Private research institute partly financed by public funds
FIESP	Federação das indústrias do Estado de São Paulo	São Paulo Industry Federation	São Paulo industrial federation
FORLUZ	Fundação Forluminas de Seguridade Social	Forluminas Pension Foundation	CEMIG employee pension fund (CEMIG is an electric distribution company controlled by the Minas Gerais state government)
FPM	Fundo de Participação dos Municípios	Municipal Participation Fund	Revenue-sharing mechanism through which the federal government transfers a percentage of its tax revenue to municipal governments
FUNCEF	Fundação dos Economiários Federais	Caixa Econômica Federal Pension Foundation	Caixa Econômica Federal (CEF) employee pension fund
FUNDAÇÃO COPEL	Fundação COPEL de Previdência e Assistência Social	COPEL Pension Foundation	COPEL employee pension fund (COPEL is an electric distribution company controlled by the Paraná state government)
GEIPOT	Empresa Brasileira de Planejamento de Transporte	Brazilian Transportation Planning Company	Defunct federal agency for transportation planning
IADB	Inter-American Development Bank		Multilateral financing agency
ICMS	Imposto sobre Circulação de Mercadorias e Serviços	Tax on Goods and Services	Charged by state governments
INEP	Instituto Nacional de Estudos e Pesquisas Educacionais Anísio Teixeira	Anísio Teixeira National Educational Research Institute	Department of the Ministry of Education responsible for educational statistics and research
INPC	Índice Nacional de Preços ao Consumidor	National Consumer Price Index	Consumer price index

Continued

Acronym	Original name	Name in free translation	Description
IOF	Imposto sobre Operações Financeiras	Financial Transactions Tax	Charged by the federal government
ISS	Imposto Sobre Serviços	Tax on Services	Tax on services charged by municipal governments
LLX	LLX Logística		Private logistic company—owned by the bankrupt EBX Group
LOAS	Lei Orgânica da Assistência Social	Social Assistance Organic Law	Law that regulates social assistance benefits paid by the federal government
MDS	Ministério do Desenvolvimento Social	Ministry of Social Development and Hunger Alleviation	Ministry for Social Development
MMX	MMX Mineração	MMX Mining Company	Private mining company—owned by the bankrupt EBX Group
MPX	MPX Energia	MPX Energy Company	Private energy company—owned by the bankrupt EBX Group
OECD	Organisation for Economic Co-operation and Development		Multilateral organization
OGX	Óleo e Gás Participações	Oil and Gas Participations	Private oil and gas company—owned by the bankrupt EBX Group
ONIP	Organização Nacional das Indústrias de Petróleo	National Oil Industries Organization	National oil companies federation
OSX	OSX Holding		Private shipbuilding company—owned by the bankrupt EBX Group
PACS	Programa de Agentes Comunitários de Saúde	Community Health Agents Program	Preventive healthcare program managed by the Ministry of Health
PASEP	Programa de Formação do Patrimônio do Servidor Público	Program for Civil Servant Asset Accumulation	Tax paid by employers to finance employee benefits

Continued

Acronym	Original name	Name in free translation	Description
PDP	Política de Desenvolvimento Produtivo	Productive Development Policy	Industrial policy adopted by the federal government
PIS	Programa de Integração Social	Social Integration Program	Tax paid by employers to finance employee benefits
PISA	Programme for International Student Assessment		Worldwide study by the OECD in member and non-member nations of 15-year-old school pupils' scholastic performance on mathematics, science, and reading
PITCE	Política Industrial Tecnológica e de Comércio Exterior do Governo Federal	Industry, Technology and Trade Policy	Industrial policy adopted by the federal government
POSTALIS	Instituto de Seguridade Social dos Correios e Telégrafos	Correios Pension Foundation	Postal service employee pension fund
PROUNI	Programa Universidade para Todos	University for All Program	Federal government educational program
PSDB	Partido da Social Democracia Brasileira	Brazilian Social Democracy Party	Political party
PT	Partido dos Trabalhadores	Worker's Party	Political party
RAIS	Relação Anual de Informações Sociais	Annual social data report	Inquiry on labor market statistics made by the federal government
REAL GRANDEZA	Real Grandeza Fundação de Previdência e Assistência Social	Real Grandeza Pension Foundation	Furnas employee pension fund (state-owned power-generating company)
SIAFI	Sistema Integrado de Administração Financeira	Integrated Financial Administration System	Computer system used by the federal government to manage its budget
SIGA BRASIL	Sistema de Informações Orçamentárias do Senado Federal	Federal Senate Budget Information System	Computer system used by the Senate to analyze information stored in SIAFI

Continued

Acronym	Original name	Name in free translation	Description
SIOPS	Sistema de Informações sobre Orçamentos Públicos em Saúde	Public Health Budget Information System	Databank with public health information
SISTEL	Fundação Sistel de Seguridade Social	Sistel Pension Foundation	Telecommunication company employee pension
SPE	Secretaria de Política Econômica	Economic Policy Secretariat	Department of the Ministry of Finance
STN	Secretaria do Tesouro Nacional	National Treasury Secretariat	Department of the Ministry of Finance
TELOS	Fundação Embratel de Seguridade Social	Embratel Pension Foundation	Embratel (a telecom) employee pension fund

Index

Note: Page numbers followed by *f* indicate figures, *t* indicate tables and *np* indicate footnotes.

Printed in the United States
By Bookmasters